Hide, Horn, Fish, and Fowl: Texas Hunting and Fishing Lore

Hide, Horn, Fish, and Fowl: Texas Hunting and Fishing Lore

Edited by Kenneth L. Untiedt

Publications of the Texas Folklore Society LXVII

University of North Texas Press

Denton, Texas

10 9 8 7 6 5 4 3 2 1

Permissions:
University of North Texas Press
1155 Union Circle #311336
Denton, TX 76203-5017

The paper used in this book meets the minimum requirements of the American National
Standard for Permanence of Paper for Printed Library Materials, z39.48.1984.
Binding materials have been chosen for durability.

Library of Congress Cataloging-in-Publication Data

Hide: horn, fish, and fowl: Texas hunting and fishing lore/edited by
Kenneth L. Untiedt. — 1st ed. p. cm. — (Publications of the Texas Folklore Society; 67)
ISBN 978-1-57441-320-5 (cloth : alk. paper)
ISBN 978-1-57441-446-2 (e-book)
1. Hunting—Texas—Folklore. 2. Fishing—Texas—Folklore. 1. Untiedt, Kenneth L.,
1966- II. Series: Publications of the Texas Folklore Society; no. 67.
GR110.T4H55 2011
398.209764—dc23
2011034657

Hide, Horn, Fish, and Fowl: Texas Hunting and Fishing Lore is Number LXVII in the
Publications of the Texas Folklore Society

CONTENTS

IV. *You Hunt What?! Unusual Prey and Other Things We Chase*

V. *The One That Got Away (or Should Have): Anecdotes and Funny Stories*

PREFACE

Some people seem to be born hunters. I recall a story F. E. Abernethy told me one time about his grandson, Jack, who accompanied Ab on a trip to the woods one day as he was readying his lease for hunting season. As they were walking along, Jack suddenly turned to his grandfather and said, with a mischievous smile on his face, "Let's get ourselves lost in the woods." Those were not his exact words, I'm sure, but the sentiment shows how he obviously felt completely comfortable in nature and seemed to have hunting in his blood from an early age. Others, like me, are brought to it—not kicking and screaming, necessarily, but slowly, and much later in life. I imagine that there are still others (probably many) who never take to hunting—or fishing—at all.

This Publication of the Texas Folklore Society contains articles that consider our inclination to hunt for wild game and fish streams and open waters for food, even now that we no longer need to do so for our basic survival. Some authors provide very serious examinations of the things that drive us to hunt, while others invite us to laugh about hunting trips gone bad and fishing forays that never should have been. The works contain hunting and fishing terms unique to the people who share the activities, and even some practices—or places—that have been lost to time. These endeavors that are holdovers from ancient times continue to bring people together; sometimes they are family members, getting together over many generations and great distances as part of customary rituals, and others are strangers from varied walks of life and professions with only their shared activity as common ground.

Thad Sitton brings us two interesting articles, both filled with fascinating research of the cultures associated with types of hunting many of us don't think about much anymore—fox hunting, and man hunting. Both works are valuable records that help maintain the lore of those activities. Wildwood Dean Price also contributes two articles, one on traditional river fishing, and another on a rather humorous hunting experience. W. C. Jameson provides a look at a different kind of hunting: the hunt for lost treasures. Whether it's deer, hogs, coons, javelinas, or fish—big or small—most of us have fond memories of spending time with relatives or friends, communing in nature and trying to connect to an earlier time when our livelihood depended on finding, killing, and preparing our own food.

As always, I thank the many contributors who wrote articles for this book, and there are quite a few this time. I also thank my friends and colleagues at Stephen F. Austin State University, and the administrators here who support the TFS, including Mark Sanders, the Chair of the English Department, and Brian Murphy, Dean of the College of Liberal and Applied Arts. Of course, I am grateful for the folks at the UNT Press who help us put these books together each year. Janet Simonds, our office secretary, helps with formatting the submissions, corresponding with contributors, and helping to compile everything from the original articles to hard copy photos into the final manuscript. Even when we're not actively working on a book, she keeps our office running smoothly so that I can not only address things that are related to the Society, but also focus on my "day job"—teaching classes and serving on various committees and other administrative duties that all professors must do.

This book is dedicated to my new friends at Sugar Creek. I value their camaraderie, their sage advice, their humor, and their appreciation of folklore. I look forward to many more opening weekends and the opportunity to take part in rituals that originated long before I came into camp, and getting to know the men who value a good hunt, a hot chili dog, and the anticipation of the first frost-covered morning of deer season: Drew Louis, Ladd Hardy, Alex Louis, and Joe T. Rogers (those pictured here, clockwise from the left), as well as the other hunters who've called Sugar Creek home: Chuck Davis, Donald Gardner, and others I know only through the stories that keep their spirits alive. Thanks especially to Marilyn Davis, whose offer to join the group will never be forgotten.

Kenneth L. Untiedt
Stephen F. Austin State University
Nacogdoches, Texas
May 25, 2011

THE HUNTING DRIVE

AND ITS PLACE
IN OUR LORE

Len Ainsworth quail hunting, Garza County, 2010

GONE A' HUNTING

by Len Ainsworth

Bye 0, Baby Bunting

Daddy's gone a' hunting

For to get a rabbit skin

For to wrap his baby in.

That's likely not the way it was written, but that's the way I remember the lullaby sung by my mother—and the only one I tried to sing to my kids. Fortunately, they were *too young to remember how badly I sang. I probably remember my mother singing it to my sister, five years younger; surely I* wouldn't remember her singing it to me as a baby. But the theme of hunting has resonated in our family for several generations. My maternal grandfather, Papaw Charley, was a great hand for singing and hunting, and mother must have heard the lullaby many times, sung to her younger siblings.

My paternal grandfather gave me his .410 gauge shotgun when I was ten years old, and my parents let me go dove hunting alone with a handful of shells in the mesquite brush extending into our small West Texas town. I had to stalk my quarry carefully with the single-shot gun, and get close and locate one perched on a tree limb without other branches in the way. More than once I have been fooled by a nesting dove acting hurt and fluttering ever farther from her nest and then suddenly flying away. But a few unwary birds did fall. I don't remember coming home on those first hunts with more than one bird at a time. I suppose I was so excited that I didn't keep looking after I got one, or perhaps I used up my few shells getting it. I'm sure my mother or dad helped clean the first few birds, and they were cooked as the prize they were. I learned early that you were to clean and eat your kill.

That wasn't true of all game, of course. My dad often shot small animals that we considered varmints: prairie dogs, skunks, rabbits, and ground squirrels. Crows, and since we had chickens, hawks, also came in that category. Both of my grandfathers had stories of hunting, of coyotes that had preyed on young stock, bobcats, and in much earlier days, antelope and deer that shared the open prairie. My maternal grandfather had an octagonal barrel 45-70 Winchester that as a boy I couldn't hold steady because of its weight. My paternal grandfather, too late to hunt the buffalo, nevertheless had a pair of horn covers (the black shiny portions) from a young bull that he had taken from a skeleton on the range not far from Colorado City, Texas. And he told of the numbers of bones he had seen piled for shipment. This is simply to say that hunting has been a link among members of our family, and among generations.

Some of my good memories include going hunting with my dad, walking in the scraggly hills east of town. We shared his .22WRF, taking alternate shots at rabbits and at tin cans and other small targets. That slide action Remington with a burl walnut stock keeps a place in my gun cabinet. The old rim fire rifle isn't legal for deer, but its cartridge holds more powder than a regular .22 long rifle casing, and it *has* dropped a couple of antlered bucks. Absorbing the jolt of dad's larger bolt action deer rifle was accompanied by absorbing his frequent admonition that the high powered rifle "shoots today and kills tomorrow," requiring knowing what was behind the intended target. Other memories are as a young boy walking with my dad along the banks of the North Concho River on winter nights, him with a headlight and .22 rifle, hunting raccoons in the big pecan trees, for their skins. We usually came home with a few pelts that he had skinned out where the coon fell from the tree. The skins were stretched to dry on our barn wall and represented several dollars each. The season for taking and selling furs began the first of December, but my dad was convinced that the "hair wouldn't slip" after the first cold spell in November, so we usually had a few drying hides on the wall a little ahead of the official opening. So "Daddy's gone a' hunting" had literal as well as symbolic meaning for me.

For the first sixteen years of my life my hunting range, as well as the rest of my physical world, was centered in the North Concho River valley, extending outward only a few miles in any direction from the small town of Water Valley, Texas. I became intimately familiar with the hills to the east that extended to make the higher, flat divide with the Colorado River watershed. The low hills were places for hunting, trapping, and exploring with rifle, friends, and dog. I walked a trapline in those hills a few days a week during the two-month winter fur season during the middle years of World War II.

A young teen cousin came by bus from Pecos, Texas, to visit during one of those wartime summers. The next morning he suggested a walk into the hills, and I agreed readily. I was delighted when he produced a pistol that he had brought with him, unbeknownst to the bus drivers, his parent, or mine. We shot the pistol several times, and then hid it in some rocks as we returned, knowing full well that it would have been forbidden. That evening my dad called the two of us together and asked how we planned to pay for a cow. He claimed we had been seen shooting and that the landowner had a cow killed. We tried denying everything, but to no avail. So we retrieved the pistol and worriedly delivered it up to stern warnings and, finally, an admission that we had apparently done no damage except to our reputations.

To the west of town were larger ranches that were occasional hunting venues when in my teens. North and south the river was attractive for hunting, fishing, and occasional camping. The river ran through a county park, but we ranged far beyond its borders. Permission to hunt, fish, or explore was seldom asked of landholders by me or my boyhood companions, and was even more rarely refused in those 1940s of my youth.

Hunting is a noun, a verb, an adjective, a destination, a concept. It's a little hard to describe to non-hunters. It can be an adventure, it is exciting, it can be boring, and it can be dangerous. It is a challenge, and can bring satisfaction, embarrassment, or chagrin. I can get the same feelings of excitement sweating in the edge of a cotton field on a fall afternoon waiting for a dove to come whistling past, as in a deer blind on a cold morning, or slogging through a muddy field wondering if the next step will flush a pheasant. Hunting can become boring when the game fails to appear, but the exercise gained, and watching the scenery change, make it worthwhile. Chagrin isn't uncommon when an animal or bird slips by from an unexpected direction. I don't know anyone whose heart doesn't thump harder than usual on a quail rise, when a covey whirs up in several directions. And it is challenging when an unseen turkey gobbles just out of range, but won't come to the call.

Weather can be extremely hot in the September sun in West Texas and freezing cold on a December tramp across frozen Panhandle fields for pheasant or quail. Hunting allows for daydreaming in a deer blind or on a dove stand, yet requires concentrated attention to be successful in those same venues. It can be startling when a cock pheasant explodes from almost underfoot, out of a grassy spot that wouldn't seem large enough to hide a sparrow. Hunting can afford satisfying and memorable moments, as when I perceived an erect weed stem to actually be a tail feather that became a bird in flight when a pause in walking caused the cock pheasant to launch.

Hunting is a celebration of life in being outdoors, in company or alone. It comes from watching the darting, slip-sliding flight of the mourning dove, from the unexpected direction of flight of a single quail, or from the glide of a pheasant that seems to go on forever, and then whose location fools you because it has run many more yards after landing. It can allow time for reflection, although I think more about hunting when I'm not hunting than I think about other things when I am hunting. The act of hunting and the outdoors demand attention, and when one starts to daydream or forgets to pay attention there is often a price to pay, from not seeing a pheasant slip away to stepping into an unseen hole. Hunting in our western part of the state puts me closer than many for seeing the sway of the lacy leaves of a mesquite, the motion of a butterfly's wings, the smell of wild sunflowers, and the colors of a sunset.

Hunting is a primal instinct or reaction. It recognizes an appreciation for life and acceptance of death. One can appreciate the beauty of wildlife and the variety of their ways of survival and still enjoy the hunt. It is satisfying to be successful in hunting, even as we know that success comes at the expense of an animal or bird. There is the momentary pang as I retrieve a quail, or look long and hard for a bird that seemed to be wounded but can't be found. But men and women have hunted since before history, and accept that life itself is uncertain and that no concept of fairness exists in the natural world. My parents' insistence upon our cleaning and cooking our kill stemmed from more than just not being wasteful. It also recognized the completion of the act of hunting.

We learned a serious and lasting lesson on the potential danger in hunting and safety when my dad was accidentally shot on a deer hunt when I was a teenager. Shot in the side by a falling rifle, on a Reagan County ranch nearly a hundred miles from a hospital, he recovered because of quick action by an uncle, a rancher's wife who packed and bound the wound, ambulance attendants, and a skilled surgeon. The bullet from the rifle, at point-blank range, entered my dad in the back above the kidneys, struck a rib, splintered, clipped the edge of a lung, and exited in the front. Relegated to the back of the pickup truck because of a leg in a full cast from a football injury, I was no help in the rescue. My uncle piled me into the back and lifted my father into the seat. He then drove to, stopped, opened, drove through, stopped and closed three different pasture gates by force of ingrained habit, as he sped to the ranch house and a telephone as fast as he could. I rode in the ambulance with my dad to the hospital, while the uncle went back through those same three gates, gathered our camping gear, and followed. The surgeon on duty had Army experience in the European theatre and was all too familiar with gunshot wounds. Recovery was quick and complete. A few years later, an itching sensation higher up on his back encouraged my dad to go to a doctor, who removed a bullet sliver that had worked its way out to just below the skin. The traumatic occasion never dampened my dad's desire and appreciation for hunting, nor mine. It has made me more careful, however—much more careful.

Another unforeseen danger in hunting came in the possible loss of potential daughters-in-law. Older son Price brought a former law school classmate home for a long weekend. That weekend happened to fall on the opening of dove season. Vicki agreed that she would like to go with us, but didn't want to shoot. It was still hot and rattlesnakes a consideration. She didn't have boots, so we rigged her up some snake leggings, actually some canvas "puttees" of World War I vintage. The canvas covered the top of shoes and laced up to just below the knee. We went to hunt in the Roaring Springs area of Motley County, just after lunch. Eschewing a hat, she acquired a light sunburn during the long afternoon. Vicki helped Price find wounded birds in tall cover, some of which was needle grass. Some of those needles worked their way under the shoe covers and produced a painful irritation. Fortunately, we didn't see any snakes. Vicki approved of dove hunting for Price, but declined further invitations to accompany us. She did go once again, for a quail hunt. After an early start and a hundred-plus mile drive to Hall County, an all day hunt and a sleepy return, she apparently decided to give up quail hunting as well. She has continued to be supportive of husband Price's hobby and wished him well as he celebrated his half-century mark with a pheasant and grouse hunt in South Dakota. The couple spent a few days in France to mark her similar milestone, so perhaps she didn't mind not hiking after the grouse.

When younger son Charles brought his friend Jennifer to meet the family, it was again the opening of another dove season. She came prepared, with shotgun, to join us. We went south of Tahoka, in Lynn County, taking up stands along one of the few lines of trees in a vast farming area. Birds came to us over a low rise and across a field of Johnson grass. It was a good, apparently safe location, isolated until a few young boys took up spots just below the rise to the right front of us. So, we had to be careful where we shot. The boys were shooting away from us, toward the rise, until one followed a missed bird and let fly toward us. The bird shot rained down, and the landowner ran toward the boys, yelling and banning them from the area. Jennifer quietly noted that she had been hit. While we tried to assure her that the distance was such that no damage would be done, she pulled her collar down a bit to show that a pellet was imbedded in her skin at the collarbone. She and Charles picked the single shot out, leaving a small indentation. I was most thankful that it hadn't struck an eye, and worried that we had lost more than a hunt. But Jen accepted it all in stride, declined offers to beat up the careless hunter or to have her sue him. Instead, she has become a regular hunter, willing to sit long hours in a deer blind to select only a trophy size buck, and bring it down with precise shooting. And she and Charles are training the next generation, as their boys are beginning to hunt with them, stressing safety from experience.

A regular twenty-two caliber rifle in my gun case is a continuing reminder of an earlier life. Anxious to move up from a Red Ryder BB gun, I bought it with some of the first money I ever earned as a preteen, by piling prickly pear. It is a Stevens Springfield bolt-action piece with a clip that inserts under the forearm, in front of the trigger guard. That rifle may have been my first experience in comparative shopping. I looked at .22s in most of the San Angelo stores, Sears, Wards, Western Auto, and sporting goods stores that specialized in guns. My choice was based on more than just cost, but that was a big factor. The one selected was one of the least expensive guns examined, and it has not increased in value as have some others from that time period. I suppose my dad bought the gun for me and I repaid him, although I doubt that any forms had to be completed at that time. A few years later I bought a pistol, and forms did have to be completed, and one had to be older than my fifteen years to purchase a handgun. When I went to pay for the pistol and the clerk had to refuse to sell it to me, a man who was shopping in the store, unknown to either the clerk or me, simply said he would sign for me. He did so, and I walked out with the pistol, which I still have. Times were simpler over a half-century ago.

The rifle got a lot of use, the later pistol very little. I was instructed to use only .22 Shorts, the smallest load, when hunting or shooting near our home in the small town of my boyhood. My dad warned about being careful where one aimed and stressed that the range of the rifle could endanger others. Nevertheless, I was allowed to hunt rabbits and shoot at targets with the small cartridges in the near vicinity of the house, in the mesquite covered acreage now crossed by Highway 87. I learned about the power of even the small shells when one of my friends, also about age twelve, shot my rifle at a bird on the electric line (that we called a high line) coming to our house, and clipped the line in two as neatly as can be imagined. We had to call on the company for repair. Fortunately, a lineman lived in our town and soon made the reconnect. Since he was also a neighbor, my friend and I got a lecture from him as well as separately from our parents.

As might be expected from a boy, the rifle got a little rough treatment. I didn't have a gun case, so it rode in various places in whatever vehicle we traveled in, and the stock got a few dings. Once, sitting on the high bridge over the river, I was shooting at gourds that were washing down the North Concho as the river was rising after a rain. I was in high school by then and a couple of girls had also come to watch the river rise. I digress to note how we took any opportunity to break the daily routine. Just possibly so as to maintain their attention, I was firing rapidly as there were many targets on the rolling crest. When the clip emptied, I pulled the spring holder to eject it. And it did so, right into the river below me. So, my rifle became a single shot for some time. Apparently, one wasn't supposed to break or lose the clip, as replacements weren't available locally. I was delighted, years later, to find a clip in an antiques store.

The rifle resided in many closets over the years, being used some, but giving way to a much lighter plastic-stocked model when my boys were old enough to begin to learn to shoot. One winter, perhaps thirty-five years after its purchase, I carefully stripped, sanded, and refinished the stock. It has been used hardly at all since, but still shines in my glass fronted gun case. The case shows the guns, but has a cable securely locked through their trigger guards as another reminder of how times have changed since my grandfather's rifle rested openly on the steer horn hat rack in his home—that was always unlocked.

Because deer were scarce where I grew up and no other big game was available, I hunted birds. That meant shotguns. My dad claimed to not be a good wing shot, so I tried to be. Doves on the wing still cast serious doubts on that ability from time to time. The

.410 was, of course, adequate for dove and quail but had the distinct disadvantage of being a single shot. It also put forth a small pattern that called for accuracy. It served its purpose well, as a gun for me to learn with, and for two of my younger cousins to learn on as they grew up, and for my two boys as they began to shoot. As with the .22, however, the gun was fairly long and heavy, so a lighter, easier to operate lever action .410 became their "learning" gun. I realized that the old gun was too long for the boys when a small "pump" knot showed up about an inch from the end of the barrel. One of the boys must have touched the ground with the muzzle and then fired without noticing it. It still shoots all right, but now gives an excuse for missing, in that the pattern may have been affected.

With no noticeable trace of modesty I used it to down a pheasant on the wing at over forty yards a few years ago and loudly drew attention to the feat. Since the limitations on punishment must surely have expired by now, I confess that I mistakenly bagged a hen rather than a cock. The attention of my hunting companions quickly shifted from my aim to my more general eyesight and powers of observation, or lack of same. That was my helping of crow for the day. Other than such an occasional mistake we carefully follow game laws and restrictions. We recognize the damage done by poachers, out of season and night hunters, and the need for conservation. We recognize, however, that our ancestors hunted under different situations and conditions. Hunting for meat, my grandfathers would have been little concerned with limits and seasons. My dad applied his own common sense, even if it conflicted with the existing regulations. Trapping a few quail from a covey, for instance, to provide a meal seemed a forgivable transgression. But times have changed. We want our children and grandchildren to have opportunity to hunt, and for game and hunting venues to be plentiful. We trust that carefully developed game regulations will help that happen.

I've shot a twelve-gauge Browning automatic for more than forty years. My wife asked our dentist friend, an avid hunter, to recommend a shotgun for a Christmas gift for me. He suggested the Browning as one that would last a lifetime, and I believe it will. Only the safety spring has had to be replaced, from clicking it on and off so many times. Even with a recoil pad the Browning "light twelve" will punish a shoulder if it isn't snugged in tight, a lesson taught to me more than once. Although it looks the same as it did years ago, it seems to grow heavier over a day's hunting, so a similar, but lighter, twenty gauge gun is beginning to get a little more use.

A new bride, my wife went deer hunting with me the first winter we were married. I was in service, on leave from Ft. Bliss. We went to my parents' home for Christmas. Deer were reported on a ranch just a mile or so up river from town, so we went out well before daylight to take a stand. It was so cold we could barely stand it, even huddled together. About dawn we heard a crackling of ice and leaves as a deer walked past. By the time I could get a rifle up, it was gone. Another never appeared. Peggy was finished. She has never again wanted to go on a hunt, except to eat at camp for ladies night. She has gone bird hunting with me a few times, staying in the car with a magazine, wondering why we were taking so long. When I hunted with my dad, uncles, and/or cousins, we sometimes set up a tent, an unwieldy ex-army model that took a half-day to erect and another half-day to take down. It could be kept reasonably warm and made good storage.

One night at each of those outings we hunters cooked and the wives came for dinner cooked on an open fire. We never cooked the recent game, if any, tending to steaks instead. And our potatoes, if not world famous, were at least worthy of a few stars. We "discovered" that if spuds were sliced into a paper bag with substantial amounts of flour, and pepper and salt, they could be uniformly coated by vigorous shaking. Then fried in an inch or so of hot grease they were better than any hash browns or French fries available—then or now. That, of course, was before cholesterol was suspected of being able to make inroads on good tasting food—just as steak sizzling in a little bacon fat in an iron skillet on hot coals has become similarly suspect. My gravy included the crusty residue of the steak, and was always pronounced good. It wasn't as good as my Grandma Ethel could make, but she had decades more experience gained cooking for crews of March Ranch cowboys. But the memory of that steak gravy look and taste is still good.

I began to take our boys hunting when they were small. We hunted deer along the North Concho River near Carlsbad, Texas, where an uncle had a ranch leased. We hunted birds in different places, on the South Plains, off the caprock near the double mountain fork of the Brazos, and in the Water Valley area. Both boys liked to hunt, and still do. We camped out a few times on the North Concho, putting up a small tent and cooking on a campfire. And we stayed with my parents and in San Angelo a few times each, as our base.

Sons Price and Charles, 1979

One of my best days of hunting came on one of the campouts. We pitched our tent near the river, and it was cloudy, cold and damp when we rolled out of sleeping bags at about dawn. We walked toward where the turkey were believed to be roosting, and arrived before good light. But we missed the birds; they were leaving as we arrived and we didn't get a shot. So, we took the Jeep and started driving around the pasture. We spotted the birds going away from us, probably seventy yards away nearing a fence. I stopped and jumped out and grabbed my rifle. As the birds got close enough to the fence to begin to fly over I got one in my scope and fired. The gobbler fell. That was a lucky shot, but the boys were impressed. We had loaded the Tom and started on around toward camp when we spotted a covey of Bob Whites. I stopped, got out my shotgun and got three of them, one on the rise and two singles before the rest disappeared. We continued back to camp and had breakfast. Then we started in the Jeep again. Out away from the river in sparse brush we saw a buck moving, but slowly. I stopped, pulled the rifle out of its case, used the steering wheel as a rest, and got off a shot. I aimed properly at the heart area, but missed my aim. Perhaps from the vibration of the Jeep, or of my heart, the bullet traveled a little further right and cut the buck's jugular vein as neatly as it could have been done with a knife. The deer dropped instantly and bled out right there. We loaded the deer into the Jeep and went back to camp. By that time my dad had arrived at camp, from his warmer bed at home, and had coffee heating. While he skinned the deer and bragged on it as being the best eight-point seen in that area, we cleaned the birds. All was completed by noon. We went back to town and only returned the next day in a drizzling rain to take down our camp.

The boys were raring to go when the next season rolled around. We set up camp well away from the river, near a ranch road and a field with some green. Our luck wasn't so good that trip. Younger son Charles tried some of his cousin Charley's chewing tobacco that, coupled with the sway and bounce of the Jeep on the ranch roads, put him out of commission for an afternoon. It also caused him to give up chewing at an early age—perhaps forever.

We heard a deer snort a couple of times during the night, and had high hopes. However, I missed two or three shots at deer the next morning, and we found neither turkey nor quail, illustrating the feast or famine aspects of hunting. Other hunts in that area accounted for other game, however. Older son Price shot a deer with his new rifle one afternoon, and Charles and I got three turkeys as the light was fading one evening.

The spirits of competition and cooperation are present when hunting in groups. They are intensified in family hunting groups. Hunters compete to bag the most birds or clay pigeons with the fewest shots, or to fill their limit more quickly than their companions. Those same hunters will defer to the individuals having game birds coming more directly toward them, even if within range of both. Pheasant hunters routinely trade positions in walking fields and in alternating walking and blocking roles. Younger hunters often defer to older to take the role of "blocker" at the end of long rows of cut grain. Yet, there is competition to get off the first shot, which can lead to some interesting claims. Four of us were in a Jeep on a ranch when someone spotted a deer. A cousin and I bailed out, quickly took aim, and fired. Someone asked, "Who fired?" We each answered "I did." The buck had fallen, kicking, from where he stood. As one, cousin Charley and I said, "It's probably yours." When we dressed the animal we learned that both bullets had found their mark; either would have been fatal. Competition yields bragging rights to the one who catches the first fish, the most fish and the largest fish. In the field they go to the one that drops the pheasant with the longest tail feather, the most quail, and biggest buck. Cooperation includes hunting for each other's lost game, and helping with dressing and cleaning without regard to who brought down the birds or animals.

It is interesting what we remember about hunting, even when events are long past. Price recalled one time when were hunting with Boyce, a friend, as follows:

> I don't remember if it was dove or quail, but I don't
> think we saw either (or cougars for that matter). We

practiced shooting a .22 in a small limestone canyon to pass the time. We all heard a shot ricochet up the canyon wall, and Boyce (who had been seated well behind the shooter) said something about the high whining sound. As he finished we heard a small thump, and he said that the bullet had landed next to him. He looked around on the ground for a moment and picked up the deformed bullet head. I think of that incident each year on November 22nd, although that had to have been over thirty-five years ago.

We also caution each other about danger in crossing a fence with a gun. Each of us hands his gun to another before climbing over a fence, or pushes it under and lays it on the ground before crossing. Other than just common sense, those actions probably stem from a long-ago story of a cousin, in far away 1930s California, who accidentally shot and killed himself crossing a barb wire fence. Cautions extend to driving to and from hunting as well. Vicki was driving their boys to Gonzales to meet Price at a quail lease one afternoon. Price was hurrying to meet them when he rolled his SUV. He was in his seat belt and hardly injured, but his bird dog was thrown from the vehicle and killed.

We have met some interesting people while hunting, from the Hispanic ranch hand who loaned me a large switchblade when I was skinning a deer with a small pocketknife, to the pediatrician who constantly urged pheasant hunters to walk faster across High Plains grain fields, the dentist who was perhaps the worst wing shot in the state, a college administrator whose motivation to go hunting was pre-dawn sausage, gravy, and biscuits at a greasy spoon cafe, to an Arkansas truck driver. The latter invited me to go coon hunting with him and his dogs. When I asked about bringing my boys along, he reluctantly agreed, probably concerned that they couldn't keep up. But we all thrashed around the woods and underbrush at about the same speed along the edge of the Ouachitas in South Polk County deep into the night. The dogs finally treed, and we caught up to them. Clyde handed me his rifle and flashlight and shinnied right up a tall tree after the raccoon. When he got the animal out onto a light limb he began to shake the tree violently. The coon fell out and the dogs pounced on it. Clyde slid down the tree much faster than he had gone up, and dispatched the raccoon. We have laughed many times about seeing that large man grunting with a "whumphing" sound, climbing that tree much like a bear would have, with arms and legs around the trunk. Convinced the boys could keep up, Clyde then insisted that we go back out early to hunt squirrels. So, after a few hours sleep and fortified by strong coffee, we went out again before daylight, into larger woods. As it became light young Charles, probably eight or nine years old, popped a running squirrel off a limb that must have been over forty feet above us. Although it was with a .410, it was still a good shot, and impressed Clyde, who thereafter was ready to take Charles fishing or hunting whenever we went to Arkansas.

Each boy has suggested incidents to illustrate our family involvement in hunting. Charles, in the true oral tradition, tells a story on himself. I had put the boys in two different locations to watch for deer while I returned to camp to start supper. I heard gunfire at the field where Charles was located, and then met him walking back to camp. He relates that I had placed him in a stack of tractor tires in the corner of a field. About eleven years old, he waited with only his head above the tires. He says he fired the 30-30 with open sights eleven times at a deer that came onto the other side of the field—missing every time, having no clue as to distance, but in memory he thinks it may have been five hundred yards. He would have fired more shots, but ran out of ammunition. The one who most liked this tale was Charles' son at age nine, who found it hilarious that his dad would miss eleven times. Now, it may have been only four or five times, as surely I wouldn't have left the boy eleven shells, but it is his memory and his story.

That story related closely to another. Driving along the highway, we spotted several deer in a field where we could hunt, at some distance west of the road. I stopped the car, got my rifle from the trunk, leaving the family in the car alongside the highway, and in street clothes went over the fence and worked my way along some brush toward the deer. I fired three times. In the car, hearing the shots, Peggy reported that Price exclaimed, "Son-of-a-gun, he got three of them." His idea of my prowess was as far off the mark as I was, missing my first two shots without even startling the deer, but getting a small buck with my last shot. I had not been a much better judge of the distance than had Charles in his tractor tire blind.

Those hunts on the North Concho were occasions for family to be together. We were with my parents, then with my mother, and later with her and Bud, her second husband—and with uncles and cousins from time to time. We were serious but sporadic hunters. We didn't have expensive rigs or large hunting leases. We hunted largely on the kindness of others, those who had land, owned or leased, for ranching purposes. Perhaps they shared with us the idea that wildlife doesn't truly belong to anyone, but to all. We never hunted in the tall fenced places where game was fed and handled as a commodity. We never had permanent blinds or guides, but simply tried to figure out where the game might be at a given time and sought them, sometimes successfully and sometimes not. Shared times may be developed in many ways, and hunting is one of those. And it is surprising how many specific memories come from those sporadic hunts.

A college student, Charles stayed a couple of days with his grandmother and step-grandfather. He went hunting in the hills of Coke County, and brought down a small buck that he field dressed and brought back to town. Bud had him hang the deer from a pecan tree overnight to age and cool out for butchering. Charles said it was like a good history lesson, as the older couple told him how they butchered hogs and cured them in the days of their youth. They helped him cut up and trim the deer, and enjoyed doing it. Cleaning deer wasn't always as much fun. Many years earlier Peggy was to cook her first Christmas dinner for the family, then totaling eight. My sister and family came a couple of days early and my parents were coming Christmas day. On Christmas Eve afternoon my dad went out driving and spotted and shot a deer. He field dressed it and brought it home and stored it in the ice house at his grocery store. When they set off early the next morning for Lubbock, he brought the deer along. Peggy was not thrilled to have my dad, brother-in-law, and me in the carport skinning and, in and out of her kitchen, butchering the buck. The house was small, crowded with people and residue from two young children and their gifts, and it was too cold for much outside activity. She prevailed against cooking any of the venison that day, but we stocked the freezer.

Earlier, I mentioned cleaning and eating one's kill. Over the years I have tried some unusual game. The first I remember is a 'possum my grandmother roasted, in a covered iron pot, in their fireplace. She baked sweet potatoes with it, and they were easily the bulk of my meal. Almost all the 'possum went to feed the chickens.

Len with Sandhill Cranes, Lubbock, 1962

I tried wild rabbit, at an uncle's ranch out of Ft. Stockton, where I also trapped and ate my first quail. There have been many dove, pheasant, some turkey, and a well-remembered wild duck. That duck probably caused a severe cold, since I dropped it over a partly frozen pond, and had to wade out to retrieve it and shiver in wet clothes for an hour or so after. I didn't care for the dark duck meat, even though it was cooked with dressing. Neither did I care for Sandhill Crane, but we dutifully baked and tried to eat one of the big birds that I brought down.

Another meat that I tried to eat, without success, was raccoon. As a teenager in a pear grubbing camp, I took my .22 and a head-light, and accompanied by two men from the crew, went night hunting. As we walked up to a windmill, standing stark in the night sky with a large concrete water tank beside it, I spotted eyes shining atop the tank. The raccoon continued to be held in the light as we approached and I shot it. The two men skinned the animal and asked the cook to serve it at breakfast, which he did, cutting it up, flouring it, and frying it like a chicken. It didn't taste like chicken. With each chew the first bite seemed to grow larger, and it was my last. I did try armadillo, in another pear camp and from another cook; it may have tasted like chicken, as it was at least edible. I had squirrel and jack-rabbit in other camps, though I ate little of either. And I suppose I've eaten a little of the prover-bial crow, but infrequently.

Peggy has valiantly assisted with the final cleaning of game, par-ticularly birds, over the years. Perhaps she was diligent because she didn't trust that all of the shot had been removed. She has cooked several kinds, protesting all the while that she doesn't care for any wild game although she eats her share of quail and turkey, if not of dove or pheasant. We have had venison, and gift cuts of elk and buf-falo. No bear yet. One was killed on our place in Arkansas, but we were in Lubbock and couldn't claim a roast. I suppose frog-legs count, too, as the boys shot big bull-frogs around a ranch pond much faster than I could clean them, and we all tried that supposed delicacy. As I write, there is a breast of pheasant, wrapped in bacon, baking in the oven. It had been in our freezer for more than a year, but still looked fresh and now smells good. As we eat it, I'll remember again leaving with both grown sons on a mid-December, frosty cold, fog shrouded, early morning drive for the pheasant season opening day breakfast at Providence Church, north of Plainview in Hale County. I'll remember the shot that brought down the bird. And I'll remember going there in years past with a now deceased friend, and at other times with other friends. Even though I may overcook the meat, it'll still taste sweet.

As time has gone by and both boys have families of their own, our opportunities to hunt together have become fewer, but no less memorable for me. We have gotten together for pheasant hunts, for one goose hunt near Houston, for quail hunts, and opening day for dove is a family tradition, whether we are together or not. It seems we begin calling each other more often as dove season approaches, and after opening day to see how each of us fared. We frequently hunt separately with other friends, and hunt alone also. Even when we hunt dove together in the early fall we are likely to be spaced widely apart, spending only the travel time as time with

Grandson Charley Ross (age 9), his first buck

each other. But it is still a shared experience, and one that is and has been important to me.

Our oldest grandson shot his great-great-grandfather's .410 when he was ten. There are others to try it yet, and time for them to be connected in the talk of the hunt of that day and those of years before. The latest manifestation of the generational bonding via hunting is a picture of our nine-year-old grandson with his first buck, a heavy bodied ten-point Whitetail, taken earlier this season. The picture was transmitted directly from the field by his dad, via Internet technology, allowing us to share in the excitement in almost real time. And the event will be fixed in memory through future conversations and, I'm sure, by the mount that his parents will have made.

As hunting spaces dwindle and distance and time impinge on occasions for getting together, ostensibly to hunt but also to be involved with each other, each time becomes more memorable for me. My most recent trophy is the tail fan of a big turkey, taken the past spring. It was almost too easy, except that it required a three-hundred-mile trip. A neighbor and I drove from Lubbock, stopping for award winning barbeque at Dickens, to his son's place on the Brazos River near Rhineland. We picked up decoys and drove on a nice ranch road to an elevated fiberglass deer blind, about a hundred yards from an automatic feeder, and unloaded our guns and ice chest. I drove the pickup around a stand of trees, walked the fifty yards back, and we set out the decoys, climbed into the blind and made ourselves comfortable in two swivel chairs. It was a pleasant spring day, so we didn't need the propane heater already in the blind. We opened the window slots on three sides, ate our lunch, drank soft drinks, and watched. When we spotted a turkey a few hundred yards away, across a field, we began to use the hand held, battery operated, recorded sound, turkey call. That one paid us no attention, so we went back to the chips and Cokes. Two other Toms showed up in about an hour, far away but easing toward us. Our call must have been heeded, because one came close enough and got in the open enough for my twelve gauge. I suppose a purist could have used a .22 or a scoped deer rifle, or even the old .410, but I wasn't going to miss and have my neighbor recall it and give me continuing helpings of crow in the future. It was a big turkey, going over twenty pounds, providing a couple of nice turkey breast roasts in the freezer.

The hunt was far too easy, and the beard isn't long enough to brag about, but of course I kept it. It will be a conversation starter with kids and grandkids until dove season comes again, just a few months away. Hunting has been an integral, constant, enjoyable part of my life, and of our family generations before and after.

Lions in Botswana

MAKING A DRIVE IN BOTSWANA

by Francis Edward Abernethy

Making a drive has been a hunting custom as long as man has been a man—and even before. When a community's survival depended upon a successful hunt it was important that early man hunted for game in the most efficient way. One way was to form a long line of hunters spaced ten or twenty feet apart. They moved forward, side by side, making a drive and flushing and killing any game that started in front of them.

Men still make drives. Quail, pheasant, and grouse hunters line up and seine the grasslands, shooting the birds that rise in front of them. Sometimes four or five men will space themselves in a line a hollering distance apart and make a drive to flush deer out of their brushy hiding places.

The point is that making a drive is a contemporary hunting custom among humans that is steeped in antiquity, and I believe that it is also a much older instinct. After a trip to the Okavango Delta in Africa in June of 1996, I wrote Thad Sitton the following letter (dated 11/26/08), in which I discussed my views on the genetics of hunters:

> Did I ever tell you about the time in Botswana, when we came on this pride of lions preparing for a hunt? We had been tracking them for over an hour in a Land Rover. We finally came upon them just after sundown in a long clearing at the edge of a field of man-tall grass. I guess there were about a dozen lions in all. About half were full-grown females and the rest were adolescents and teenagers. They were all flopped around, sniffing each other, playing grabass, taking naps—totally

unconcerned. They greeted each other with friendly social sniffs and ambled around, never in a hurry, quite calm, seeming to swap the gossip of the day.

Then on some invisible (to us) signal they began sauntering along the clearing, with singles stopping in place about every six to eight feet. They looked disorganized, but in the end they were stretched out in a discernIble line, grownups at both ends and scattered through the middle. Most were sitting. Some of the young lions were lying down, dozing. At another imperceptible signal the pride of lions all came awake, arose, and casually ambled off to our left and into the tall grass.

I had lost track of time, but it seemed to me that all this lining up took around twenty to thirty minutes, maybe less. This mixed pride of lions, as trifling and lazy as they looked in the process, became a deadly pack of hunters, seining the grass and scrub brush for game.

That was the last we saw of that pride, but the hunters were successful; they killed a kudu down near the pond below the camp, and we could hear the roars of the old males as they came to the feast. They were still hanging around the kill talking about the hunt when the sun came up. Just like folks!

I was sitting on a deer stand yesterday afternoon—like a big cat at the edge of tall grass—when I heard a twig snap. My head snapped around, my nostrils instinctively flared, and I could feel the muscles of my ears pulling them back to attention. I will bet that my pupils contracted at the same time. Just like a cat.

Ab in a tree, listening like a big cat

Riley Froh

THE DECLINE OF THE POACHER AS FOLK HERO IN TEXAS

by Riley Froh

Either poaching develops good hunters or else great hunters make good poachers, but the two fit together exceptionally well. However, one cannot be both a poacher and a sportsman. Certainly, trespassing on private property to take game and fish is best done by the slob hunter, someone who thinks only in terms of himself, neither caring for the future of wildlife nor the condition of his country, a selfish person of limited vision for the greater good of his surroundings. But the poacher is a legitimate folk character, larger than life and invoking all kinds of images in Texas—some, unfortunately, favorable.

The most seductive image of the Texas poacher is the subconscious connection in the public eye with the legendary and romantic archer Robin Hood, who slew the King's deer with deadly accuracy and robbed the rich to provide for the poor. This thief is acceptable in history only because of his time, and he hardly transfers to today's market. Toleration of such habits in the twenty-first century is out of place. In the framework of Merry Old England, catching game illegally represented a steed of a different hue. It all started when Robin dropped a fine buck out of need, dispatched a King's forester to save his own life, and then remained in Sherwood Forest out of necessity as a wanted man, an outlaw, and a first-rate poacher. Here he would operate in the heart of Britain's version of the Big Thicket, righting wrongs inflicted on the "people" while staying alive by hunting. Maid Marian was sort of in and out of camp, so to speak, to provide other needs. Old Rob was a happy man as long as he could outwit the Sheriff of Nottingham.

There was a brief time when the twentieth-century poacher in Texas operated out of the need to feed his family. The public excused it as "gleaning in the fields." However, except for some instances during The Great Depression, this picture is as false as a typical politician's claim of possessing a compassionate nature. If every law-breaker who cites children's hunger as a reason for taking game by criminal means got a job instead of going hunting, his children would eat better. To accept hunger as an extenuating circumstance today is a sympathy born out of silly sanctimony; this technique is the very thing defense attorneys have used for decades to defend their clients, and it works every other time because so many jurors enjoy soap operas.

For an excellent visual example of the admired Texas poacher, watch the outstanding movie *The Return of the Texan*, set in the 1940s and based on Fred Gipson's wonderful novel *The Home Place*. (Hollywood has always understood "The Texas Mystique." Producers and directors put *Texas* or *Texan* in the title as a drawing card, and no other state will serve as well. *The Texas Chainsaw Massacre* comes to mind.) In *The Return of the Texan,* Walter Brennan (Grandpa Firth) sneaks onto the Richard Boone (Rod Murray) ranch to take a turkey. Of course, our sympathies are with Brennan, a retired Texas Ranger still using the old Winchester '73 of his glory days. On the other hand, Boone plays a rich, selfish, mean, and grasping land owner, and the actor does a fine job playing this villain. Brennan is his likable best. His shot to break the turkey's neck gives him away, but on foot he easily eludes Boone, who is slowed down on his horse by the hill country brush. Still, Walter can't resist firing a few shots, and kicking up dust enough to spook the horse and get Boone thrown. And so here we have the poacher as folk hero. Never mind that it was Boone's land and that Brennan was trespassing.

Actually, what is clear to me from having observed for years the contradiction of such folk heroes is that they simply like to break the law. Poaching is only one degree in their shadowy lives. Typically, game thieves operate at night, so they frequently hold down fairly good day jobs. They delight in the added thrill of illegality plus the chance of being shot at by the land owner. Curiously, boldness rather than stealth might also be their stock in trade. They can be strangely nonchalant when stopping by woods on a snowy evening—or any other time for that matter. But little boys in Texas on the school playground used to talk about them as though they were war heroes, great athletes, or even champion ropers and riders. They wanted to grow up just like them, noble outlaws of field and forest. And many did.

My good friend Billy Bob was just such a man. A wild teenager, he was thrown out of school at sixteen (yes, dear reader, principals used to be able to toss out recalcitrant youths whose antics disrupted the educational process). Delighted with his freedom, he got a job, promptly got married, fathered a child, and began running women, drinking, carousing, and poaching, sometimes all at the same time since he always carried one or two guns. His take of game became prodigious, his conquest of women even more so. Both activities can have a predatory side when approached the wrong way.

Night or day, he was a road hunter. "People wonder why I drive so slow," he told me. "That's how you keep from stirrin' up the game." His eye was so sharp at distinguishing quail and deer against their built-in camouflaged backgrounds that I often wondered if he had strange powers, some sixth sense at discernment; but as I studied others at their trade over the years, I concluded that this trait was common to master illegal hunters.

Nerves of steel are a must, for when you leave your vehicle on a dark night, doors open, motor running, lights cutting the night while you vault over a "bob-war fence" to go after some downed or wounded trophy buck, you just might draw a crowd, especially if you had just fired a high-powered rifle to announce your presence. But that was the *modus operandi* of so many of these characters. See—I told you they were often admired.

And the true poacher is just as quick to take a fish as to blast a buck. They had great luck "fishing" for catfish. Of course they did. They worked along the bank, feeling up into holes and grasping their prey by the gills. For good reason this method is patently illegal: the catfish loses his sporting chance. On the other hand, grappling requires nerve, strength, and agility. Think about it. Who knows what one might grab along a river bank? "Water moccasins won't bite underwater," Billy Bob assured me. I wouldn't count on it. I still get the shivers thinking about it.

Another crooked practice is called "telephoning" the fish. This requires an old crank wall phone, which is the same instrument of torture reportedly used by county sheriffs throughout the South. Lawmen attach wires to the most sensitive areas of a suspect, give their machines a crank, and get a confession without leaving a mark on the "guilty" party. "Calling up" the fish employs longer wires, and any poacher worth his salt knows exactly where to find the prey.

Telephoning is the poacher-preferred quiet method. However, explosives are sometimes used. Dynamiting is much more common in Louisiana than in Texas for the simple reason that a Cajun is much more apt to pull such a stunt ("Hell no, me no coonie, me from Port Ar-ture."). Blowing up fish is one thing Billy Bob never did, even though he is serving as an example of a brash Texan devoted to taking game and fish illegally.

Of course, Billy Bob had his rivals. Henry, the furtive hunter I observed for a lifetime, stayed in character to the end. Henry would sneak onto someone's property, but only if it was a sure thing. He took most of his illegal game on legal leases. Henry was a Depression Baby, a member of the Greatest Generation during WWII, who never got over the times of poverty when as a teenager he shot out of season just to eat. But he became a fanatic hunter after the War when he could afford to buy plenty of meat. He just liked to kill deer.

On his lease at Hondo, he noticed that by the glow from the Hondo Drive-In Movie a mile away he could skylight nice bucks where they crossed a tank dam. Henry dropped many a fine deer at midnight. Of course, when the hunting resumed legally at sunrise the next day he was up in his stand to take another. He was very adept at using family members' tags to kill more than his own limit of two bucks a year. He also had other ways of getting past a warden's game check, but strangely, he was tolerated by others on the same lease who played by the rules. It was just a different time with different attitudes. There were always those of us who disapproved, but we were in the minority at the time.

Henry had a capacity for timing to get the best leases. He had a small place sandwiched on each side by big ranches, and he exploited this situation to the hilt. "I can kill a deer a day out of that stand," he said, and I think he may have. Like most poachers I have known, Henry had a one-sided philosophy: he possessed no capacity for understanding animals who would "steal" from him. Coons figure that corn put out for deer tastes just as good to them. And they can go the deer one better. Rather than having to wait for the timer to go off, those mischievous, bandit-eyed burglars climb up and shake out a meal at all hours. Henry employed an incredibly mean-spirited defense against these clever fellows. He nailed treble-hooks from his fishing box to the tree limbs leading to his feeder. These fish hooks bit deeply into the coon's paws, drawing out chunks of hide and hair from their cute little feet when they tore themselves away. The triumphant joy Henry expressed when he showed me those bloodied grapples haunts me to this day.

Henry and Billy Bob usually worked alone. Poachers hunting in pairs provoke double trouble. Weldon and Joe worked together in the maintenance department of a Hill Country college, right on the edge of some of the finest deer country around. "The whole state of Texas is my deer lease," Weldon trumpeted, and it pretty well was. For years he and Joe blazed away at all hours of the day and night, using .22s when the sun shown and larger calibers under the moon. They really were experts at creeping through the brush in their tennis shoes. Joe told me he could move like an Indian in the woods, and I watched him and he could. Both were devoted and dedicated alcoholics and they set records consuming strong drink while taking game. A fellow worker told me that you

had to be careful when moving anything around in the maintenance office, for bottles hidden by these two characters would fall
out of the most unlikely places.

They had a running feud with two game wardens who knew
them by name and face. Stopping Joe and Weldon became an
obsession with the law men, but their goal was never achieved.
The pair of poachers knew every trick in the book. One time they
even played a practical joke on the wardens and got away with it.
Locating an old lever-action Winchester rusted and battered but
still serviceable, they bought the thing for a song. Each pair of
protagonists stalked the other and the hunters were on the look-
out for a stake-out. Armed only with their throw-away gun, Weldon
drove and Joe did the shooting, firing the whole magazine into a
cedar break. He then slung the gun into the brush. Weldon
burned out with great screeching of tires and noise. He stayed just
under the speed limit and skidded to a halt at the road block. The
wardens searched the vehicle top to bottom, finding neither
weapon nor game. Chagrined, they let the two suspects—who
were rubbing it in excessively—go free. I would like to be able to
say that Joe and Weldon were later apprehended during one of
their capers, but such is not the case. Justice is often incomplete
this side of the grave.

In the end, the joke was on the pranksters. I had seen that gun
they tossed away and knew what it was really worth. It was a collec-
tor's item, a gem of a find. I later searched unsuccessfully for that
rifle along Devil's Backbone many times. It may still be there, a
silent reminder of a time long gone.

It was John Barleycorn and not the long arm of the law that
finally stopped these two freebooters. They stole grain alcohol
from the biology lab at the college, mixed it with ground up pep-
permint, and went on a real drinking spree, much of which they
couldn't remember. Their kidneys were never the same, and they
suffered other maladies related to their excesses. Gradually, their
health failed, and prowling the woods just never provided the old
appeal. But they retired from the game as legends in their own

time, admired by too many and condemned by too few for the good of the community and game laws of the state.

In an attempt to justify their flaunting of the law, Weldon and Joe played the role of two modern-day Robin Hoods by providing wild turkeys to poor families at Thanksgiving. Of course, for the same time and expense they could have purchased them at the local grocery store instead of stealing game from land owners and the Great State of Texas. But that wouldn't outwit the game wardens or maintain the authenticity of their roles as poachers with hearts of gold.

One of the biggest prizes for the Texas poacher is to sneak onto the world famous King Ranch. I suspect that a few have accomplished this feat but not as many as brag about having done so. I also doubt that as many illegal hunters have vanished in this vast acreage as legend would have it. Still, the place does have its secrets. There are isolated mesquite thickets in the heart of the ranch where a body never would be found. It's a fascinating piece of property.

One low-class fellow I know for sure has hunted the King Ranch illegally, using a .22 with a nipple from a doll's baby bottle on the end of the barrel for a silencer. Another who is telling the truth about taking a deer on the place crept in from adjoining property, but I don't think he ventured very far. In both cases the trophy bucks they harvested set records. The risk was great but the rewards proved excellent. My advice would be that crooked hunters choose to trespass somewhere else. The Ranch is incorporated now, more businesslike, and security is even tighter than in the old days. The best approach for slob hunters is to lie about having hunted on the property. Few sportsmen are going to believe a braggart anyway.

One sound way to avoid the game laws of Texas is to be above the law. If the noted historian J. Evetts Hailey can be believed, Lyndon Baines Johnson was a known practitioner of this privileged approach. On his ranch he maintained a modern tower complete with elevator for illegal night hunting. A powerful search light froze the bucks in their tracks in the darkened oat fields. Supposedly, he really enjoyed demonstrating to a variety of dignitaries his power to do as he pleased more than to show off any hunting skills. Curiously, this deplorable behavior impressed the gentry more than it should have, but such is the nature of some politicians, and such was the nature of poaching in Texas down through the 1950s.

No one ever crossed Lyndon Johnson over his Whitetail hunting. It was in dove season where he was challenged about taking more birds than allowed and blasting them after sundown. His challenger was a law enforcement officer who took his oath of office seriously, regardless of the political nature of the law breaker or the number of friends he had in low places. It took Johnson seven years to get this dedicated warden fired but the reward for vengeance was great. The conscientious law man was two years away from a pension, and he lost it all. There was no widespread indignation from the public, which largely took the view that the game warden was a hard-head. All he had to do was to look the other way.

Refreshingly, times have changed. Currently, the best known combination of Texas good-ole-boy hunters, Governor Rick Perry and writer and singer Ted Nugent, hunt strictly by the book. Nugent sits on the board of the NRA and Perry publicizes sportsmanship. Both men represent a striking contrast to the cynical flaunting of the game laws so common by the rich and powerful fifty years ago.

The jury is still out on exactly what happened recently on the Armstrong Ranch, which, incidentally, lies across the road from the King Ranch and is just as famous for feudal living at its very best. It appears that former Vice-President Dick Cheney and his party were hunting quail legally when Cheney blasted his attorney in the side of the face. The official version is that it was an accident. Still, the victim was a lawyer and some feel Cheney has a mean look. Texans have always had a tolerance for husbands who shoot their wives' lovers. Perhaps the statute could extend to shooting lawyers who professionally do to clients what some men do to other men's spouses. But few in Texas got as excited about the Cheney shooting as the rest of the nation, since it's not that big a deal to catch a few birdshot on a hunting trip in the Lone Star State.

Texans do get worked up about poachers these days. The only thing constant in history is change, and attitudes about hunting have altered greatly in Texas. The poacher label is now synonymous with terms such as wife beater or child molester. The poor illegal hunter is besieged by lawmen, citizens of all walks of life, informants, boy scouts, and brownies.

To understand the demise of the poacher as folk hero in Texas, follow the money. Gradually, between those wonderful, restriction-free days of the 1950s and the present, deer became an important cash crap for landowners who began to look at poachers the way rural Texans have always despised any predator; it didn't take long for managers of deer herds to view an illegal hunter as no better than a coyote. No rancher in Texas has the toleration of the coyote that folklorist J. Frank Dobie promoted. The modern poacher has to watch his step.

Moreover, Texas Parks and Wildlife maintains billboards with all the right catch words. Dial "Operation Game Thief" to report illegal hunting. In the background is a shady looking character of no attraction. Poachers are poachers, but a thief is a crook.

The funniest thing is the deer decoy trick, all caught on video tape. The game wardens call the model Bucky; they place Bucky in the most desirable and likeable spots on the country dirt roads frequented by both poachers and slob hunters. There he stands, bold and appealing, just beckoning for a low-class person of even lower degree than usual to blaze away. The concealed warden pushes a remote and Bucky will turn his head to watch the vehicle. The cameras roll and in no time a pickup will slide to a halt, reverse back, and the driver will fire at this once in a lifetime opportunity to bag a real prize. It's all caught on film: the double take by the shooter; the second shot; the second double take; and finally just as the wardens skid to a stop on both sides, the third ineffective shot. Sometimes the lawbreaker has a son or daughter in the cab being trained in methods of illegal hunting. The cha-grinned hick is caught and preserved on celluloid in his infamy, right there in front of the family. Oh, what a lesson for both father and child. There is visual proof of a clear choice to poach or not to poach. He can't effectively plead that he didn't see the decoy but rather was shooting at a knot on a tree. He is cited not for shooting at a deer but for discharging a firearm from the cab of a vehicle on a public road. He's snookered no matter how good his lawyer is. And it ain't entrapment. All he has to do is to obey the law. The poacher quickly loses his charm when caught red-handed.

But comic relief soon fades in the reality of enforcing the game laws. All too often a warden dies in the line of duty, and logically this is to be expected. Unlike other law enforcement jobs, the game warden is faced with an armed suspect almost every time he makes a stop. Oh there are a few unarmed illegal fishermen, but not many. Most of these are packing, too. It's the manly thing to do. For a number of reasons, those who break the game laws blaze away at wardens. Sometimes, they're hyped up on drugs or alcohol—or just overrun with emotion; it's not much of a step to fire on somebody "messin' with 'em" at a cer-tain point.

The public is no longer amused. Juries are no longer sympa-thetic. Sentences are growing longer and longer. The poacher is finally seen for what he is: a person of low degree, despicable rather than admirable, and not the stuff folk heroes in Texas are made of.

It is no surprise that our state—with its unique history of vio-lence and individuality, its cult of doing whatever you're big enough to do, its long ties to the frontier mentality, and its Alamo image—leads the nation in the number of game wardens killed in the line of duty. Seventeen have died between 1919 and the fall of 2010. Maine is closest with fourteen. The average nationwide is five. But trigger-happy poachers better take note. Texas also leads the nation in handing down and carrying out death penalties. The public is tired of the rising crime rate. Now that poachers are lumped in with other lawbreakers of all stripes in the public mind, the free ride of the slap on the wrist is over. If you want to dance, you are going to have to pay the fiddler these days. No more cases of manslaughter. The charge from now on is going to be murder. The illegal hunter who in 2007 killed the last warden shot in the line of duty is now facing the death penalty; and there is little public sympathy for his plight.

Still, it wouldn't be Texas if we could simply conclude that the poacher as folk hero was over forever. Gradually, hunting in Texas and the nation is becoming too expensive for the middle class. I am beginning to hear rumblings among average sportsmen of good manners about their lack of opportunity to follow their favorite pastime because of skyrocketing costs for leases and out of state fees. I hear talk of "hunting where I damn well please" from outdoorsmen who would have never uttered such a sentiment a few years ago. If hunting does become a privilege only the rich can enjoy, as it was in Jolly Old England in the time of Robin Hood . . . well, *Quien Sabe?*

Frank Mayhew

NOCTURNAL WOODPECKER

by W. Frank Mayhew

The "afternoon" was only slightly half-over and already that day's sun, which could only be described as weak, waning, and indifferent, was seen scurrying over the southwestern horizon. Hiding in the lengthening shadows, the cold-weather gods, with little to fear, boldly strode forward, announcing their evil intentions for the approaching night. Their single digit temperatures were already audaciously nipping at the heels of the few fading remnants of that pusillanimous sun.

It was going to be a cold night, a very cold night, exactly what I had been hoping for. Looking forward to a few days of peace and solitude, I had set up camp the day before, deep in the East Texas woods. This trip had become an annual event for me.

My family had long ago come to recognize that a few of us need some time alone, to sort out all that has gone before, and to plan for that which we know will be coming. For me it is a time of rationalizing and rejuvenation. As I mentally go over the recent events of my life I begin to rationalize their causal behavior patterns, both mine and other peoples'. Once I reach a level of acceptance, the behavior and the events are then filed away to be retrieved only on an as-needed basis. To a psychologist this is called a coping device, and this particular device is called "compartmentalization." The psychology community is split as to whether compartmentalization is a good thing or a bad thing.

As far as I am concerned there is no debate; compartmentalization has allowed me to deal with some very traumatic events without allowing the events themselves to control my life. There is not and never will be continuous crisis in my life; I simply cannot live that way. The completion of the rationalization process is a signal that I am now free to absorb all that Mother Nature has to offer. This second process, the absorption or rejuvenation process is a very spiritual time for me. A state of blissful solitude is essential for both phases, reflection and mystical, and while both are valuable the later stage is most important to my well being.

Using a four-wheel drive Jeep, and its heavy electric winch, I would set up my small canvas-covered camper as far back on the Sabine Hunting Club lands as possible. My camper which, according to the manufacturer's propaganda sheet, could sleep seven adults, came equipped with a three-burner propane stove, a small sink with a ten-gallon water reservoir, a hand pump, and a small propane-powered refrigerator. As the reader will see, the refrigerator, or rather its power source, will play an important role in the story that follows.

As stated earlier, the refrigerator is powered by propane gas, and in order to conform to certain safety regulations the burner for the refrigerator can only be accessed from the outside. A small, louvered aluminum door, located on the back side of the camper, protects the burner and its electric ignition system. The heat from the burner is vented through the louvers.

For several years I had used a small, isolated hill as my campsite, as it afforded good drainage from Texas' predictable winter rains. Once again I positioned my camper on the edge of this little knoll.

Transporting all of the needed essentials, including an ample supply of liquid refreshments and several good books, there was little need for me to "go out," and even less need for anyone to "come in." If everything went as planned, which it seldom did, I would usually enjoy several days of glorious solitude before anyone discovered I was there. Once discovered, it was as if others assumed a single camper had to be in need of company, so here they would come, usually bearing little other than hunger and thirst. Most were willing to forgo their own previously planned activities in order to keep me from dining or drinking alone. Such great sacrifices had to be rewarded, I suppose.

Cold weather has always enhanced the camping experience for me, if for no other reason than it serves to discourage visitors. In the past, on very cold clear moonlit nights I would ease out of camp and make my way down an old log road to a nearby beaver pond. By staying in the shadows, and by paying attention to wind direction and avoiding the noisy gravel-covered lanes in the road, I usually could make it to the pond without alarming anything that might be stirring at that time of night. Also, by staying in the shadows, my eyes were fully adjusted to whatever level of light was available.

There is a whole world of nighttime activities that many of us never have a chance to see. For instance, I have stood completely mesmerized as a magnificent owl silently lifted off from one of the huge sentinel cypresses which ring the beaver pond. With a six- or seven-foot wingspan the great owl still managed to maneuver through the trees in absolute silence. The only clue that death was on the wing was a brief tremulous cry heard as the owl lofted its small, hapless prey back to the same perch from whence it had come.

Another time on a bright moonlit night I stood at the edge of the pond watching a beaver on its way to work. He deftly skirted a raft of sleeping Mallard ducks as he made his way towards a leak at the end of a dammed-up culvert. As he neared the culvert I detected a presence in the roadway above the culvert, and there standing in the road were several deer. What made this so amazing to me was that not more than a minute or two before I had scanned that very area, and saw nothing. What was even more amazing was the fact that in order to reach that spot those deer had to have passed within ten to fifteen feet of me, and I had not spotted them or them me.

I am continually amazed at how some animals can move ever so quietly, even through dense brush. However, I have come to believe that contrary to the popular stereotype, cats are not necessarily the stealthiest animals in the forest. For my money, except for their somewhat exuberant loquaciousness, especially during the breeding season, owls are the quietest animals. I have watched huge owls launch themselves from rather small limbs without disturbing the limb at all. Their ability to move silently through the trees is legendary, and quite often lethal.

Late one day, while on what had proven to be a non-productive bow hunting excursion, as I was on my way back to camp, I decided stop and wait out the last rays of light. For my "stand" I selected an old fence post which was a foot or so shorter than me. When nothing of merit had appeared I decided to head on back to camp. Just as I was pushing off from the post I sensed, or "felt" a disturbance in the air behind me. As I looked over my shoulder my vision was filled with the sight of a huge owl, wings cupped for landing, talons extended, not more than a foot or so from my head. The owl was attempting to land on "my" post. One of us yelled an obscenity or two. Since I was a few inches taller than the top of the post, as I conjured up what could have happened, it suddenly occurred to me that my quivering knees meant that I must be really tired, so I sat down at the base of the post and rested a while before trying to walk again.

While owls—and cats and deer and several other animals—can lay claim to being quite stealthy, few people will challenge my contention that except for the occasional human, feral hogs and armadillos are, without a doubt, the noisiest of animals. Pound for pound nothing makes more noise coming through the woods than an armadillo. But armadillos are usually solitary animals. Hogs are not. They are highly social, and very competitive, and of all the animals observed around the beaver pond, pigs are by far the noisiest drinkers.

On this, the first night of my trip, as is my custom, I made my way towards the pond. When the temperature is bitterly cold, as it was this night, it has been my observation that, except for man, most animals have the good sense to conserve their energy. And after an hour or so at the pond I was reminded of that observation, as I had not seen a single living thing.

I decided to curtail my trip to the pond and return to the camper for another of my favorite camping activities, reading. By closing the camper's interior curtains separating the two end sleeping compartments, a single stovetop burner usually provides semi-sufficient warmth for such a reduced interior. A small coffee cup filled with Crown Royal provides another kind of "interior" warmth.

Donning an overly large L. L. Bean woolen "camp robe," I was basking in the warmth from the stove, and the Crown. I gathered my reading material and settled back on what the camper manufacturer euphemistically calls a couch. Engrossed in my reading I reluctantly became aware of a staccato knocking sound coming from just outside the camper, a sound similar in rhythm to that made by a woodpecker. Since I wasn't aware of any woodpeckers that "peck" at night I decided this had to be something else entirely.

From my Marine Corps days I knew that sounds carry extremely well on cold, clear nights, so this sound could very well be from much farther away and could conceivably be from something completely unfamiliar to me. Nevertheless, I grudgingly put aside the robe, slipped on my boots, and went outside for a better listen.

Without a hat or coat or scarf or gloves, I certainly didn't tarry long, but needless to say, other than my chattering teeth, I heard nothing. Rationalizing (there's that word again), that what I had heard must have been a freak wind, or maybe just the camper settling (although since the ground was already frozen I really didn't think that was a possibility), in very short order my curiosity nevertheless departed and I returned to the Crown and robe.

I quickly settled in and once again was lost in my reading. So engrossed was I in the material, I had completely forgotten about the "woodpecker," and then suddenly there he was again, tapping out his monotonous tune. Very quietly I closed my book and silently sat it and the Crown cup on the bedside table. I then sat very still, listening, for a very long time, just to make sure I was definitely hearing something. There it was again, and again, rhythmic in cadence, but pattern-less in timing. While unpredictable in tempo, still, it almost seemed as if I could "feel" the impact of those sounds against the camper itself. After draining the dregs of my cup, I again put aside the robe and grimaced as I once more slid my feet into a pair of very cold boots. However, this time I also put on a pair of insulated coveralls, and a wool "go-to-hell" cap, and a pair of woolen mittens. With a heavy duty flashlight in hand I quietly eased out of the camper, determined to once and for all identify the source of these very irritating interruptions.

First, I stood by the Jeep listening intently. Nothing!

Next, I walked several hundred yards up the road to where I knew there was a large tree stump, where I sat quietly, and listened. Nothing!

After that I walked the other direction towards the beaver pond where I leaned back against a large hickory, and listened. Nothing!

Returning to the camp I methodically circled the camper, shining the light up in the trees and out into the woods. Nothing!

Finally, yielding to the lure of the Robe & Crown I went back inside the camper. This time however, except for the cap and gloves, I kept my cold weather gear on. Not even bothering to try to read I sat very quiet, and very still, listening and sipping. Nothing!

Whether it was the warmth from the fire or the Crown, my mind began to once again 'rationalize' the problem away, in hopes I suppose, that I would not need to conduct any more cold weather investigations. I had almost become convinced that in some strange way I must have imagined all of this, when that damned "peckerwood" started up again. Forgoing my hat and gloves I rushed out of the camper, sweeping the area in all directions with my light. As I stomped down the back side of the camper out of the corner of my eye I detected a slight movement from underneath the camper. Something or someone was under the camper! Ignoring my basic instinct when facing the unknown, which is to "aggressively study the situation from a safe distance," I flopped down on my belly and shined the light underneath the camper, directly into the eyes of a large Catahoula.

Now for anyone who might not know what a Catahoula is, it is a hunting dog, usually dingy yellow in color, with large brown or brindle colored spots. Noted as much for their pleasant demeanor as for their superior tracking and trailing abilities, Catahoulas are favored by many deer hunters.

This particular Catahoula didn't seem particularly upset that I had disturbed his reverie with my belly flop and my bright light. He made no attempt to flee. In fact, he even seemed pleased to see me, so much so that he began to wag his tail, and a long tail it was. It was so long, in fact, that on some of his more enthusiastic wags the tip of his tail would tap the bottom of the camper. Here was my "woodpecker."

As I lay there trying to figure out why he had chosen that particular place to bed down, I realized he was directly below the gas vent from the refrigerator, which was without a doubt, the warmest place to be found around the outside of that camper on that very cold night.

Not wanting to bring him inside the camper with me, but not wanting him to freeze to death either, I opted to put him in the back of the Jeep. I also loaned him one of my son's blankets, for which he acknowledged his gratitude by tapping his tail on the side of the Jeep. Fortunately, this could not be heard from inside the camper. This time when I returned to the camper I didn't even bother with the stove. I simply bid the cold, the Catahoula, and the Crown all a good night and crawled into my sleeping bag.

When the alarm went off early the next morning I sneaked a peek at the thermometer I keep by the front door and saw that it was a "brisk" minus nine degrees—*inside the camper.* I quickly lit all three burners on the stove, turned them up on high, sat the already prepared coffee pot on one of the burners, and promptly jumped back in bed. A little later in my half-dream, half-awake state, I imagined that the "woodpecker" had returned. As I raised my head I realized that what I was hearing was the coffee percolating.

In a few minutes, as the inside of the camper became quite pleasant, I began to stir. Pouring myself a cup of coffee, I sat back on the edge of the bed. I had to smile as I realized I had used the Crown cup from the night before. Before getting dressed I wanted to at least brush my teeth. (If I don't do anything else, in the way of a morning lavatory, I will always try to brush my teeth.) This would prove to be somewhat difficult on this morning.

After several futile efforts to coax a frozen toothpaste tube to give up some of its gel, I held the business end of the tube over the business end of the coffee pot. I was quite pleased at my ingenuity, until I realized I did not have any water with which to rinse my mouth. Other than the water used to make the coffee, I had not had the foresight to "pump" any into another container, and the water in the reservoir was frozen solid.

Coffee is a poor substitute rinse, but it was all I had.

Fortified with clean teeth, and several cups of coffee with just a hint of Crown, I was ready to enjoy another of my passions, which is to walk through the winter woods. As is my custom, I usually take some sort of gun along; otherwise, any local people I might encounter might look at me funny. I do like to hunt, so the gun is really not just for show. However, many times, as was the case on this day, hunting was not my primary objective. I often also take along a small 35-millimeter camera and have managed to get some quite interesting photos, although I do not consider photography to be a major interest and certainly not a hobby of mine. To me these walks are really spiritual in nature (no pun intended).

As I was leaving I opened the Jeep to see if the dog wanted to go too, but he indicated he didn't, so I went alone.

As the first light of dawn began to emerge, a very vigorous north wind also made an appearance. At first it was up high, in the tops of the trees, but finding little to irritate at that altitude it continued its search at ground level, managing even to stir some of the frozen, frost covered leaves which, for mutual support I suppose, had gathered up in great piles on the ground.

Even with the earflaps of my "go-to-hell" cap pulled down as low as they would go and my woolen scarf pulled up over my nose, in just a few minutes my eyes began to water and my exposed cheekbones began to sting from that bitingly cold wind. Fortunately, I had had the good sense to stuff a full-face balaclava in one of my pockets.

Using the trunk of a large pin oak tree as a shield from the wind, I hurriedly donned the light brown, cotton balaclava. The first exposure to the wind convinced me that I might need more than just the balaclava. I managed to stretch the gray, woolen, go-to-hell cap enough so that it would fit over a balaclava-covered head. To complete this fashion statement I also wrapped the camouflage-colored scarf around my neck. With just the area around my mouth and eyes exposed, I now felt quite comfortable and continued my soul-solacing journey.

Earlier, when the wind was still quite high up, I had observed that the small limbs of some of the trees made a clacking sound as they were being buffeted about. Now, as I was leaning against the Pin Oak I heard what could only be described as groaning or moaning sounds, coming from deep within the tree. It was if that old tree, like old folks everywhere will do, was complaining about the cold.

Later, as I stood in a dry creek bed, looking and listening to everything around me, I realized that so far, other than myself, I had not encountered one living thing. I had to laugh as it dawned on me that all of the "dumb" animals were probably still in their warm shelters; it was only the "superior" human who, for no logical, discernible reason, had chosen to subject himself to these bitter conditions. Darwin may have had it all backwards.

Thanks to a dog of dubious antecedents and his involuntary imitation of an imaginary nocturnal bird, my hunt for peace and solitude was unfulfilled on this trip. After one more day and night of "hearing" all kinds of strange noises, I decided it was time to break camp and head back to the real world.

A day or so after I arrived back home a neighbor commented to my wife, "I see you guys have a new dog! What's his name?"

My wife said, "Well, my husband calls him Peckerwood!"

L. B. Harris with Northern Pike, 2007

FISHING TEXAS: A PASSION PASSED ON BY MY DAD

by Jim Harris

In any one genre of Texas fishing, I'm going to come up short, lacking in enthusiasm and skills to hold any fishing records. Say, large mouth bass fishing in tournament-quality lakes. I've done some of it over the years, and even been in the same boat with professional fishermen piloting bass boats that cost $40,000. But I've not done enough of it to say I fished that way with a passion and wanted to do it night and day.

Or fishing for large catfish in a river. I've done a little of it, even in some places using old gallon milk jugs tied together with fifty yards of trotline weighted down with treble hooks loaded with chicken gizzards. I can truly enjoy floating down a slow-moving river checking lines, some of them hanging from a tree branch, but I wouldn't say that I ever developed an insatiable desire for that kind of fishing, either.

And I enjoy wading out into the surf with a floating shrimp bucket tied to a belt and casting a handful of lead weights out into the gulf as far as my 1950s saltwater rod and reel will allow me. In those salty waters, I've caught my share of speckled trout and a fair number of red fish over the years in this summertime ritual, but I never dreamed about the sunburned arms and the spray in the face on winter nights. If I ever had dreams about the jellyfish that one year grabbed hold of my right calf while I waded in the surf, those dreams were nightmares that I thankfully forgot by morning.

How about fast-water fishing below dams? Yes, I've been on the banks of water moving so fast a small boat could be turned into kindling in a matter of minutes. And despite the swiftness of the river, I've caught long and heavy fish in such places. Even as a kid, I've taken home bass and catfish from waters flowing out of dams and enjoyed the time, but today I don't time my summer vacations so I will be in such places when the locks are opened.

There was a period of time when I was in high school that I had a bow and arrow fixed with a spool and line that allowed me to shoot and retrieve carp and drum in the shallows of lakes and rivers. But I quickly tired of that fish-in-a-barrel sport.

By most standards, the kind of Texas fishing I have done over the years would not qualify me for any trophies or medals from an angling organization. And my fishing experiences probably wouldn't serve as the basis for writing an authoritative fishing manual sold in Bass Pro Shops or a philosophical and meditative fishing memoir like Thomas McGuane might write.

However, the fishing experiences I have had across the state of Texas have served as a testiment to the incredibly rich variety of fishing experiences to be had in the Lone Star State, and despite the fact that I came away from those experiences without any sort of savvy that would allow me to give up my day job and start guid-ing for a living, my fishing experiences in different Texas waters have been some of the most rewarding and pleasurable times in my life, times I recall with nostalgia akin to that longing most humans associate with first-time experiences, such as driving a car for the first time or going on a first date, for instance.

I've been fishing for over sixty years, and I have wet a hook in the northeast and the southwest corners of the state. I've fished Lake Texoma in the north and Amistad in the south. I've caught fish in Ray Hubbard Reservoir in East Texas and Spense Lake in West Texas. I've fished large bodies of water, such as Whitney and Possum Kingdom, and I've fished ponds on ranches and farms. I've eaten catfish from the Red River along the border with Oklahoma and from the Rio Grande in the Big Bend. For over a decade I had a house on Cedar Creek Lake southeast of Kaufman, and there I spent many weeks, not just days, landing sandies on calm summer days when you found the fish by watching for the turbulent surfaces where sand bass schooled.

Wherever I have fished in Texas, I have always thought I was in the most beautiful place on the earth, even in some settings urbanites might deem ugly and unfit for human habitation. For instance, I've stood in the mud on the banks of the Pecos River near Mentone, an almost uninhabited and despoiled little burg west of Kermit. The Pecos there is a mesquite and salt cedar-infested stretch of river that can smell like rotten eggs in the summer when the water flow slows to a trickle.

But I love the Pecos at that point just below the New Mexico line in Loving County, the least populated one in Texas, with only sixty-seven residents in the 2000 census, fifteen or so of them being in Mentone, the county seat. Whether I was at the abandoned and nearly empty Red Bluff Lake south of Guadalupe Peak or on the banks of my uncle's stock tank northeast of Dallas, or on a South Padre Island dock, I've always wanted to be no place else or be doing nothing other than trying to entice a fish, small or large, onto my hook. Fishing Texas is just that sort of experience for me, and I still do some sustained, serious, and intense fishing every year, although today much of it is in places other than Texas.

They say most of our major life patterns stem from experiences in our youth, and I think that must be the case with me when it comes to the love I have for fishing. Fishing was one of the first—and certainly most memorable—recreational activities I shared with my father when I was a boy.

Dad was a dedicated and deeply committed minister, a Baptist preacher whose life revolved around the various churches where he served as pastor, counselor, spiritual advisor, and friend to hundreds of men, women, and children in several parts of Dallas County. Church activities were at the center of most of the things our family did. Even summer vacations to exotic places such as New Mexico or Colorado would include some kind of church-related activities.

However, since his death in the summer of 2008, the things I most remember doing with my dad that did not include church were the fishing trips we took to Grapevine Lake, or the lakes at Texoma, Whitney, Lavon, Mountain Creek, and others. And it may seem a little odd, but the most memorable sermons I remember him delivering were those that used the passage from Saint Matthew that used the expression "fishers of men." He referred to that passage in the Bible dozens of times over the years.

Perhaps the list of fishing holes I visited in my youth will tell you the region where I was raised. I was born on my grandfather's cotton farm northeast of Dallas, but I attended public school in Dallas, first in Cockrell Hill and then in the south part of Oak Cliff. To my country cousins, I was definitely a city kid, but in recent years when I've been with the few of those cousins who have survived the barbs and nets of time, I've found myself discussing fishing with them and longing to convince them that my life has really been anchored in the country, along the muddy creeks and around the cattailed tanks that were always within walking distance of their farm homes.

It was my dad's stories about his growing up fishing in Texas that first got me interested in angling. Dad was brought up by his mother and older siblings in the Trinity River bottom lands near Combine, Texas, southeast of Dallas. His father had abandoned the family in the 1920s, and my Granny Harris struggled to provide for her six children, Dad being one of the two boys expected to carry some weight in providing for the four younger sisters.

Living in the country, one of the things the Harrises did to put food on the table was to go fishing in the Trinity, in small creeks that fed the big river, and in a variety of ponds and small lakes that filled the rich bottomlands. Today I see his life then as akin to the lives of the rural characters found in William Faulkner novels, people who also lived in the rich soil of wooded lowlands.

For my dad, fishing during his youth was both a utilitarian and a recreational activity. The latter of those two motivations dominated his leisure time and his fishing experiences for the remainder of his life. For the twenty-five years he had a house on Cedar Creek Lake, crappie fishing was his passion. He liked nothing better than taking his boat down to the Chief Dock, motoring out to below one of the lake's long highway bridges, tying up to a concrete column, and hauling in one- and two-pound crappie until his basket was full.

Crappie fishing was not only his passion, it was also another of the activities at which he excelled. Dad could catch more crappie than anyone I was ever around. He knew just how to hook the small shiners he preferred. He knew just how to place the line where the fish congregated. He knew just how to jig the bait to make the fish think they were in the presence of a tasty snack feeding around the mossy concrete columns.

Dad was so good at catching fish, my wife Mary wrote a poem about his angling skills:

> "Gila Trout"
>   —near the Cliff Dwellings
>
> The Gila Wilderness
> works miracles
> for some
> like Dad
> my husband's father.
>
> Sometimes I pray to the trout or
> lost Indian
> of the cave
> to no avail.
>
> No hook of mine
> nor prayer
> will lure
> the trout
> from shadowed waters.
>
> But Dad has
> Indian patience,

prayerful occupation,
and quietly
acquires trout after trout.

Our line may only
be inches apart
but the lost Indian
whispers and tells
the trout—choose his.

Mary's poem was printed in a small chapbook we published through our family's non-profit company called The Hawk Press. We titled the book "Fishing North America" because we had friends from all over America and Canada who contributed poems to it.

One of the last places my dad and I fished before his death in 2008 was in northern Saskatchewan. He was in his eighties both times we drove up to the fertile lakes and rivers of Saskatchewan, but Dad was still an excellent fisherman. On those two trips to Canada, he caught as many walleye as I did even though I had been fishing the region for fifteen years before he lowered a line into the cold waters.

What he had learned in a lifetime of fishing Texas waters he carried to places such as Lac La Ronge, Deschambeau Lake, and Jan Lake along the Manitoba border in northeastern Saskatchewan. And lordy, lordy did he catch fish from the rented Lund boats the two of us used for two different weeks. Every day we ate fresh wall-eye, and every day we caught and released dozens of fish. On more than one day, we landed over 100 walleye and northern pike. We caught more than enough to tire us out and make us sleep well each night when we had finished our grilled, fried, broiled, baked, or boiled fish dinners.

In Canada Dad was in fishing heaven. He had never even thought about the possibility of catching fish in such quantities. It was a kind of heaven for me just watching him bring in fish after fish after fish each day we were on the water. I will never forget it, and each of the two times I have gone back to fish Saskatchewan since his death, I have spent part of at least a day thanking the fish gods for giving us such a good time there together.

And from now on I will continue to thank the small gods of the lakes for enticing me to learn to fish in my youth. I can remember walking as an eight-year-old to a small creek that paralled Fort Worth Avenue in west Dallas, a tiny stream buried in dense woods and containing so little water no fish could have inhabited it. But in the three-inch-deep water, I put my hook and hoped for fish. After the first futile attempts, I learned that even though I could catch no fish in the creek, I could tie a piece of raw bacon onto a string and haul crawdads out of the water and into the air.

When I was eight or nine years old I wanted to walk to wherever there was water and fish or pretend to fish. After rains when the water flowed over the curbs of my neighborhod streets, I would go stand just out of the rush and lower a hook into the muddy waters. Maybe the water in the street had come from a creek where fish swimmed, I surmised, and they might be carried into the concrete rivers.

I now believe that probably it was enough just standing beside the waters and wishing that I was not only near that which gives us life, not only near that from which we all come, but also near the descendants of those living things that chose to remain below the surface.

Today, most of my fishing is done in places other than Texas, in my home state of New Mexico and in my adopted country of Canada. In the last few decades I have fished the Kenai River in Alaska and the waters off Bora Bora in the South Pacific. Several times I've fished trout lakes and rivers in Colorado. I've camped many nights beside the quality waters of the San Juan River near Farmington, New Mexico.

However, it was fishing in Texas as a child that shaped my attitudes about sport, about the sport of angling, and about the longing deep in all humans to be beside the still and turbulent waters from which we came.

John C. Wolf

THE ANGELINA CAT AND COON HUNTING ASSOCIATION: A SORT OF MEMOIR

by John C. Wolf

In 1966, I had just reached my 23rd birthday. Contrary to the expectations of a good many of my high school teachers, I had completed an M.A. degree and had been gainfully employed as a psychologist at a state residential mental health facility in deep East Texas. Life was good. The future beckoned. The time had come for me to begin to assume my rightful place in the adult world. Some of the more promising young men were finding their places in that world by joining the Jaycees, while others were joining the local Masonic or Elks Lodge.

Some of my friends from college were continuing their foray into the political world we had begun on campus in the Young Democrats by becoming actively involved in the County Democratic Party (in those days nobody openly affiliated with the County Republican Party). As an ex-athlete (defined as one who valiantly attempted successful participation in high school, and even briefly, collegiate athletics), I briefly considered devoting time to recreational league softball and basketball, but was reminded by friends that the only thing worse than being an almost never used substitute in high school was continuing that level of non-participation in places where I had to pay to *not* play. Marriage, further graduate study, and military service were still waiting for me, but for the time being, I was searching for direction, for an outlet, for identity.

Then one day a colleague in my workplace provided me with the opportunity I had been waiting for. As I grew up in East Texas in the '50s, there were plenty of chances to be outdoors. I had been a Boy Scout and had hunted a lot, mostly dove and quail, but on occasion also deer and duck, and in the 1960s East Texas was still by and large unfenced. My friend took time out from his duties as a "custodial engineer" to invite me to join a social club in which he was already a well-established member.

And so, I became a member of the *Angelina Cat and Coon Hunting Association*—membership by invitation only. Dues were $2.00 per year. The "Angelina" portion of the association's name had obvious origins. We were located in Angelina County, Texas. I assumed that I understood the remainder of the title.

The adventure began. My friend, Charles, suggested that I meet him at his home the following evening. I was to be introduced to his coon dogs and ride with him to my first meeting of the Angelina County Cat and Coon Hunting Association, hereafter known as the "Association." I explained to him that although I had a variety of firearms for hunting, I had no dogs of any sort, hunting or otherwise. I was assured that a lack of dog ownership would be no impediment to membership. And strangely, he added that I need not bring any of my hunting firearms along on my first expedition into the unknown world of East Texas "cat and coon hunting."

At about 6:30 p.m., I rolled up to his house. I did not see Charles, but I did see two of the mangiest animals that ever posed as dogs, lounging on the porch. I immediately had some reservation about their usefulness in hunting; when I, a stranger, stepped onto the porch the result was that one of the dogs began snoring even louder than before, while the other dog raised one ear, rolled over into a shady spot, and resumed his inactivity. On the way to the Association meeting, I learned from Charles that I had just met Sam and Red.

The Association meeting took place around a fire in a small clearing on the edge of a big stand of woods. I was to learn many things around the fireside of the Association meetings, but the first thing I learned that particular evening was that Sam and Red were indeed NOT the mangiest animals that ever posed as dogs. There were a lot of other deserving candidates for that honor present that evening. And what was even more important, I learned that as far as cat and coon dogs were concerned, appearances can be very deceiving. When the sun went down and the dogs, of many varied colors and markings, were unloaded by their owners, the sleepy and disinterested looks disappeared. Instead, the dogs were now quivering, whining, and straining against their leashes, all the time leaning expectantly toward the rapidly darkening tree line.

The Association membership gathered slowly but steadily, pickup after pickup pulling up to deposit both men and dogs into the small clearing. Coffee was brewing by the time I arrived, and as with the loaves and fishes, seemed to always be available for the entire duration of the meeting. The membership varied in age, from rather youthful representatives like Charles and me to those of more indeterminate age. There did not appear to be any age limit, and there most obviously was no dress code. I noted that this organization fit my budget if nothing else. Boots and jeans or coveralls were the order of the day (or as it turned out, the order of the night). The business meeting of the Association was rather brief. Someone asked if there was a list of dogs present that evening, and was informed that such a preliminary could easily be accomplished during the hunting portion of the meeting. No one seemed to be particularly interested in the human membership, present or absent.

I was keenly observing the surroundings, and it was soon obvious that the main business of Association meetings was the hunt itself. One thing struck me immediately as being unusual about this hunt. The hunters, or rather the human members of the Association, did not appear to be armed with anything except a liberal supply of chewing tobacco and cigars. I did not see a single firearm among the group. This struck me as strange, because I had a difficult time imagining that the quarry, when located, would surrender and volunteer to return to camp. I was quite young, as I said earlier, so I was more inclined to ask questions then. I asked a nearby Association member, an apparent authority to judge by his age, where the guns were kept. His response was that he wasn't sure who had brought a gun that evening but he was sure that someone had. Another even older appearing Association member offered that a pistol would be as effective as a shotgun or rifle. One question often leads to another. I wanted to ask how it was determined that the single member who was armed would happen to be present at the precise location and time when the quarry was located, since timing is often everything in successful hunting. As a boy growing up in East Texas, I began hunting as soon as I was allowed to carry a .22 rifle, thus qualifying me (I thought) as an expert on hunting. However, I bided my time asking that question.

I did inquire, however, about one puzzling point of the Association and the hunt. I couldn't imagine how much of a sporting challenge hunting cats would be, as it had never seemed to me that cats were especially difficult to locate even without leaving the city limits. So, I felt bound to ask about the cat hunting portion of the Association, especially regarding whether the owners of the cats objected to such a practice. A perceptive veteran member answered, "Why sonny, we don't hunt housecats! We hunt bobcats!" One question does often lead to another, so I felt confident in posing the logical follow-up question, "How often are you successful in getting a bobcat?" I was quickly advised, "I don't recall any of us finding a 'cat, at least not since I have been a member." "How long have you been a member?" I asked. "Oh, about twenty to twenty-five years, I guess," was the response.

Apparently, no one had asked the next obvious question: Why then, did the name of the organization include the reference to "cat" hunting? Several heads quickly skewed around toward me incredulously. "Why sonny, that's why the name of our association is the ". . . cat and coon *huntin'* association. We hunt for them 'cats. When we start *finding* a bunch of them 'cats, maybe we'll change our name."

The niceties of the formal meeting having been so rapidly disposed of, the hunt began. There was a special bustle of men and animals, and suddenly, the dogs were loosed with a single command: "Hunt." Off went the dogs into the dark night, as indeed it was by then. Quite soon nothing was seen of any of them, although their barks and bays were very clearly heard echoing through the dense woods. Amazingly, the human members of the Association rapidly returned to the fireside, where a fresh cup of coffee and additions to an already extant wad of chewing tobacco happily fortified them quite satisfactorily. Soon, storytelling and reminiscing were in full display, while the sounds of the dogs clearly resounded around and about us in the night. Then came <u>Revelation Number One</u> for the evening: The hunters in the Angelina Cat and Coon Hunting Association all had four legs and a lengthy tail! The two-legged accomplices were simply present for the convenience of the real, four-legged hunters. In looking back I realize that the coon hunt is an old-fashioned Southern social event that migrated to East Texas along with other customs, and that the interaction among the members of the hunting party is that of a fraternal order, with no less ritual but decidedly less pomp and flourishes than is found in collegiate or community organizations.

After a time of fraternal fireside interaction, the sounds of the dogs changed and the casual attitudes of the humans changed accordingly, as we all quickly rose and began a rapid pursuit of the now stationary barks. Striding along through the night, we eventually came to the locus of the sounds, a tallish tree on the edge of a thick stand of timber. Having now been a member for most of a complete hunt (or so I thought), I was emboldened enough to inquire, "Who gets to kill the raccoon now that we have found it?" Amid the barking and general cacophony of sounds now emanating from the dogs at the foot of the seemingly topless tree extending well into the darkness, I thought for a time that nobody had heard my question. However, I learned that the members, even the younger ones, were simply trying to prevent embarrassing me with having to respond to such an absurd question with what that they felt could be nothing but a response perceived as unkind and condescending.

Undeterred, I repeated my question. After a time, Charles, my friend who had sponsored my membership in the Association, edged over to me, while the rest of the group busied themselves in discussing whose dog "struck" first (that is, found the scent trail first) and whose dog barked "treed" first (that is, whose dog was the first to tree the so-far invisible quarry). He suggested that perhaps I might wait until later in the hunt to pursue an answer to my question. Eventually, one of the members did arrive, armed with an old single-shot shotgun, which he quickly discharged with what seemed a rather casual disregard to the location of the object of the hunt. I must admit that the sound was loud and the effect was immediate. The echo of the gunshot had hardly died away when the Association members whose dogs comprised the actual hunting party began summoning their animals to join them as they left the area, enroute to I knew not where. It occurred to me that perhaps this rapid dispersion was a courtesy to the shooter, who had obviously not hit the subject coon or apparently anything else but a lot of night sky.

Without thinking, I asked Charles, "How far are we from the spot where we left our vehicles?" I had noted that the time was almost 11:00 p.m., and my enthusiasm was beginning to wane a bit in anticipation of an early morning arising to be at work at 8 a.m.

"Why?" responded Charles.

"Well, now that the hunt is over, I just wondered how long will it take for us to get back to your house?" I asked, although I quickly added, "I have really enjoyed this first hunt."

Charles was not an overly expressive sort of fellow but he smiled a bit, and replied, "Oh, the hunt ain't over. We usually keep going until the dogs get tired, or we do. But don't worry, we'll be home in plenty of time for you to get cleaned up and get to work on time!"

That indeed did prove to be true. The dogs seemed to enjoy the evening, night, and eventual early morning just fine, despite what I observed to be dismal shooting by the hunting party that resulted in no actual coon casualties beyond one obviously slow raccoon who strayed too far from an available tree and became a testimonial to Darwinian selection for the quality of foot speed.

The final gathering of the hunt, in the growing dawn, revealed that dogs and humans alike moved more slowly but with satisfied looks on the faces of participants regardless of species. Some dogs had not yet returned from their wanderings, but their owners showed no displeasure even when their prized partners failed to respond to the calls, often an air horn or car horn or simple yell, repeated a number of times. By now, I was more generally aware of where we had been moving during the hunt, and I knew it was a goodly distance from where we had started.

"What about the dogs who are still out?" I asked. I was assured by several hunters whose dogs were still absent that they were not worried and that the dogs would wander back to one of the nearby roads sometime during the day. Anyone who found them would know whose dog it was and would just "bring Ol' Ben home" on their way to wherever they were going. I knew then why everyone had a large box in the truck bed—to haul dogs even though they had not brought any animals with them that night. Some of the dogs were beginning to resume their previous posture of lassitude, as they jumped into the truck beds, or in some cases, into the truck cabs. Most looked ready to return to their previous duties of guarding front porches.

The final gathering of hunters of the Association for my first venture presented me with a wonderful opportunity to thank everyone for their hospitality and patience with one so new to the theory and practice of old fashioned 'coon huntin'. "Think nothin' of it," I was assured, "See you next time." I did allow that perhaps my next time might not be the next night, when apparently another hunt was scheduled. I wish now that I had just left my comments at that. Of course, I did NOT. Then came <u>Revelation Number Two</u> for the evening: When new to an organization, it is best not to talk too much, at least not right away. "I really enjoyed the hunt, and I'm sorry that the hunting was so bad tonight!" I blustered out. I was quickly assured that the hunt went very well, as usual. "But, the shooter had such a bad day; he didn't kill any of the coons that the dogs found and treed. Surely, he has better luck than that sometimes," I deferentially added.

One of those members of indeterminate age but of apparent endless experience in these hunts finally answered, "Well, son, that's sort of the reason that we call this the Angelina Cat and

Coon *Hunting* Association. When we start killin' the coons, we'll probably change the name to the Angelina Cat and Coon *Killing* Association!"

I relearned a valuable lesson that evening that I had somehow forgotten since my days working in the fields with my uncle on his small farm. It is very difficult to learn when *talking* a lot. It is much easier to learn when *listening* a lot. I also recalled that some knowledge is most painfully acquired but retained in direct proportion to the discomfort associated with its acquisition.

I have searched for some especially profound insights I may have gained during my participation in the night meetings that occurred in the year and a half I was an active member in the Angelina Cat and Coon Hunting Association, but I don't believe profundities were the product of my journeys through wood and field so long ago. I did finally arrive upon <u>Revelation Number Three</u>: It takes a while to "git the hang of coon huntin'."

Those orchestrated wanderings provided, instead, a small glimpse into the reality of East Texas in that time and place, with a group of men who simply loved the outdoors, especially in the night, and who prized the company of one another and their dogs, away from jobs, financial concerns, and family and health issues. The meetings offered them the opportunity to roam an environment where each was for a time free. The all-male composition of the Association attested to an important function of the group—a "boy's night out." It was refreshing to have joined an organization which delivered to its members precisely what it promised. I was to learn over time just how extraordinary that outcome really was. I have no idea what the long-term effects of the Association activities might have been on the raccoon population, but I imagine the East Texas coon to be rather adaptable, possessing the same love of outdoors and freedom evidenced by the hunters, and which the festivities of the Association only briefly interrupted and perhaps even nurtured.

My retrospection did result in <u>Revelation Number Four</u>: Appearances are often deceiving. On first blush, neither the human hunters nor the dogs were very impressive to the eye.

However, both first impressions turned out to be considerably inaccurate. First, I was confused about who the hunters were. The four-legged animals are the hunters in coon huntin'. The two-legged animals are merely willing accomplices in the process. Second, these four-legged hunters are built for performance, not show. When the time came for them to hit the trail, they became beautifully coordinated machines with both individual and group personalities. They were tireless, in perpetual motion, and surprisingly working cooperatively in the course of the hunt. Finally, the two-legged hunters also functioned perfectly as a sort of team, each complementing the other. They, too, were built for the job, dressed for the surroundings, and although individuals, also worked well together.

As an aside, I am reminded of a rather common story directed toward cat and coon hunters and the process of the hunt. This story has been told by storytellers such as Jerry Clower, and it goes something like this: Seems that the dogs had treed the raccoon in question one evening, and as is customary, some (but not all) members present that evening arrived to do the scorekeeping honors, to record which dog "struck" first and which dog "treed" first. As fortune would have it that evening, the designated shooter for the night had not yet arrived, and after a time, the dogs were frantically still barking "treed," as indeed the coon in question remained. Attempts to dislodge the quarry by tossing sticks and other objects up into the pine were unsuccessful, but as the tree was regrowth and thus not especially tall, one of the youthful members volunteered to climb up and dislodge the coon, or so the story goes. Up he went and, rather quickly, all sorts of noises of distress ensued from both hunter and quarry, including a high-pitched yelling from the young hunter. You probably recall how the rest of the story goes, as the hunter yells, "Shoot him! Shoot him!" In response, the designated shooter, who had finally arrived, yelled back, "I can't shoot. I might hit you." The punch line follows, as the voice from above yells, "Shoot up here anyway. One of us has to have some relief!"

Now, this humorous story is well known to many, hunters and non-hunters, and of course around the campfire it inevitably surfaced when a new member was welcomed to our Association. However, during my tenure in the Association I had the opportunity to meet several adult raccoons up close, including one mama coon who had been trapped by my friend Charles with two of her offspring, and I know of NO coon hunters, past or present, who would be foolish enough to climb up into a dark tree anywhere near an adult raccoon. Nonetheless, the old adage, attributed to one of the greatest storytellers of all time, J. Frank Dobie, applies, "Never let facts get in the way of a good story." During my time in the association, I did learn to appreciate a good story told by expert storytellers who showed their love for a lifetime vocation. From a friend of mine and a friend of many, many others, Kenneth Davis, I have learned that what I was participating in at that time so long ago was a "communal activity," whereby tradition is passed from generation to generation, not in written but oral form.

I was to have other nights of adventure and revelation before my year-and-a-half tenure as a member of the Angelina Cat and Coon Hunting Association ended with marriage and a new job. Not surprisingly, I found that newly wedded wives did not share the same love of dogs and all-night outdoor "hunts" that some husbands brought to the marriage. Indeed, much learning was yet to come in the course of time, but none more memorable than what I gleaned during my nights in the forests of East Texas in the company of honest and generous comrades, tireless canines of uncertain lineage and keen senses, and remarkable forest critters.

POSTSCRIPT:

In those remarkable eighteen months, we humans never saw a cat, and so I suspect that name of the Association remains unchanged today. If the real hunters ever saw one, they kept it to themselves.

John Wolf skinning the closest thing to a coon he could find

The author with her father and brothers and the 17-point buck, 1983

DENTISTRY, DEHORNING, AND MORE: SOUTH TEXAS WOMEN'S HUNTING STORIES

by Mary Margaret Dougherty Campbell

Traditionally, hunting has been the domain of men who hunted to put food on the table. As late as the 1950s drought, when life was especially difficult for ranchers in South Texas, my dad and his family ate more venison than beef. After the drought, until the day he died, my dad refused to eat any more deer meat—except for the occasional piece of fried backstrap. He gave away the meat when he or any of us kids shot a deer so it wouldn't go to waste. Even though he didn't enjoy eating the meat, Dad nevertheless enjoyed the hunt, which was a tradition in his family. Everybody hunted, even his mother. However, hunting remains an activity dominated by men, who now hunt more for sport than for survival. Their sport has its procedures, rules, and rituals the men take for granted, even when they initiate women—wives, girlfriends, daughters—into the rites of hunting. When family members participate in the tradition, the folk culture, they are strengthening family bonds that today's society tests daily.

Growing up on a ranch, I heard my share of hunting stories around the kitchen table and the campfire, but the stories were told by men about their own experiences. At age fourteen, I shot my first deer, a spike (a male deer who only has two short antlers that will not grow and spread so is, therefore, a cull deer) and had my own story to share, but I didn't. Over the years, I began to hear my grandmother and other women tell their hunting stories— generally in the company of only women—stories that have existed but have not been as commonly recounted as those of the men, especially in mixed company. Today, it's not just the men who enjoy the sport of hunting. As Francis Abernethy points out in his Preface to *Between the Cracks of History*, "If we wish to study the world and mankind in all of their dimensions of time and space, then folklore is the teacher to whom we must turn."[1] Indeed, the women's stories are part of hunting folklore and, therefore, deserve their place in the study of hunting lore.

Many women who hunt grew up on a ranch where hunting was part of life, some hunting from an early age, others choosing not to participate in the hunt. After I shot my spike, I did not shoot a rifle again until I was in college. When I went to another part of the state to further my education, I began to appreciate my background and noted how different it was from the other girls' who lived in my dorm, mostly city girls. I realized I had taken for granted living on the ranch and all that kind of life entailed. Thus, I began taking greater interest in the ranch, spending most of my college holidays with Dad. During Christmas break, he and I hunted. He drove the pickup and I knelt on the propane tank in the back, looking out over the cab.

My favorite hunting story from those days is the time I shot a seventeen-point buck. Yes, seventeen points. They say that if you can hang a ring from a point, it counts. The man at The Dinero Store, where the local buck contest was being held, verified the count by placing a metal ring on each protrusion—seventeen in all. Until I arrived with my buck, our friend Richard Beall had been winning the contest. In fact, this was after Christmas, and Richard's deer had been winning the contest since Thanksgiving weekend. When the man told me my buck would beat Richard's, one of Dad's evil little smirks came across his face. You see, we hadn't actually gone to the store to enter the contest; Dad just wanted the man there to see the deer and place his ring on the horns. Dad signed me up in the contest, and a few days later, I won. The prize was a hunting knife, which I didn't need because Dad skinned and cleaned my deer with his pocketknife. The only reason Dad signed me up was so I'd beat Richard, which delighted Dad. He really liked Richard, but Dad liked to play tricks on people when he could. I gave Richard the knife, but I don't think it consoled him much.

Georgia Lowe from Tilden, also raised on a ranch, never developed interest in the ranch and ranch life growing up. Like me, it took going away to college for her to appreciate her roots. Her second year in college at Texas A&M, Georgia decided she wanted to hunt. She had made friends who hunted, so she decided she wanted to try it. She said that growing up, hunting "wasn't a big deal" to her. She had never even shot a gun. Her dad, Dolf, glad that she was now showing interest in hunting, readily agreed to take her. Dolf recalls helping Georgia choose a gun on the first day he took her hunting:

> I handed her a .243 that I'd had forever. "Nope." I handed her a .22-250. "No, no, I don't like this one. Let me see the .243 back." So I gave her the .243 back. "No," she said. "Here, here's a .222." I bought that gun when I was twelve years old. "If you kill a deer, it's yours [the gun]."

Apparently this .222 would suffice. So, they went to the pasture, climbed into the blind, and waited. Georgia recalls the cramped quarters in the blind, saying the blind was so small that the two of them "were crammed in." Georgia sat on the stool; Dolf squatted and held the gun for her, but eventually gave it to Georgia and told her to point it out the window, which she did. Dolf says, "And we're sitting there, and there's a couple of does and a couple of javelinas, and I'm looking and thinking, 'Holy sh—.

Here comes a deer, and you could see him coming down the road, and he's just walkin' and bobbin' his head." As Dolf watched the deer, he realized, "that's a 10-point buck with a drop. How lucky can you be?" A "drop" is a tine that grows down rather than up, which is rare and, therefore, highly desirable.

Of course, he spoke none of this aloud. As the buck came closer and closer, he wondered how he could get his daughter to shoot the deer without her getting buck fever or wounding the deer and its running off. He tapped Georgia on the shoulder "and

BAM! She hit the side of the window of the blind and the deer at the feeder [below the blind] were like 'Whoa! What's goin' on?'"[2]

Georgia admits that she "made all kinds of noise. I even hit the blind with the gun" moving it to the other window. Georgia broke one of the "rules" of hunting—that of being quiet in the blind, which Dolf expected her to follow yet had neglected to tell her. Dolf silently dismissed the noise and told her that a buck was coming and to get ready to shoot. "I'm ready. I'm ready," Georgia nervously said.

The buck walked back into the brush before she could get a shot off. Georgia remembers she didn't have her glasses on, nor did she have her contact lenses in, so she couldn't see very well, especially looking through the scope.

A few minutes later, Georgia exclaimed, "Dad! Dad! There's another one! There's another one!"

He told her, "Shoot him! Shoot him!" Georgia didn't realize it was the same buck. When recounting this adventure, Dolf said, "I've been married twenty-five years, and I don't argue. I know better. 'Yeah, that's a whole different buck.'" And it was getting closer. Dolf knew that the buck would eventually see the feeder and throw his head up. He instructed Georgia to aim for the white spot on the buck's neck. He recalls, "So, she's all ready, and [the buck] gets closer and closer and he does just what I think he's gonna do: he throws his head up, and I tell Georgia, 'Shoot! Shoot! Shoot him now!'

> 'I can't, Daddy, I can't!'
> 'You gotta shoot him now!'
> 'I can't, Daddy, I can't!'"

The buck continued to move toward the feeder and blind, walking down into a creek and back up on his way toward them. The buck had not yet noticed the white ranch pickup parked by the fence down the hill, but Dolf knew that Georgia's last chance to shoot this buck would be when the buck spied the truck and threw his head up once again. When that happened, Dolf again told her to shoot. She aimed at the white spot as instructed, which Georgia remembers was all she could really see through the scope, just fuzzy colors, so she *could* distinguish the white part. She aimed at it and shot. "I got it! I got it!" Georgia admits hitting the deer was "total luck" because she couldn't even see it. She observes, "It had ten points and a four-inch drop tine. I was pleased." Dolf kept his word and gave her the gun. She says that "hunting is so much fun I'm ready to go again!"[3]

Also raised on a ranch in McMullen County, Mattie Swaim Sadovsky has hunted all of her life. It didn't take going off to college to kindle her interest. One particular season, Mattie remembers that her grandfather, Rodney Swaim, had spotted a buck he wanted Mattie to shoot. He had a feeder behind his house and watched the deer who fed there, and this one buck he thought would be a good one for Mattie. Actually, there were two nice bucks regularly feeding there, but this particular buck had Mattie's name on it, so to speak. Her grandfather told her he would call her over the next time the buck came to the feeder. Mattie got that call one day, but it was her grandmother Bobbie calling, saying the buck her grandfather wanted her to shoot was there and to hurry over. So, Mattie hurried over, being careful not to make too much arrival noise. She asked her grandmother if she were certain this was the buck she was supposed to shoot, and her grandmother assured her that it was, so Mattie shot and killed the buck. When her grandfather got home, he asked Mattie why she had shot that buck. Mattie said, "That's the one you wanted me to shoot." You guessed it—it was the wrong buck. Mr. Swaim had assumed his wife could distinguish between the two deer.[4]

D'Anna Woodmansee's father, Steve Woodmansee, was a game warden in Live Oak County. D'Anna's interest in hunting developed when she was in about the sixth or seventh grade. She recalls, "Daddy was so proud that I had expressed an interest in hunting" that he took her every chance he got. But, she observes, "There was a distinct difference between a seasoned Game Warden and a prissy twelve-year-old girl. He liked it stark and serious. I liked it warm and more along the lines of a morning where Daddy finds the deer within the first ten minutes, points, and I shoot." The particular hunting excursion that readily comes to mind when she thinks back on those special times she spent with her father happened one cold South Texas morning when D'Anna was twelve years old. The temperature on the bank in Three Rivers read "16 degrees." She remembers that reading distinctly. They were heading out to the Dougherty Management area. Upon arrival, they unloaded all of D'Anna's stuff (the "gear" she usually took on those hunting trips: a CD player and headset, hot chocolate, whatever food her mother had packed, and a book—none of which a man would bring because these items are not specifically part of the hunting ritual) "into this tiny one-man blind and settled in." As D'Anna and her father waited, the sun slowly came up, making the frost on the grass and trees sparkle in the sunshine.

But, before the sun rose all the way, D'Anna grew bored. She recalls the experience:

> So I turned on the music. The Eagles' *Hell Freezes Over* was the album of choice. Daddy kept telling me to turn it down because I was going to scare off the deer. We'd sit for a while and then I'd complain because it was too cold and Daddy would patiently and sweetly tell me just to suck it up. To try and break the cold a little bit, Daddy had brought along a small propane tank that had an open flame burning off of it. Keep in mind, my full-grown Daddy and I are shoved into a one-man blind with an open flame and ALL my stuff and I'm complaining because it's cold. So Daddy tells me to put my foot over the flame to try and warm my feet up. So, I'm jamming to the Eagles, trying to warm my feet, and Daddy pokes me and points out the blind window down the sendero [which is a strip of land cleared of brush and trees]. Out on the horizon, at a perfect distance, was a beautiful, full, tall-horned, old buck—just the kind that would look great on

my wall amidst my other conquests. Then the adrenaline kicked in and I got really engrossed in watching this deer to see where he was going, preparing my shot but still warming my foot over the open propane flame… Then I noticed that it was getting a little brighter in the blind. Then my foot got really hot. Then the flame got really big. By this time, in slow motion it seems, I realize that my foot in my rubber hiking boot has caught on fire! Daddy starts screaming. I start screaming. The deer, and any other deer in a fifty-mile radius, runs away. We keep screaming and bumping around, two people in this one-man blind full of my stuff, trying to figure out what to do with my flaming foot. So, I do the only logical thing I can think to do: I grab my foot. Luckily I had on gloves. They were my really nice gloves which, needless to say, I never wore to church again because they were melted to my shoe. And I didn't get a deer that day. And Daddy learned that next time we'd take a contained flame.

D'Anna said that when she grabbed the flame on her boot, she was able to snuff it out—thankfully! Needless to say, setting one's boots on fire in the deer blind goes against the hunting "rules."[5]

Alyssa Webb grew up in Victoria County. She recalls "truck hunting" with her father, Tom Webb, which she defines as, "You know, where you park the truck and open the window and hope the deer don't notice you down the right-of-way." Tom Webb grew up in a hunting family, generally hunting in blinds. But, as Alyssa points out, "Lo and behold, he had a girl. He never let it slow him down; he taught me to hunt and shoot and always took me hunting with him." She has treasured memories of truck hunting with her dad in the evenings. She says, "We'd sit in the truck and roll down the windows and wait. When something worth shooting came out, be that a deer, hog, coyote, or bobcat, my dad would whisper for me to be very quiet, and he'd line up his shot." Afterward, they would take their "trophies," as she called the kill, to her grandparents' house for cleaning. She would usually try to sneak away from *that* activity into the house where her grandmother would give her a treat.

She remembers that most nights her dad didn't shoot anything and that she never shot an animal. She shot at "cans, targets, etc. but wasn't too keen on the idea of killing a deer—although [she] loved to eat fried venison." She remembers "falling asleep across the seat and waking up when [they] pulled into the driveway at home." She doesn't remember when her dad started taking her hunting with him, but she "couldn't have been very old—maybe even three or four. [She doesn't] know many men who are patient enough to take a small child hunting, but [she has] the best memories of hunting with [her] Dad."

Their hunting adventures didn't stop when Alyssa was a child, although as she grew older, her school activities demanded more and more of her time, leaving her less time to spend hunting with her dad. When she was in college, she decided it had been too long since she "had made the time to go with him." Her grandfather had "a huge blind built, complete with a staircase, windows—the works." When she and Tom were in the blind, Alyssa fell asleep, just like she had done as a child in the truck. Tom told her, "Some things never change, but I am so glad you came."[6]

Alyssa's mother, Karen, also shared a hunting story involving Tom Webb. Karen had hunted with her father since she was a child, so when she married Tom, hunting was not foreign to her. Whereas Tom's family generally hunted in blinds, Karen's hunting experiences had been from the ground, behind a tree. Karen remembers that after they married, Tom "decided to let [her] go hunting with him and nothing doing [she] had to get in the tree blind, alone." She is not very fond of heights but was eager to hunt, which she says "was comical in itself as [she] is not exactly graceful." She settled in and waited for the deer—that never came. She recalls that time passed "very slowly" and finally "darkness fell." From the blind, she could see when Tom's truck started and she was relieved to know that soon she would be down on the ground, out of the blind, "that tiny prison." To make matters worse, she was a bit nervous about being alone in the pasture after dark. As she waited for Tom, she noticed that the headlights were driving *away* from her rather than toward her. She had no way to communicate with Tom because this incident occurred before cell phones. After "a few tears and a few panic attacks," she saw the headlights coming her way. When Tom picked her up, Karen learned that Tom had headed home after hunting, stopping by his parents' house on the way. Once he arrived home, he wondered why Karen wasn't there. Then it dawned on him that he had forgotten her in the blind! Karen says, "Needless to say, that was the first and last hunting trip [she] took with him."[7]

Carolyn Orsak grew up in rural Live Oak County, but since her father had no interest in hunting, she did not hunt at all until she began dating her husband, Buddy Orsak. They would go to his lease and "sit in the blind and there were even a few occasions that [they] would take a rifle!" Eventually, she did kill her first buck and "got hooked," after which she would go sit in the blind by herself. As her kids got older, however, she quit hunting, "but would still go along and sit in the blind with them and crochet while waiting for the deer to come out." "Now," she says, "they pack up all their hunting gear, and I pack up my needles and yarn and off we go!"[8]

Some women who are not fortunate enough to grow up on a ranch, or even in the country, where hunting is a part of life, wind up marrying men who hunt, as Carolyn Orsak did. Georgia Lowe's mother, Carolyn Lowe, is another such woman. Carolyn grew up in San Antonio. Her dad and grandfather hunted; in fact, she remembers her grandfather "always had a lease." She had spent some time in the country but "didn't have much exposure to hunting and country life." Soon after she and Dolf married, Carolyn decided she would like to try deer hunting. Dolf agreed to take her. The first day they went, Dolf describes as the "prime time to kill a deer…the wind was in my favor, the sun to my back, all the good signs that you're supposed to have." They drove to a field where Dolf thought they might see some deer that afternoon, and as Dolf predicted, two or three big bucks were standing in the field. They didn't sit in a blind like Georgia and Dolf had done; instead, they sat by a fence on the edge of the field. He recalls

> I'm from the country and [Carolyn] is not, and I'm thinking she should know something she doesn't know how to do, like walking up to a barbwire fence and putting your gun on the fence to use it as a rest. You're supposed to know how to kneel down and use the right knee and all that stuff; well, she didn't know how to do that. So she flipped and flopped and messed around and hit the fence and hit the gun. The barbwire just started shattering down [the length of it], and the deer all perked up and jumped out of the field. She finally got ready and said, "I can't see! I can't see! [pause] OK, I'm ready." And I said, "OK, let's go. All the deer are gone." So she gets mad.

That was Day One. Two days later, Dolf and Carolyn tried again. They arrived at a field and, Dolf says:

> The wind, the sun, everything good. We were looking around the field for deer when I saw a pretty good buck. Same thing. So she gets mad, and I'm like, "Let's just go." I get up. "Let's just go." She said, "What about that buck over there?'" I said, "What buck?" She said, "That buck" She could see that this one had horns—not real big ones, but it had horns. [Dolf holds up two fingers on each hand above his head.] And I'm like, "If you think you can hit that blankety-blank thing, go ahead and shoot." So, she did. She shot it and broke its neck...So she immediately jumps up and said, "Now you go clean that blankety-blank thing." That was the end of her hunting career.[9]

Carolyn doesn't recall this last comment, but she said that when she hit the deer, Dolf said, "My God! You got it!" She said the deer stood "a good distance away"—Dolf verifies 175 yards—and her father didn't believe her when she told him about shooting it because "it was that far." She told me, "I can't tell you what kind of gun it was; I don't have a clue. I was just handed a gun with 'Here. This is what you need.'" As it turns out, both Georgia and Carolyn shot their deer with the same gun. Only Dolf could tell me this. For Carolyn, "The thrill is over." She has had the experience of shooting a deer but now would rather just watch them, photograph them. However, she maintains that she wouldn't mind shooting another one, but it would have to be a big one.[10]

Stephanie Ingham is another woman who was not raised in the country. Whereas Carolyn Lowe grew up in San Antonio, Stephanie comes from a small town. She maintains that "many women who have picked up hunting were probably outdoorsy kids," which she was—building forts and tree houses, fishing and dredging their lake for crawdads, tad poles, fish, and bugs, etc. She's another one who married a hunter, C. Y. She says she doesn't "care much about the guns or get into the brands and terminology;" she leaves that up to her "gunsmith and personal buyer," C. Y. Her story involves her first—and only—deer she has shot. Stephanie says it would have been a six-point buck, but he had "lost two spikes in a fight." She says, "I took him at 100 yards away . . . open scope [no scope] with a Chinese SKS (7.62 x 39)." For someone who doesn't know the

Stephanie Ingham

terminology or much about guns, she sure got that specific, which tells me that C. Y. edited her story before she sent it to me. To get back to Stephanie's story, she "missed the first time . . . [H]e scurried in a circle, but right back to the same spot where [she] got him the second time." With Stephanie, it's not exactly the *story* of her first hunt so much as it is the aftermath. Like my dad, Dolf Lowe, Steve Woodmansee, Tom Webb, Buddy Orsak, and all other hunter/fathers and husbands, C. Y. was thrilled Stephanie had an interest in hunting. Since that first hunt, C. Y. has "upgraded [her] to a DPMS Sportical LR308." She observes that "as soon as a man knows you like to hunt, even just a little bit, he uses every opportunity to buy ya more stuff. All it took was me saying that I could not see out of the scope, which called for buying this new bigger gun with an adjustable scope and butt stock."[11]

When Mattie Swaim married Reagan Sadovsky, they already shared a passion for hunting. Rather than feeling the need to take the initiative on his own to buy hunting gear, guns, or other equipment for Mattie, all Reagan had to do was ask Mattie what she wanted for Christmas. She told him she wanted a new deer blind and feeder for her Christmas gifts from him—and she got them. Mattie and Reagan even have his-and-hers wall mounts in their home.[12]

Thus far, the stories have been told by and about women who hunted solely in the company of a father or husband. The Streadl family of Alice has three women hunters—mother Jeanette and daughters Lori and Kim—who often hunt alone and who all have hunting stories. When I was collecting their stories, a group of us sat around my kitchen table. Jeanette's story of a deer who refused to die was the one I was to record, but as her story drew to an end, I could readily tell hers was not the only story that was going to be told, so the tape continued to roll. As typically occurs when people sit around a table visiting, one story led to another, which led to another, which led to another.

The first Streadl story, Jeanette's, occurred in about 1988 on the Lundell Ranch in western Jim Wells County, where her husband Alvin was ranch manager. Family friend David Hale went out to the ranch from time to time in the afternoons and on Saturdays to hunt with Jeanette. This particular Saturday Alvin was supposed to be at the ranch in Webb County, so Jeanette and David had the hunting on this big ranch to themselves. They drove to a pasture where they always saw deer, and saw one as soon as they entered the pasture. Jeanette told David to "Stop. There's a deer under that tree." They couldn't tell if the deer was a buck or a doe because of the trees and brush, but Jeanette said, "Let's just shoot and take names later." That was the last day of the season, and they still had a number of doe tags, so it didn't matter if they shot a buck or a doe.

David shot first and missed. He then told Jeanette to shoot because he really couldn't see the deer clearly enough. She shot it—"in the butt." The deer didn't go down. David got out of the truck and shot again, this time hitting the deer in the leg. They both continued to shoot, but the deer refused to die. Jeanette remarked, "This deer must have had nine lives because we shot everything we had in our gun. We shot it in the butt, the leg, the jaw, everywhere but in the shoulder." David told her to shoot the deer again—because it *still* wasn't dead, but she had run out of bullets. So, David reached in his pocket for a bullet, loaded it, and shot one last time, finally killing the deer, which turned out to be a doe, by the way. Unknown to David and Jeanette, Alvin was already back from Webb County, and all the time they had been trying to kill this doe, Alvin had been watching them through binoculars from the top of the hill, laughing. Jeanette remembers that Alvin "finally comes down and asks 'How many did y'all kill?'" to which David answered a simple, "One."

"One? And twenty rounds of shots?" Alvin managed through his laughter.

For all of their effort and ammunition, Jeanette said the only meat they got from that deer was one ham and the backstrap.[13]

After the laughter subsided at the table, Jeanette said, "Kim killed a deer the day she came home from the hospital with Logan," launching Kim into her favorite hunting story. Kim's son Logan had contracted pneumonia at six weeks of age, spending the week between Christmas Day and New Year's Day in the NICU, followed by an isolated room. When Kim arrived home and got

Logan settled, she announced she was going hunting. About ten minutes later, she returned. Jeanette said to Kim, "I thought you were gonna kill a deer."

"I did. I'm done. It's dead."

Frustrated after her week's ordeal, Kim didn't waste any time. She drove to the deer blind, parked directly beneath it, and climbed into the blind. Before she even got settled in, she saw a ten-point buck with a drop tine and shot it. That was that.[14]

Kim's story reminded me of a story my mother told about my grandmother, Nonnie Dougherty. Nonnie's favorite hunting was for turkey. According to my mother, not long after she married my dad, Nonnie invited her to go turkey hunting one afternoon. Mom was surprised at Nonnie's approach. They didn't even leave the house until almost dark, when they drove down to the Lagarto Creek, got out of the old army Jeep they used on the ranch for hunting, and walked down into the creek. Nonnie instructed Mom to sit with her under the trees on the bank. As the turkeys came in to roost for the night, Nonnie shot her turkey.[15] That was my grandmother—not exactly in for the sport of the hunt but for the kill, the meat.

Both stories have hunters with a pragmatic approach. Nonnie and Kim knew what they wanted to accomplish and simply did it. They could enjoy the hunt another day. I do know that Nonnie actually did hunt from a blind when her lady friends came to visit, so she did enjoy the hunt when she didn't need a bird for the supper table, and Kim continues to enjoy hunting, as well.

After Kim's story, Jeanette said, "Lori finally killed one, one time."

"Me?" Lori asked, astonished. "I've killed a bunch of deer a bunch of times." So, Lori began one of her stories: "One time, Daddy got *really* mad at me." She was sitting in a blind one afternoon, reading a book (she packs as much stuff as D'Anna Woodmansee to the blind) while waiting for deer to come to the feeder. In the meantime, cows wandered up and started rubbing on the blind, making it sway. Next, horses showed up and began eating the corn from the feeder. Eventually, Lori saw a deer come to the feeder and eat corn right along with the horses. The deer was a spike, and Alvin had told the girls to "Shoot every spike you see." So, Lori knew Alvin would expect her to shoot this spike. The problem was, though, that the horses were in the way. One particular horse was directly in line with the spike, eating head to head, with the horse's behind toward Lori, the deer facing her. She decided that if the spike ever turned his head sideways, she would shoot. That opportunity came. Lori reported that she "dropped it right where it stood," but the horses went crazy.

When Alvin arrived, he asked, "What was eatin' here?"

"Nothin," replied Lori.

"*Lori Lynn.*"

"OK. It was Snip."

"#?*! You coulda shot my horse!"

"No, she wasn't in my scope."[16]

How fortunate for Snip—and Lori. Once again, the woman didn't follow the "rules" the man assumed she must follow.

Lori Streadl and her first deer

Sometimes it doesn't matter if women have grown up hunting or not, many women—and men—have stories about what I call the "oops" shots, the shots where the shooter thinks the crosshairs are in perfect position, but something happens and the bullet winds up somewhere it's not intended. Even though the majority of the other stories here are deer hunting stories, Betty Jennings of George West shared a turkey hunting story. She said that C. M. Porter of Mathis was "very particular about his turkeys," rarely allowing anyone to hunt them. He fed his turkeys before feeding wild animals became popular. He decided to take Betty turkey hunting, but he limited her to *only one*. Mr. Porter and Betty were hunting from the pickup, Betty using a .243 rifle. They saw two turkeys standing together "a good ways apart," according to Betty. She put her rifle out the window, took aim, and shot her target turkey through the neck—and the other turkey behind that one in the breast! Betty said, "C. M. laughed, thought it was funny, but only let me take *one* of the turkeys home. He *kept* one of them." Well, he had told her *only one*.[17]

An "oops" shot story of my own took place several years go on the ranch where I grew up south of George West. On the first frosty morning of deer season—the optimal time to hunt—Bruce McCumber, Richard Beall (the deer contest loser), and I met at the ranch house and were all three seated in the cab of Bruce's pickup at the top of the hill overlooking the pipeline sendero as the sun began to rise. We sat, watched, waited, and whispered but saw no movement, only frost glistening off the golden grass and brush. Eventually, Bruce suggested we move on. It was a big ranch with several big pastures, so we figured we might have better luck if we drove rather than sat.

About 10:00 we came up the bank from crossing the Lagarto Creek in the West Pasture when Bruce eased the pickup to a stop and killed the motor. Simultaneously, Richard and I saw the spike off to the right. Richard quietly opened the door and slipped out so that I could rest my .243 on the window ledge. The spike was facing us about seventy-five yards off, looking right at us. This would have to be a neck shot. I found my spot on the cross hairs, clicked off the safety, and curled my finger around the trigger. POW!

Bruce said, "What was *THAT*? It looked like snow!"

Richard said, "Yeah, I saw it! What was it?"

I wondered how Bruce had managed to slip nips of whiskey while we had all three been in that not-so-roomy cab all morning. Snow? In South Texas? Granted, the morning had begun frosty but had turned sunny and pleasantly cool. "I don't know what y'all are talking about. As soon as I pulled the trigger, I shut my eyes."

Bruce and Richard both shrugged as Bruce got out of the pickup. The deer was down, so we walked toward it. As we approached the spike, we could see what Bruce's snow was. Richard said, "Jack (that's what they call me), you've done a nice dental job on this spike," to which I replied a confused, "Huh?"

Apparently, as I pulled the trigger, the spike dropped his head enough so that my bullet went straight through his mouth rather than directly through his neck. My bullet sent his teeth flying through the air like snow. Since then, I've been know in some circles as the Deer Dentist.

Another strange-shot story involves my friends Judy Hinnant and Lynn Harris. Several years after my deer dentistry, I received a call during the Thanksgiving weekend about 5:30 in the afternoon from Judy, who was sitting in a pickup at the end of a sendero on her mom's ranch north of Alice, watching for deer. Lynn had come from Navasota for the Thanksgiving holiday to hunt with Judy, who is definitely not a serious hunter.

I know this because I went hunting *once* with Judy at her mom's ranch, about eighteen years prior. Judy was driving the pickup, I was in the middle (no gate opening), and Kenneth Kay was riding shotgun (the gate opener). Like all South Texas ranches, that ranch has senderos cut through the thick brush at regular intervals. Judy, never one for patience, would gun the motor toward a sendero, then slam on the breaks, bringing the pickup to a screeching halt in the middle of the sendero, throwing Kenneth and me virtually into the dashboard every time. At first, we thought she was just playing with us and would settle down.

Lynn Harris in her camouflage gear

Wrong! Eventually, Kenneth and I admonished her for such driving and assured her that if any deer *had been* in the senderos, we were undoubtedly scaring them back into the brush. She giggled and gunned the motor again, throwing our heads against the back window. Needless to say, we were not successful in our deer quest.

But, a more dedicated hunter, Lynn realized quickly after her previous year's hunt with Judy on a four-wheeler, with an experience similar to the one Kenneth and I'd had, that she needed to separate herself from Judy and opted to sit in a blind. This separation didn't particularly bother Judy; it just bored her, thus the phone call I received from the pasture. My cell phone battery was losing its charge, so we didn't talk long. What I knew at this point was that Lynn was in the blind and Judy was bored.

The next day, Judy called to report that Lynn had been successful with the previous afternoon's hunt, laughing as she said it.

When I asked her why she was laughing, she said, "Lynn got a ten-point buck."

"OK," I said, "what's so funny about that? Getting a big buck like that is a good thing."

She said, "But you don't understand. She shot its left horns off!"

"WHAT?"

"Yeah, when she shot, the deer turned his head, and she shot the horns off that side!"

"No way!"

"Yeah! When we called Tommy to get him to meet us at the house to help us skin it, he thought we were lying—until he drove up and Lynn was standing there holding half of the deer's horns in her hand." He shook his head in disbelief.

Discussing the width of the buck's spread, Tommy said, "You know, Lynn, that spread is as big as you want it to be!" Lynn, realizing what he'd said, nodded and grinned.[18]

Judy with Lynn in the truck with the electric corn feeder

Eventually I got the rest of the story: While Lynn sat patiently in the blind scanning the edges of the sendero for Mr. Big to emerge from the brush, Judy was driving around in the pickup, wearing her thumb out from pushing the button on the electric corn feeder (remember her small threshold for boredom). As quiet as the day was, the diesel motor on the pickup, coupled with the intermittent sound of the electric feeder made Lynn keep thinking she was hearing a John Deere tractor, which worried her that the deer might be too scared to wander out of the brush.

After quite a while, Judy called Lynn on the walkie-talkie to say that she thought she was looking at a buck Lynn might want to shoot. Judy says, "She summoned me to the deer blind to pick her up. I was speedy quick in getting over to her." No doubt!

Judy remembers that Lynn "shimmied down the blind in her camouflage gear and off we went to the scene of the soon-to-be slaying.

"As I turned the corner, I said to her, 'There it is. I think he's a nice size buck.' That is when I was informed that he was a shooter." A "shooter" is a buck worthy of being shot for whatever reason the game manager on the ranch deems important—his size of horn rack, his age, etc.

Lynn asked Judy to get her a little closer to the buck. As Judy brought the pickup to a stop, Lynn positioned her gun through the open window and shot. When she got out of the pickup and saw the deer lying on the ground, she was disgusted: "Hell, I shot a doe."

Judy's response was, "Oh no! You've shot Bambi's mother!"

As they walked up the sendero to the deer, Lynn shook her head, saying, "I know my eyesight is not what it used to be, but I didn't think I'd mistaken a doe for a buck!" Then she caught a glimpse of the horns on the ground and turned the deer over in disbelief.[19]

Lynn says, "My buck was a ten-point, then a five-point. He is now a ten-point again and hanging on my wall. I dehorned that buck with a .30-06."[20]

The spread width she decided upon is a modest 14.5 inches. She proudly notes that the "right beam length is nineteen inches. He's not that wide but has a lot of mass" (which means the horns were thick in circumference).[21]

Hunting is a part of our culture and the stories part of our lore. Current hunting stories become old stories as they are retold over the years around the campfire, at the hunting lease, or around the Thanksgiving table when hunting season is in full swing. Joyce Gibson Roach defines folklore as "all the ways a culture has of accomplishing its life (folk-make, folk-do, folk-think-believe, folk-speak, folk-be) and the means used to accomplish that life."[22] To a great many people—men and women alike—hunting is a significant aspect of their life, and they pass along the tradition through their stories of the activity, as well as through participation in the activity, especially fathers taking their daughters and husbands taking their wives hunting, not only because these men are excited the females are interested in something of interest to them but also because, on some level, they realize they are passing on a tradition important to future generations.

Joe S. Graham maintains in his essay "Toward a Definition of Folk Culture" that "Humans use their culture to organize their world and make it more livable" and that "Folk culture . . . is usually passed on in face-to-face interactions in informal situations."[23] Since we live in a world where time spent with family is waning and the demands of the world are waxing, fathers and husbands taking their daughters and wives hunting serves as a means of carrying on face-to-face interactions in a natural setting, away from the demands of the world. Further, these families cherish the hunting time, the time they spend together in the quiet of the blind or leaning against a fence on the edge of a field. Indeed, Francis Abernethy says in his introduction to *The Family Saga* that he "could have had a chapter on hunting and fishing tales from the families [he] encountered that believed these sports were at the core of their family's identity."[24] The cover story of the July/August 2010 issue of *Texas Trophy Hunters*, written by Pam Zaitz, reveals the value of the Zaitz family time at their South Texas hunting lease as she tells the story of her finally bagging "Lefty," an old deer she had been watching for several seasons. Zaitz, her husband, and their two sons all hunt, enjoying and appreciating this shared family activity and interest.[25]

Rhett Rushing observes that "Any time you find two or more people with anything at all in common, then you've found a folk group. It's more a consideration of shared experiences and desires. . . ."[26] Certainly, then, Pam Zaitz and her family constitute a folk group, as do Carolyn Orsak and her family, as well as the Streadl family. Girls who hadn't taken much interest in the hunting tradition return home from college realizing its importance and wanting to participate in that part of their folk culture, as depicted especially in the stories of Georgia Lowe and me. Although D'Anna Woodmansee and Alyssa Webb began hunting with their fathers at a rather young age, as they grew older, they recognized, albeit probably on a subconscious level, that this hunting activity is a part of their lives, their background—who they are—and have the desire to immerse themselves in it to become whole.

All of the women whose stories appear here have become active participants in the hunting tradition at one time or another. Some women may not actually sit in a blind or carry a gun, but they want to participate, and they do so by driving around in the pickup pressing the feeder button, like Judy Hinnant, and taking hunters to the blinds, sitting and watching the deer to appreciate them while the "hunters" sit in the blind. It's participation, still, but in another form. Carolyn Lowe experienced the actual hunt but now prefers participation by observation and appreciation. Carolyn Orsak crochets.

The "oops" shots make good stories, and bring laughter to the listeners, as well as smiles to the tellers' faces as they reminisce about the experiences and feel the joy as they see the listeners smiling and laughing. These stories, indeed all hunting stories, should continue to be told, especially orally because, as Douglas Southall

Freeman points out, when discussing a Southerner's attempt at setting down on paper some of his stories, "Spontaneity was lost in the polishing of paragraph."[27] Storytelling is an oral art form, a tradition which tends to lose valuable elements when set to paper, elements such as gestures, facial expressions, voice inflection, and the like. Setting the stories down on paper is important for the collection of the particular lore, but it's in the oral telling that the stories truly *live*.

Although women's hunting stories have traditionally not been as readily told as those of men, they have always existed. We could go into a discussion of society's gender acceptance differences throughout history at this point, but we won't. Suffice it to say that women's hunting stories are being told more and more—even making the cover story of a men's hunting magazine—in circles of both women and men, and that women's hunting stories deserve their place in the story of hunting lore.

I'll give you one more story to close, another Lori Streadl story. A year or two ago, Lori went with her boyfriend Val, a hunting guide, down to a ranch between Freer and Encinal, where hunters from Houston had come for the weekend. The hunters wanted to shoot some wild pigs, so they loaded up on the high rack of the hunting truck while Val and Lori got in the cab. They came upon a pig that was "huge," according to Lori, weighing several hundred pounds. She said when the hunters started shooting, "it sounded like World War III up there." Like her mother and David Hale's experience with the doe who refused to die, these hunters kept shooting, but the pig wouldn't die. Finally, Lori leaned out of the cab window and told them to shoot the pig in the head to kill it, to which one of the hunters responded, "What do you know? You're a woman!" This remark did not set well with Lori (remember, she shot the spike beyond her dad's favorite horse). Finally, Val got out of the truck and put the pig out of its misery by shooting it in the head with his pistol.

The next day, as Lori and Val sat in a deer blind, Lori asked Val if it would be okay if she shot a pig. He said that would be fine. Val had his video camera along that day to film the deer for the ranch as Lori waited to shoot. In a while, they heard a loud noise that turned out to be a herd of pigs running down the road into the corn field. Lori selected a sow and shot as she moved along with the herd. Lori had been telling Val she is a "One shot, one kill" hunter, which is exactly what she proved to be. And Val got it all on film. After she shot the sow, Lori turned to the camera and said, "That's how it's done, boys."[28]

ENDNOTES

1. Francis Edward Abernethy. "Preface." *Between the Cracks of History: Essays on Teaching and Illustrating Folklore*. Publications of the Texas Folklore Society LV. Francis E. Abernethy, Ed. Denton: University of North Texas Press, 1997. *ix*.
2. Dolf Lowe. Personal interview. 28 May 2010.
3. Georgia Lowe. Personal interview. 27, 28 May 2010.
4. Mattie Swaim Sadovsky. Personal interview. 28 May 2010.
5. D'Anna Woodmansee. Personal Facebook message. 13 Apr. 2010.
6. Alyssa Webb. Personal Facebook message. 6 Apr. 2010.
7. Karen Webb. Personal Facebook message. 27 May 2010.
8. Carolyn Orsak. Personal email message. 15 Apr. 2010.
9. Dolf Lowe. Personal interview. 28 May 2010.
10. Carolyn Lowe. Personal interview. 27, 28 May 2010.
11. Stephanie Ingham. Personal email message. 7 Apr. 2010.
12. Mattie Swaim Sadovsky. Personal interview. 28 May 2010.
13. Jeanette Streadl. Personal interview. 19 June 2010.
14. Kim Streadl. Personal interview. 19 June 2010.
15. Anne Mangham. Personal interview. 29 May 2010.
16. Lori Streadl. Personal interview. 19 June 2010.
17. Betty Jennings. Personal interview. 7 Apr. 2010.
18. Judy Hinnant. Telephone conversations. 27, 28 Nov. 2004.
19. Hinnant. Personal email message. 3 June 2005.
20. Lynn Harris. Personal email message. 3 June 2005.
21. Harris. Personal email message. 23 June 2005.
22. Joyce Gibson Roach. "Defining Folklore for My Students." *Between the Cracks of History: Essays on Teaching and Illustrating Folklore*. Publications of the Texas Folklore Society LV. Francis E. Abernethy, Ed. Denton: University of North Texas Press, 1997. 12.
23. Joe S. Graham. "Toward a Definition of Folklore Culture." *Between the Cracks of History: Essays on Teaching and Illustrating Folklore*.

Publications of the Texas Folklore Society LV. Francis E. Abernethy, Ed. Denton: University of North Texas Press, 1997. 27–29.

24. Francis E. Abernethy. "An Introduction." *The Family Saga: A Collection of Texas Family Legends.* Publications of the Texas Folklore Society LX. Francis Edward Abernethy, Jerry Bryan Lincecum, and Frances B. Vick, Eds. Denton: University of North Texas Press, 2003. 1–4.

25. Pam Zaitz. "End of Season Surprise." *Texas Trophy Hunters.* July/Aug. 2010. 28–29.

26. Rhett Rushing. "Beginning Within: Teaching Folklore the Easy Way." *Between the Cracks of History: Essays on Teaching and Illustrating Folklore.* Publications of the Texas Folklore Society LV. Francis E. Abernethy, Ed. Denton: University of North Texas Press, 1997. 55.

27. Douglas Southall Freeman. "Foreward." *A Treasury of Southern Folklore: Stories, Ballads, Traditions, and Folkways of the People of the South.* B. A. Botkin, Ed. New York: Crown, 1949. *ix.*

28. Lori Streadl. Personal interview. 19 June 2010.

THE
LORE OF
HUNTING —

DEER, HOGS, COONS, AND EVEN FOXES

Bob Dunn as a young hunter

DEER LEAVES

by Bob Dunn

I'm not sure of the first time I went to the deer lease; probably it was in 1970, when I turned nine years old. It seemed that it was just always there. Early on, I called it "deer leaves" because that's what I thought the grown-ups were saying.

I remember waking up one morning after Dad's return from the hunt to find a deer hanging from a tree in the front yard of our home in Garland. Back then, the neighborhood butcher shop would process the kill for us, but later medical concerns over cross-contamination of retail meat market equipment led to a law prohibiting the practice. After that, we did our own butchering, and we always had backstraps to chicken-fry and plenty of meat to barbecue, though we never mastered sausage making.

Besides being a great place to hunt, the lease was an easy, two-hour drive from home. Dad worked nights, so we could leave after school on Friday and still have some daylight left when we got there. In those days, I thought more about landmarks along the highway than of time and distance. Shortly after leaving Garland we would pass Big Town, where we'd sometimes see Santa arrive by helicopter for a pre-Christmas visit. Then we'd drive into downtown Dallas, which would disappear as the roadway dipped into the "canyon" and the only tunnel I knew existed.

After we came out, we would cross over the Trinity River, which always seemed just a trickle winding its way through its wide flood plain. Next, onto the Turnpike, with its hibernating Six Flags amusement park, stirring me to ask "can we go next summer?" We usually didn't. Then on to Fort Worth, where the highway was elevated and you could look out over the city—so different from Dallas, which had no such elevated vista. And through Cowtown, on west to Weatherford and the Parker County courthouse, where we made a turn and were finally on the home stretch, to Graford. This

Palo Pinto County town is so named because of its location between Graham and Weatherford.

It was a hunting town with a downtown full of deer offices always open to welcome hunters, who mostly came out for a day or two. The deer office we stopped at was typical. It had a map of the ranch being represented, and its walls were posted with hundreds of photos of deer bagged over the last several years. I remember a sign near the photo display stating, "I shot all these deer in downtown Graford" with a note signed "The Cameraman."

There were a couple of tables for food, drink, cards, dominos, gun cleaning, knife sharpening, or whatever demands might be made on them. And there was something to sleep on—a bed, a couch, or a cot—a gas heater or two, and plenty of ashtrays. During deer season, someone was nearly always there, or there was a note saying where the attendant was and when he would be back. Since we always held a season lease we would mostly just stop in to socialize; Dad might play a few hands of cards if there was a game going.

Then we'd head for the camp, down a farm-to-market road that took us a couple of miles east of town to the main gate of the lease. A few minutes after passing through the gate, we passed a vacated homestead, with a classic two-story house, barns still holding surreys and implements of another time, a corral built of native stone, and, of course, the life-sustaining windmill towering over and feeding a mossy cement water trough.

Most vehicles could make it through the low creek bed that led into camp; those that couldn't would find another place where they could get a better angle. The ranch was about 10,000 acres, parcels divided among the season lease holders, and an area set aside for the day hunters. The camp area was maybe a couple of wooded acres, with camping spots shared by friends and family groups. Individual sites apparently were decided by seniority, and groups came back to the same spot year after year. Trees offered protection from the elements, and some ancient wiring and fuse boxes provided electricity. There might have been a water faucet, but we usually brought water from home.

The only permanent structure in the camp, except for the out-house, was a shack for the gatekeeper, who would check hunters in and out and record the number of deer taken. I remember that the outhouse offered a winter home to hundreds of daddy long leg spiders.

We always stayed in a big, second-hand Sears "Ted Williams" tent Dad had found somewhere. I'm amazed that we were able to keep up with all the parts while it sat idle in the garage ten months each year awaiting the next hunting season.

We usually set up camp two weeks before opening day, and this involved towing our '63 Volkswagen Bug loaded with most of our provisions. It could get around anywhere on the lease with "a running start." The car only had a few modifications: the back fenders were cut out with tin snips then folded under to allow for bigger tires, and drain holes in the back floorboards had been crafted by a .22 pistol after the Bug had stalled out once during a creek crossing.

The provisions, along with the tent, included a piece of rem-nant carpet, a full size mattress, an electric heater, folding tables and chairs, a Coleman stove and lantern, and coats and coveralls. The electric heater would keep the tent nice and warm, but we usually had a knife handy to cut our way out of the durable can-vas tent in case of fire. Looking back, that tent probably would have burned so fast we wouldn't have known it until we felt a draft.

Two friends shared our camping spot, parked on either side of our tent, forming a U-shape, with a campfire in the center. On one side was a motor home built from an old bread truck; on the other was a newish travel trailer. This arrangement was loosely duplicated in maybe ten or twenty spots around the camp. Perhaps the most popular was the slide-in camper, some with, some without the pickup. After the end of the season everything was removed from camp and we started fresh the next season.

On opening morning, we were usually awakened by a hand crank siren the ranchers used to call cows. It was quite effective if you were sleeping in a tent, though the RV guys probably didn't get the full blast. After layering on warm clothes, including thermals and coveralls, I would usually have a packaged cinnamon roll and a Coke while the grown-ups were making coffee.

With coffee downed, cigarettes smoked, weapons readied, and hunting licenses checked, it was time to load up and hunt. All types of vehicles—Jeeps, pickups, SUVs (before they were called that), dune buggies (this was before the 3- and 4-wheeler days) lined up at the gate. Dad always liked the VW Bug because it got you out of the weather and had a heater. One problem: there was no place on the Bug's exterior to place a gun. A hunter friend had removed his coveralls before the trip back to camp and placed his very nice .30.06 on the car's roof, only to be rudely reminded of his error when the gun crashed onto the rocky road a few seconds after taking off.

Once the gatekeeper checked us out, we were off to our designated hunting grounds. Day hunters turned left at the fork in the road; lease hunters turned right. It was a set-up that worked well, for I never remember a day hunter on our lease. We only ventured into the day hunt area once, to see a small plane that had crashed in the fog, killing the pilot and his wife instantly. A hunter recalled hearing the plane circling, before it came down low, clipped a tree and crashed into the ground not far from his stand. He was so upset he left, informing the gatekeeper of the accident on his way out, and never returned.

Roads in the area were kept in good condition to allow easy access to gas and oil sites. There had been an oil strike some fifty years earlier, followed by more recent natural gas production that had left evidence everywhere in the form of pipe, tanks and pump jacks. Although the roads were good, we had to cross Keechi Creek in three of the four spots, where it snaked through our area.

The lease was in a horseshoe bend of the creek, which, with a hilltop on the west, made a natural boundary. I can still look at a map and immediately find the exact location. I had a strong fear of breaking down or getting stuck and being stranded, and voiced the fear when that danger seemed imminent. "Bobby," my dad would answer impatiently, "let me know if you see rusted out cars with skeletons; otherwise we'll assume everybody has made it out alive." (That's the cleaned-up version of his cautionary order.)

We eliminated long walks to the stand in the early morning dark by driving to a point near them. The stands were nothing but a few limbs piled around a fallen tree; we never built or bought anything like blinds or feeders. We usually got to our spot half an hour or so before daylight. There was something about the darkness that heightened the senses, especially hearing, and every armadillo that scurried through on dried leaves could make one feel under attack. I was well armed, with a five-shot bolt action .243, but sometimes I wondered if it was weapon enough to protect against whatever might be approaching from every direction.

When daylight finally came the new threat was nodding off in sleep—we had stayed up late and gotten up early, and the warming sun induced dozing. Luckily, the noisy VW helped restore the senses. By mid-morning it was time to head back to camp.

On the 20-minute drive back, I would usually have to open and close a few gates. Everybody had the same schedule before dawn and after dusk, so there was a good chance you might catch a gate open. At mid-morning and early afternoon, you were on your own. These were the barbed wire gaps with no hinges, and with wire loops at top and bottom on the fastening side to catch the cedar post. The fences were well past their prime—rusted barbed wire barely gripping weathered cedar posts, old pieces of baling wire taking the place of the staples that had lost their grip after decades of service. With some practice I learned how to hug the posts together just enough to get the loop over the top. In later years I learned the value of a cheater bar hanging from the post to apply leverage. But I really learned to appreciate gates on hinges, and absolutely loved cattle guards.

Deer camp was always a busy place between morning and after-noon hunts. Hunters were usually working on their vehicles or accommodations. Lunch was usually a sandwich or something from a can.

It was common to see the game warden in camp, making sure everything was legal. There could easily be a few dozen deer taken on a good morning, each requiring a perfectly filled-out tag attached in the required manner. It wasn't hard to do, but in all of the excitement it was sometimes easy to forget. If the game warden found one not tagged correctly, there would be a rush by other hunters to make corrections before he finished the citation. Poach-ing was a big problem, and if a tag wasn't filled out correctly it could possibly be re-used. If the deer population was reduced, the number of hunters would gradually be diminished also. And hunt-ing was a boon to the local economy.

On Saturday, we almost always went to town, and Graford was a busy place in those days. At the cafe where we sometimes ate, I discovered that chicken fried steak, fries, and a slice of coconut pie was a perfect meal, and a happy relief from camp fare. And we shopped for provisions at the downtown grocery store. At the back of that long narrow building was the meat counter where the pro-prietor custom sliced the best bologna and cheese I've ever had.

The afternoon hunt was my favorite. Dad staked out a hilltop he liked to hunt, so the rest of the lease was mine. There were two conditions: I could not affect his hunting in any way, and I had to be at or near my stand at dark when he drove down to pick me up. He warned that he would not wait or go looking for me, although I'm sure he would have. But I never risked it because it was a long way back to camp.

Our lease was a few hundred acres with a good mix of cedar and hardwoods. The terrain varied from gently sloping to ledges and rock outcroppings; because the creek served as the boundary on three sides it was easy to keep my bearings. I would walk slowly and deliberately, looking for the signs I read about in hunting magazines, the quietness interrupted by the occasional report of a rifle in the distance, or the whir of helicopters from nearby Camp Wolters. Otherwise, the only noise to disturb the solitude was the flushing of a covey of quail, exploding in every direction to quickly disappear.

Saturday nights were best, whether we stayed in camp or went to town. One camp always had a big fire that served as the official gathering place. Everyone was welcome; it didn't matter if it was their first day or tenth season. There was plenty of conversation, about hunting, work, sports. One group of guys were big fans of Fort Worth Wings hockey, and all were Dallas Cowboys fans. And there were the inevitable practical jokes, but always in fun, and I don't recall lasting anger resulting from any of them.

We sometimes drove to a cafe on the Graham highway for a plate of the great onion rings they made. And from there, Dad would call home to check in—no cell phones in those days. Not far from the cafe was a roadhouse/honky-tonk. And it was there that my dad taught me the phrase "Loose Lips Sink Ships," a phrase that I didn't know then was associated with World War II.

One dark night after such an outing and approaching the camp gate, we saw a shooting star, then another and another. We parked the car in a pasture, sat on the hood and watched an incredible meteor shower, and we talked. It was a night I'll never forget—true and good and wonderful, even though it was only remotely connected to the "deer leaves."

Ab Abernethy in full hunting gear

"NOW, DON'T THAT BEAT ALL!"

by Francis Edward Abernethy

A morning deer hunt is usually over around ten o'clock. Even the most patient of hunters is ready to come off his stand and go back to the camp by that time, particularly if he has not seen a hair. I carry coffee, a pork chop, and a Snickers bar, so I can last a little longer, if I have a mind to. Under the best of circumstances, somebody has stayed at the camp and cooked sausage and eggs with biscuits and gravy for his buddies when they come in from the woods. If not, there might be a cold plate of last night's fried venison backstrap still lying around. The coffee pot is always on, and the hunters report on their morning hunts, usually as they stand backed up to an outdoors log fire.

The hunting report is casual, but it should be accurate because the others listen and learn. "All I saw was a big old black fox squirrel and one armadillo and some fresh hog rubs where that trail comes out of the creek bottom." Or, "When I finally turned around and saw him, he saw me and left the county." You learn two things with those reports: 1) where to put a hog trap and 2) don't turn around when you hear a deer walking up behind you. Reports lead to remembrances and remembrances lead to the kind of hunting tales that have been told after hunts ever since man got the genetic command to kill and eat meat or die.

A great gun story is one Fount Simmons used to tell down in the Thicket. Fount was paralyzed from the waist down, but he was a great market hunter during the time when the railroads were being built in the Thicket and the big saw mills were flourishing. He heard that somebody had an eight-gauge shotgun for sale in Newton, so he took a two-day ride up there and bought it. He tried it out on his way back and said it took him an hour before he could get back on his horse. When Fount got home he charged it pretty heavy and set it in the gun rack and told his brother Rad that

that was just the right gun to get the old buck with, the one that always skirted their field just out of range. After a light shower one afternoon Rad took the gun and eased out to the edge of the pasture and took a stand at the forks of a split-rail fence, with the gun barrel resting on the third rail. About three o'clock the folks in the house heard a mighty roar from Rad's direction that shook the trees. About six o'clock Rad came in, considerably bruised up and with his arm hanging kind of limp. He said he had the front end and the back end of the deer hanging down in the woods, and that he had spent most of the afternoon rebuilding the fence.

An old boy came up from Houston to hunt one weekend with Speck Risinger in Tyler County, and of course, since he was pretty new to the game Speck put him on a real meat stand right on this sand road. Speck called them "poison stands!" and it scared you to think what might come out over you.

Speck checked him out on the rules of the hunt, told him not to shoot a doe or any of the hounds, and left him standing there with his brand new Marlin lever-action .30-30. It was a still-frost morning, and the dogs jumped a big buck just as he was coming in to bed down and, dogs a-squawlin', the race was on. Speck fired his gun to let the standers know that a buck was running, and then he took off through the woods trying to keep them in sight. Sure enough, they were headed right toward the sand-road "poison stand."

Speck wasn't far behind when deer and dogs crossed the road, and he was waiting to hear a shot and a yell but there wasn't a sound. When he got there the man was still stuttering in the shakes of buck fever and standing with his gun at his side. He said that it was a big buck and that it just kind of trotted across the road about twenty steps from him—said he had time to fire five shots before the buck hit the brush again. Speck said he hadn't heard a shot, and the old boy swore and be-damned that he had fired five times. That was about the time Speck saw something shining in the sand and looked a little closer and found five .30-30 shells. Not a cap had been busted. The old boy had levered the shells through but had never pulled the trigger.

Chuck Davis said that on another occasion Speck saw this stander and asked him what he had seen. The stander told him that he did see four or five dogs crossing the high line, but that was all. Speck asked him, "Do you think that a deer was chasin' the dogs?"

Jim Hayes, who was teaching in Woodville at the time, was hunkered down on a stand in Sunny Dell Pasture early one cold morning and decided he had to have a cup of coffee. So real slow he got his thermos and poured a cap full and glanced down the road just in time to see a big old rocking-chair buck sneaking out to cross the road. He didn't have time to put down his cup, so he eased his left hand with the coffee out to raise the gun barrel. He got it up just to sight as the buck started into the woods again, and he touched it off. Jim said the gun roared and the whole world turned wet, hot, and coffee brown. And that old buck left the country without even raising his flag.

On another frosty winter morning Jim Snyder climbed up and squatted on a big log for his morning relief. He propped his rifle against the log, and for easy access he spindled a short roll of toilet paper on the rifle barrel. Soon after, but still in the midst of, a young buck stepped out of the woods and gazed in wonder at this large growth on a downed log in his stomping ground. Never removing his eye from the buck target, and pants down and still in a squatting position, Snyder slowly retrieved and shouldered his rifle. He raised it to sight only to be reminded that a roll of toilet paper rested between his back sight and front sight and completely obliterated the deer. The buck, amused and confused at such a picture, strolled back into the brush. Snyder went back to his business with his handily spooled roll of toilet paper.

Noah Platt used to tell of a fellow he was hunting with who took three shots at a deer trotting along just on the other side of a barb-wire fence, and each shot centered a fence post.

On a hunt at Cecil Overstreet's, one of the Moyes got so excited when he heard the dogs bringing game his way that when the deer popped out behind him into the land line he whirled around and threw his gun at him.

Another time, some young man hunting in Cecil Overstreet's pasture in Hardin County was walking down a trail to his stand when a little forked-horn stepped out in front of him. He popped back the bolt, reached in his pocket for a shell, and came out with his cigarette lighter. He claimed that he chambered the cigarette lighter, fired at the buck, and left a burn stripe all the way from his appetite to his asshole. In spite of which, the deer got away.

Closer to the truth, if that's what you're looking for, Bill Clark tells a similar story about a man hunting near Sugar Creek. This

Pat Barton and Bill Clark

fellow had been hunting an old mossy horn for several years without luck. In the early dawn on one frosty morning, he took out his new 20-gauge to test it on some squirrels. Just as he started to cross a fence he spotted his old buck nearby and looking the other way. He chambered a shell and pulled the trigger, and all he heard was the click of the firing pin. Old Mossy heard it too and hit the brush. Disappointed with his new shotgun, he broke it open and saw a roll of Tums in the chamber.

George Doland told about this Fort Worth hunter who was perched in a tree by a thick love-grass pasture waiting for nothing but a trophy buck. The prize buck showed up, the hunter fired, and the deer dropped where he stood, into the tall grass and out of sight. The hunter shinnied down the tree and headed through the tall grass across the pasture. He found the buck and pulled his knife to gut him. He grabbed his buck by his horns—and the buck indignantly rose up with the hunter hanging on and slashing at his throat. After some bloody hand-to-horn combat, the hunter finally subdued his trophy. He was sitting by his buck, trying to get his adrenalin back down and his breath back up, when he saw another buck lying in the deep grass about ten yards away. It was the buck he had shot.

These tales are not over after the hunt. They pop up every time hunters get together, and they're about all sorts of animals, including hogs.

Here's a tale I've told around the campfire, probably more than once. I don't know when I started hunting hogs. I guess it was when I first shot one and brought it home and cooked a ham for Thanksgiving dinner. It beat hell out of a turkey.

I was at Sunny Dell Pasture, hunting out of my leaning post-oak stand on Big Dry Creek when this big old sow came by just at sundown. I popped her. I guess she weighed a hundred pounds or more. Then I got to wondering what I was going to do with all that hog. I sure wasn't going to tote a whole hog back to my pickup a half a mile away, now—in the black dark. I decided to cut it up, deer fashion. I cut off its hams and shoulders and then peeled

A big ol' hog

out the backstrap. I had a mess of meat stacked around in the black dark when I got through, plus a rifle, fanny pack, and climbing hooks.

I was trudging up the hill to the ridge road with a ham in both hands and a backstrap over my shoulder when they opened up. My God but it sounded like all the coyotes in the world, and they were gathering in the edge of the woods about fifty feet away, red-eyed and stirred to a feeding frenzy by the smell of that hog's blood. And I had left my gun for the next trip! I have no doubt that my hair stood on end, like in comic strips. I could feel it. And I could feel my blood which had stopped circulating and had gotten cold. The coyotes got louder and sounded closer, and I finally got back enough in control to start moving again—but not running! I knew I'd never make it in a race.

Looking back, there were probably five or six worn-out coyotes on the other side of the hill. I doubt that they even knew I was in the vicinity. I wasn't looking back that night, however. I made it out to my pickup and would have left the rest of that hog in the bottom with the coyotes, but I had to go back and get my gun and gear.

John Artie McCall and I talk on the phone fairly regularly, usually about hunting and wild animals. John Artie is paranoid about raccoons (and hogs!). Coons steal the corn out of his deer feeders at his camp on the Trinity. They throw chairs out of his deer stands, and tear up his duck blinds. This morning he was telling me how a friend of his was losing lots of corn out of a feeder, so he raised his feeder higher than he figured any coons could reach. He was still losing corn, so he put out a motion camera. What he got was a picture of one coon standing on another's shoulders, raking corn out of the feeder for every other coon in the pasture! "Now, don't that beat all! You think a coon ain't smart!"

Hinkel Shillings and Walker foxhounds

HINKEL SHILLINGS AND THE RED RANGER

by Thad Sitton

On April 21, 1941, terrible news passed through the crowd of three thousand at the annual state field trial of the Texas Fox and Wolf Hunters Association near Crockett. The nocturnal hunters of fox and coyote—"hilltoppers," "moonlighters," or just "plain old forks-of-the-creek fox hunters"—had assembled for one of their rare daytime competitions to discover who had the best dog. Judges watched hounds with big numbers on their sides run foxes in broad daylight to see which ones led the packs. Day or night, such men never rode to hounds like the red-coated horsemen. Instead, in most of their hunting, they stood by fires and listened in the dark to the voices of a special breed of dog developed to chase foxes entirely on its own. It was a strange hound and a strange bloodless sort of hunting, in which, as folklorist F. E. Abernethy once observed, "The race is the thing, and it is the running of it that is its significance, not the reward at the end. . . ."[1] In truth, as outsiders often observed, there seemed no obvious reward to fox hunting. The game was left alive to run another night, and in any case, nobody ate foxes.

Rural sheriffs often drew the hard duty of bringing bad news of the death of loved ones, and the Houston County sheriff had just arrived to tell foxhound breeder Hinkel Shillings that his champion foxhound Dawson Stride had escaped his pen near Center, Texas, joined in a local fox chase, run himself to exhaustion, and died. Penned foxhounds were notorious for breaking kennel. When a hot fox chase came by, as in this instance, American Foxhounds like Dawson Stride often felt such fanatical zeal to join the hunt that they exerted almost supernatural pressures on their pens, some scrabbling over high board fences or climbing across electrified wires to join up. In later years Hinkel held the opinion that Dawson Stride's noble foxhound line-of-duty death was perhaps for the best, "a good way for anybody to die," but not at that time. Stricken, Hinkel slumped down on the tailgate of a pickup, his eyes filling with tears.

Other hunters also cried. Dawson Stride was famous—almost legendary. Every fox hunter across the eastern United States knew about Dawson Stride by 1941, and a rather large number of them had paid first-hand or second-hand to include his wonderful genes in their running packs. Dawson Stride had been penned up at stud for the last years of his short eight-year life, dutifully impregnating 505 female Walker foxhounds with his fabulous "get," as hunters termed his more than 5,000 direct offspring. Dawson Stride "threw" his fine hunting qualities and good looks very well, and many champions of field and bench numbered among his many children, grandchildren, and great-grandchildren. Dawson Stride's blood had impacted the entire universe of American fox hunting by 1941, and hunters who had not got around to directly incorporating it in their packs now experienced a sickening sense of vanished possibilities. Their eyes moistened not just for Hinkel's tragic loss, but for their own.

Immediately, something very unusual began to happen—unusual even for fox hunters. The Depression story of Hinkel and Dawson Stride's rags-to-riches exploits had captivated hunters just as much as the unlikely success story of undersized racehorse Seabiscuit had mesmerized track goers. In addition, Hinkel Shillings had always been generous with Dawson Stride, cheerfully taking him out to run with whatever fox hunters showed up unannounced at his Shelby County farm. Stud hound owners normally did not do this, especially professional breeders like Hinkel. Studs were too valuable, and dangers haunted every night-time fox chase. A large number of hunters at the Houston County meet had visited Hinkel and run their hounds with Dawson Stride, and now some of these men began to reach in their pockets and count their money. A movement quickly developed to buy a monument for Dawson Stride. A chairman and a committee emerged, then and there, and monument-dealer Guy Ferrell, Sr., of Beaumont, a man who had hunted behind Dawson Stride on numerous occasions, volunteered a fine 4,000-pound piece of Texas granite at cost. Hunters buried Dawson Stride at that monument in Shelby County later in April with speeches, prayers, and the sound of blowing horns, and it became the first grave in what soon became the National Foxhound Hall of Fame Cemetery, dedicated with more ceremonies on December 9, 1941, two days after Pearl Harbor.[2]

Over the years, many other great foxhounds would take their places under monuments in the little cemetery on land donated by the United States Forest Service, which at first glance much resembled many small human cemeteries scattered across rural East Texas. Fox hunters were different (some non-believers even said they were deranged), and the National Foxhound Hall of Fame Cemetery certainly manifested that difference. The monuments remain—granite and marble last a long time—monuments to Night Rowdy, Fouche River Rambler, Bandit, Mr. Jabber S, and others, many with epitaphs. Choctaw's gravestone reads, "Tough Hound, he always gave it all he had," and Climber H's, "A running hound with a running heart." Dawson Stride's own monument simply states, "He will be remembered and appreciated as long as the chase exists." On the back side of Dawson's grave, Hinkel's champion Mark S resides: "One of history's greatest foxhounds."

The "S" in Mark's name stood for "Shillings," as in the case of Dawson Stride's champion sister, Pearl S. If names mean anything (and of course they do), fox hunters like Hinkel Shillings seemed to consider their hound sons and daughters only one short step away from their human ones.

Born in 1902, Hinkel Shillings had grown up with several brothers on a 221-acre farm on one slope of Bone Hill, a famous fox hunting site in Shelby County, arguably one of Texas' most famous fox hunting counties, and the Shillings boys had listened to other men's foxhounds run foxes since early childhood. On a still night, the sound of a hot fox chase carried for miles. All the brothers had to do most evenings to hear a race was to move out onto their front porch. Hinkel began staying up all night to listen to the hounds tell the story of the fox hunt, even when hard field-work loomed the next day. Hinkel's father Isaiah, a non-fox hunter, allowed this, so long as his sleepless son plowed, or chopped, or pulled corn like everybody else after sun-up.

Fox hunters almost universally claimed that there was such a thing as the born fox hunter, and that such persons' recruitment to the sport usually came when they heard their first fox race. True hunters heard the music of the hounds—or even, as one veteran claimed, "heard the angels sing," and felt summoned to participate all the days of their lives, while everybody else just heard a bunch of dogs barking and remained totally mystified. You either "got" fox hunting upon your first exposure to it, or you didn't get it at all, or so it seemed. Hinkel did not comment on his five oldest brothers, but brother Hardy, just older than Hinkel, and younger brothers Johnnie and Bill authentically heard the angels sing and the hounds call their names on those Bone Hill nights. None of the four youngest Shillings ever recovered from the hound con-certs they had listened to on the front porch, and they became ardent, lifetime fox hunters and hound breeders.

There was fox hunting on the one hand, and all other sorts of hound-dog hunting—coons, deer, bobcats, whatever—on the other; the two were not the same. Georgian Ben Hardaway told a common story that illustrates the gulf that existed for some people between ordinary hunting and hunting of the fox. He noted in his personal history, *Never Outfoxed*:

> I was about ten years old at the time. On one par-ticular and unforgettable night, we were hunting up along Heiferhorn Creek. Our hounds were cold-trailing a coon when I heard a strange sound. My heart stopped when I heard it. In fact, every-thing stopped: my feet, my breathing, all motion ceased. I stood in the late night darkness of the

Georgia woods, and only my ears could continue to
function. The sound came pouring down the valley
where I was standing. I knew it was the sound of
hounds, but it was more beautiful than anything
I'd ever heard before. Their music sang through
my entire being like something electric and
changed everything it touched forever.[3]

If only a few fox hunters had said things like Hardaway about
the effects of foxhound voices, it would be more understandable,
but a great many people, almost all men, reported similar reac-
tions. Whatever fox chasing was, it struck some people like a reli-
gious experience, like "something electric," and they were never
the same afterward. When Alabama native O. M. Johnson went on
his first fox hunt, he became so excited at the sounds coming from
the dark that he bolted from the hunters' fire and ran with the
hounds all night long, coming back to normal consciousness at
first light when the hounds denned the fox fifteen miles away from
home. He wrote many years later, "Then I said I would not go fox
hunting any more. I have been a thousand times since." And Texan
Glen Hayden tried hard to describe how Johnson had felt, noting
that "I have stood in places with the brush popping, feet thudding,
and the wild-squalling anvil chorus of the pack drowning me in a
wave of blood-hungry melody, while my hair almost stood on end,
my throat tightened and my blood raced."[4]

Obviously, Hinkel Shillings heard the "blood-hungry melody"
very early on, and at age four or five he accompanied his father to a
neighbor's farm to view the born fox hunters' beau ideal, the pure-
blood, registered American Foxhound—in this case two Hud-
speth-strain dogs bred and certified to run the red fox. Owning
such hounds became Hinkel's goal from that point, although it
took him a quarter of a century to attain it. American Foxhounds
had been bred to match up with the "red ranger," *Vulpes vulpes,* a
fox so swift and enduring that it left coon hounds like Black and
Tans, Blueticks, and Redbones in its dust. Multipurpose hounds

like these could successfully run the smaller native gray fox, but not the imported red, now abroad as a fairly common game species in Shelby County and nearby counties. The beautiful lemon and white Hudspeths left an indelible mark on young Hinkel; he thought them the most beautiful dogs he had ever seen. He began dreaming about them at night.

Hudspeths were just one of several strains or races of American Foxhound, the foremost being Walkers, Julys, Triggs, and Goodmans. Hunters created the American Foxhound from the parent breed of British Foxhound in the decades before and just after the Civil War, mainly to cope with the speedy red fox, then spreading southward and westward from Maryland and Virginia. The Walker family of Kentucky developed the most famous variety of American Foxhound, which they modestly called the Maupin Hound after their affluent neighbor and co-developer of the strain, General George Washington Maupin (his full given name). Relatives of the Walkers began moving to East Texas in the 1850s, and—in a tremendous stroke of hound-dog-man one-upmanship—they carried with them both the foreign red fox that Texas coon hounds and gray fox hounds could not catch, and the dog that could catch it. Since they knew only the Walker family, Texas hunters naturally came to call this version of the fast American Foxhound the Walker Hound, and the name gradually spread back east and became the name that stuck.[5]

Walkers became known as the quintessential red fox hound, which said a lot about them. Such foxes set a tremendously high standard of vulpine running performance, threatening any hound that pursued them with being run to death or something rather close to it, but Walkers had been bred never to quit the chase. As Hinkel said, the Walker family "absolutely did not tolerate a quitting hound." At the extreme, red foxes had the ability to run a hundred miles in a night, and Walkers—some of them—had the ability to follow.

The wonderful hound had been called into existence by the wonderful red fox. Hinkel Shillings loved the animal that hunters called the red ranger above all foxes, and in his last years he kept a framed photo of a red fox over his TV and called my attention to it every time I visited him. "Look at that," he would say, "Isn't that beautiful?"

To understand American folk-fox hunting, hilltopping, you had to understand hunters' attitudes to the red fox. Hilltoppers admired the red fox, studied its movements and habits, transported it to new territory, raised it for release, and put out food for it in the wild; in fact, they acted like wildlife managers of the red fox even in the nineteenth century, before the profession even existed. Several times in his life Hinkel did like most other fox hunters. He acquired ten or twelve young reds, penned them in a remote location, fed them regularly (in his case with dead pullets from broiler houses), then cut holes in the fence, continued to feed, and let the young foxes gradually go completely wild. Later, he ran them with his hounds, trying very hard not to harm them.

Only a game biologist *and* fox chaser could do justice to the hunters' view of the red fox, and just such a person was the remarkable Joe T. Stevens (1920–2000). Stevens was game biologist, Walker foxhound breeder, and ordained Baptist minister, all rolled into one. He was known for sounding his blowing horn at the beginnings of church services, for his flamboyant stud-hound ads in *Hunter's Horn* and other fox hunter magazines, and for the unmatched description of *Vulpes vulpes* he wrote for *Texas Parks and Wildlife Magazine* in 1969:

> Legend would lead one to believe that the red fox is a large animal; however, he is relatively small, normally weighing from 8 to 12 pounds. His color, especially in the winter, is breathtaking. Above, his golden-yellow coat glows like flame, and underneath, his fur is a soft, snowy white. His piercing dark eyes are widely set in a rusty, dull yellow face grizzled with white. Fine jet-black fur, like stylish silk gloves, extends up to the elbow on his forelegs

and to the outer thigh on the hind legs. His strong, streamlined body is adapted for running. Apparently enjoying every minute of a chase, he can easily run in front of an onrushing pack of baying foxhounds all night, and is capable of sudden bursts of speed up to 45 miles per hour.[6]

For twenty years the Shillings brothers only listened to the red fox races of other hunters. You could not effectively pursue such a creature as Joe Stevens described with what fox men called "potlickers"—coon hounds or multipurpose, mixed-breed, farm dogs—and those were all the poor-boy Shillings had. Such dogs would of course run red foxes, but it was all very discouraging. Doubtless much amused, the elite reds simply moved out into the closest open running landscapes, turned on their afterburners, and the trail got colder and colder as the hunt went on. Eventually, the outmatched potlicker hounds began to "howl out"—to issue mournful howls at their ignominious defeats, quit, and come back, nursing deep psychic wounds. Fast, red-fox hounds could be used in gray fox races, though the dogs might ruin the hunt for other hunters, but the converse was not true.

Fox hunting in Shelby County, as elsewhere, existed at two levels of the game, depending on the species of fox the hunters chased, and for almost two decades Hinkel and his brothers remained stuck at the gray-fox level because they were too poor to acquire hounds good enough to chase red foxes. The Shillings consoled themselves by listening from their porch, by occasionally going out with other hunters on their races (bittersweet experiences, at best; the hunter needed to hear *his* hound in the hunt), and by studying and re-studying elite hound bloodlines in the three enthusiast magazines that catered to fox hunters, *Chase*, *Hunter's Horn*, and *Red Ranger*. Brooding over the pages, the brothers argued back and forth about the perfect "crossings," matings of champion foxhounds that would produce stellar offspring. Gyps were just as important as "dogs" in these calculations. Fox men were not very sexist; female foxhounds competed side by side with males in hilltopper night hunts and daytime field trials, and hard evidence suggested that they pursued red foxes just as well. From time to time the Shillings got word of some blooded foxhounds within horseback range of their farm and rode over to take a long envious look at them, exactly like dirt-track jalopy racers going to gaze at a high-performance road car they could not afford. Meanwhile, Hinkel and his brothers ran gray foxes at least two nights a week.

Non-hunters and the hunters of everything else but foxes thought this behavior astonishing about the committed fox men. They hunted several times a week, and they often stayed up all night. And all for nothing, critics thought—at least not for anything discernible to the normal eye. Aware of how others regarded them, fox chasers often kept to themselves. The blessing or curse of being a born fox hunter fell mysteriously hither and thither

Texas fox hunters

upon rural Texans, so local hunting groups like Hinkel's often assembled a strangely dissimilar brotherhood of young and old, rich and poor, educated and illiterate, townsmen and backwoodsmen, and even black and white.

It happened that the common fox in the immediate vicinity of the Shillings farm was the gray fox. Grays and reds lived in somewhat different landscapes, with reds a lot rarer. Fox hunters knew their local foxes very well, even individual foxes, to which they might give names, and they often went somewhere where their potlicker hounds would encounter only gray foxes. The gray fox, *Urocyon cinereoargenteus,* the so-called "cat fox" or "tree fox," had its own kind of charm, and some hunters like Hinkel's uncle Jim Shillings preferred to run the species. Weighing eight to thirteen pounds, almost as large as reds, grays looked smaller. They had shorter legs and shorter fur, grizzled gray on the top, vivid orange-red on the neck, legs, underside of the tail, and base of the ears. The gray fox's magnificent tail (bigger than the red fox's tail, huge, gray, and triangular in shape when viewed from the back) compensated for its slightly smaller stature. A gray fox passing at high speed looked at first glance like two very furry animals running nose to tail.

Gray foxes were nocturnal and secretive, but rather common. They preferred woods and thickets, subsisting on an eclectic diet of wild fruits, insects, and various rodents, with an occasional big-game cottontail or swamp rabbit. Slower than red foxes when jumped by hounds, grays ran twisting and devious routes around their native environment rather like bobcats, though with much more staying power. Hounds chasing grays had to bust a lot of brush, since the little foxes avoided open areas where hounds might overtake them, and commonly used "strainer" tactics on the larger dogs, passing back and forth through bramble patches, tight thickets, and even woven wire fences, which the foxes squeezed through and the hounds had to jump or clamber over. Gray foxes had smaller territories than red foxes, ran much tighter races, and so normally stayed within hearing of the listening point from which hounds had been loosed.

Beginning as teenagers, then as young married men renting their own farms, the four fox-hunting Shillings brothers gray-fox hunted with other men in the woods around Bone Hill. Almost nobody had a full pack of hounds; they had a hound or two that they contributed to the collective poor-boy pack. The Shillings were not stuck at the gray-fox stage because of a lack of hunting ambitions, however. At the beginning of the Depression, cotton prices sank like a stone, and small farmers in Shelby County relied on gardens, milk cows, and large corn patches to see them through. Meanwhile, cash in hand had become almost nil.

Potlicker hounds on the little subsistence farms worked stock and provided occasional wild meat for the pot, and they could be used to run foxes. Like most other creatures on the farm, including people, such hounds normally subsisted on ground field corn served up as crumbled "dog bread" or corn-meal mush, usually with a leavening of pork cracklings or table scraps thrown in. Gray fox hunting was cheap, money-wise, though disapproving neighbors (or even hunters' own family members) might think it prodigiously wasteful of time and precious sleep, and that nothing was accomplished by it, not even dead varmints. Landlords in particular preferred to see their rent farmers getting a good night's rest.

As at thousands of other locations across the fox-hunting universe, the gray fox hunters around Bone Hill had it down to a drill. Late on Tuesday and Friday afternoons, hunters from the Good Hope, Sardis, and Antioch communities walked or rode over with their hounds to one of the usual casting sites. They built a fire (if it was cold), loosed their hounds around dusk, then listened to them run gray foxes into the early morning hours of the next day. As occasional visitors noted, talk pretty much stopped after the dogs jumped a fox, and men stood listening—rapt, turned in slightly different directions to hear better, projecting themselves into the hunt.

A casual visitor to the Tuesday or Friday outing might just hear a bunch of dogs barking, but as the night wore on the real hunters heard the hound voices tell the whole intricate story of the fox chase—what sort of gray fox it was (perhaps even *which* fox it was), what tactics it used to "throw" the hounds, where it went to play its tricks across an intricate and well-known landscape, and above all, as the night continued, which man's dog took the lead or fell behind. The hunters were friends, and there was nothing at stake, nothing wagered, but every hunt was a *race* between hounds and between the men that owned them. Each hound/man unit operated as a team in competition with other such teams, and at key points in the race the hunter might whoop at his canine counterpart to urge it on. Hilltopping was a game hunters played entirely by ear, and some people had hearing verging on the uncanny. If the fox ran up a leaning tree and jumped out, or ran back and forth down a spring creek, the hunters—at least some of them—heard what had happened, and they heard which dogs were fooled by these fox tricks and which ones figured them out. Above all, each hunter listened to the voices of his hound to tell how it did in the race—but all the time was aware that most of his hunting buddies knew its voice almost as well as he did.

In spring or summer the twice-weekly Bone Hill fox chase might go on entirely in the dark, no fire being necessary for warmth, so the poor visitor might just stand there with these mostly silent men, who seemed to be having out-of-body experiences, while the stars swung across the sky and night waned. Eventually, the "tree fox" tired of being chased by hounds and climbed a tree, which it did quite readily, and the hound music ceased. Or at least should have ceased; real foxhounds did not usually bark "treed," a special bark, but potlicker hounds might. Then there was nothing to do but "horn" in the dogs with blowing horns, walk or ride home, eat breakfast, and get ready for the morning chores. Fox hunters usually could be distinguished from the rest of the rural population by the dark circles under their eyes.

Hinkel Shillings might have gone on chasing gray foxes at Bone Hill and Boles Field, a few miles away, for many more years, but in 1931 Hinkel's father Isaiah did something remarkable considering the state of the economy—he bought his first car. Later that year, Hinkel and one of his fox-hunter brothers persuaded their father to put the car to use in a long drive down to Livingston, Polk County, to attend the three-day November field trial of the Texas Fox and Wolf Hunter's Association. The Shillings had perhaps ridden over on horseback to visit a lesser field trial or two, although Hinkel never mentioned such a thing, but this was their first state meet—a major affair attended by a thousand or so of the general public and by several hundred hunters from Texas and beyond. Eyes perhaps blinking in broad light of day, the nocturnal fox hunters milled around in the crowd of thousands, gazing at food concessions, string bands, gospel quartets, the occasional political speaker, and, everywhere they looked, full-blooded American Foxhounds, most of them Walkers, snapped on chain lines, baying and barking with excitement.

Hinkel must have been almost beside himself, but the shy young farmer of twenty-nine probably would have been only an onlooker without the intervention of a friend of Isaiah Shillings, an experienced fox man named T. A. Harris, who took Hinkel around to all his hunting buddies soliciting subscriptions to *Hunter's Horn* magazine in Hinkel's name. Editor E. E. Everett of the *Horn* had devised something he called the premium puppy program—ten new or renewed subscriptions for a pup—to try to help poor young hunters attain ownership of blooded foxhounds during the Great Depression.

Breeders all across the United States had pledged free puppies to the magazine—probably mostly their culls, the rejected pups from each litter that the breeders would have had to dispose of anyway. Foxhounds had large litters, and their owners often made painful early decisions about which ones to keep and raise and which ones to put to death in the first day or two of life. Such men must have been happy enough to see the rejected pups live on and go to some poor boy to benefit *Hunter's Horn*, which was in its own dire straits because of the Depression.

Harris's arm-twistings did their job, and a little over a month later, on Christmas Day, 1931, Hinkel drove over to the railroad depot at Center to pick up his premium pup, the first full-blooded, registered, credentialed Walker hound he had ever owned. (A "paper hound," hunters called such a thing.) Hinkel's first glance inside her crate was not encouraging. She was sorry looking, he later admitted; she really looked like somebody's cull. But he comforted her, took her home and called her Christmas Dawson, naming her for the day he got her and for the blood of a noted stud dog named Hub Dawson that he knew ran in her veins. Hunters believed in the power of the mystic bloodlines that carried foxhound virtues down across the generations, and, as it turned out, Hinkel Schillings had not studied twenty years of hound genealogies in fox hunting magazines in vain. Perhaps he had just been lucky, but if so he continued to have that same sort of luck for half a century. Very young puppies were hard to judge, and breeder Bert Flowers of Fayetteville, Arkansas, seems to have made a big mistake; he had culled a future champion and the dam of an even greater one.

Christmas Dawson swiftly grew to adulthood in the way of foxhounds. By a year old she was big for a gyp, pretty, fast, intelligent, "game" (which was the fox men's key word meaning "enduring unto death"), and a fine chaser of red foxes. In one great leap, Hinkel had not just reached the next level of fox hunting but gotten somewhere near its upper limits. Christmas Dawson ran foxes at the head of the pack with one ear cocked to one side—her trade mark. All who saw and heard her agreed that she was a wonderful gyp, and in 1933, at about age two, she won both the all-age field trial and the best of show at the East Texas Hunt. Nor was that all of her early achievements. Hinkel had rushed to breed Christmas Dawson to a noted stud hound in Birmingham, Alabama, named Hub Stride; she had produced her first litter, and her son Dawson Stride won the bench show for puppies—foxhounds under one year of age—in that same 1933 East Texas Hunt.

Dawson Stride was bigger than his mother, a long-legged handsome liver-and-white Walker over twenty-five inches high at the shoulder, and a field competitor seemingly without fault. He had all of his mother's virtues, and more—a fine voice or "mouth," speed, gameness, endurance, and discipline in the hunt. He had a "cold nose," he followed faint scent trails far better than the average foxhound, and he even came back to his owner when the hunt ended and Hinkel blew his horn, something that many fox-crazy Walker hounds chose not to do. They heard the horn, but they ignored it and went looking for another fox. In fox men's terms, Dawson Stride was a good "homer."

Many field trial judges by day and average hilltoppers by moonlight never forgot their first sight of Dawson Stride running in front of the pack, baying his clear strong "chop" mouth, head high and tail carried high like a flag. Fox chasers had an obsession with tail carriage, and may be seen in thousands of bench show photos in the hunting magazines holding their hounds' tails in high and unnatural position. But Dawson Stride carried his tail that way without human assistance.

Dawson Stride won several lesser field trials and bench shows, and then in 1936, Hinkel counted his gas money, put some corn-bread, bacon, and eggs in a box as food for dog and man, made Dawson Stride comfortable in the back seat, and drove over to Crockett, Houston County, to enter Dawson in the Texas state hunt. Well over three hundred hounds competed in the all-age field trial, but Dawson Stride won handily, impressing all who saw him run. To feel what born fox hunters felt when they saw Dawson Stride sweep across a field, sounding his fine voice, tail flying like a flag, one almost has to be one of them, but consider the case of R. W. Sherrod. This zealous hunter followed the hounds and fox on horseback to better observe the action all three days of the 1936 hunt. Then, at the end of the third day in this Depression year, he offered Hinkel $1,500 or a herd of milk

cows (then perhaps both together) for Dawson Stride, but
Hinkel refused.

Dawson Stride continued to win bench and field competitions. Hinkel had used him to breed as early as 1934, but even
after Dawson's 1936 triumph he did not place him "at stud"—did
not withdraw him from competition. Most professional breeders
(and already by 1934 Hinkel was a part-time professional) did
that. Editor Everett of *Hunter's Horn,* proud of the exploits of
this champion premium puppy, urged Hinkel to keep Dawson
penned up. This seemed simply prudent, since reckless American
Foxhounds risked injury and death every time they went out.
They ran into barbed wire, plunged off cliffs, smashed into trees,
were struck by cars on rural roads, became entangled in wire
fences, got into steel traps, were bitten by poisonous snakes, or
suffered a hundred under mishaps—even that of falling into abandoned wells. Human threats—dog thieves and hound haters—also
sometimes lurked in the dark countryside, homing in on the
sounds of the running pack.

However, Dawson Stride loved to chase the red ranger and
loved competition, and Hinkel continued to let him run several
times a week. Many people made long trips with their most valued
hound or hounds to run with Dawson Stride, just as on-the-make
gunslingers might come into town to take on some legendary
shootist. Hinkel would just look out his front window and see
some complete stranger from Iowa or South Carolina or wherever, dog pen on truck, pulling up his driveway to open a friendly
conversation and finally get around to—however cordially—challenging Hinkel and Dawson to a competitive hunt. He wanted,
though probably not calling it that, what fox men termed a
"match race." Not always, but a great many times, Hinkel
accepted the challenge, and that night, running in the familiar
landscapes around Boles Field, chasing red foxes he had chased
before, Dawson Stride usually left the intruder foxhounds in his
dust. Honorable hounds did not bark in the race once they fallen
far behind, so the visiting hunter usually suffered hearing the

beloved voices of his favorite dogs (animals perhaps named for himself) fall silent at some point—a terrible thing to endure. The next morning, vowing eternal friendship, the would-be vanquisher of Dawson Stride would take his leave and slink sorrowfully back to Iowa or wherever to lick his wounds. As Hinkel summed things up twenty years later, "Dawson Stride ran more hard races with more different packs than any hound I knew. He seemed to like competition."[7]

Such visitors were often indistinguishable at first glance from another kind—the stranger with a bitch in heat, probably already in his dog cage, planning to breed her to Dawson Stride, *if* he proved good enough. These tended to be the real forks-of-the-creek hunters, people who did not easily write letters or use telephones. Hinkel had his stud dog ad in nearly every issue of the three magazines after 1936, and Dawson Stride had many female visitors from the ads alone. Someone would talk to Hinkel on the phone, arrange to pay his modest (at first) $15 stud fee, ship his Walker foxhound gyp to the Center depot on the train, and Hinkel would go pick her up and introduce her to his champion stud. After a day or so Hinkel would box her up and send her back to her owner.

However, the stud dog business that came unannounced to the door was of a slightly different order. Such men contemplated merging their precious hound bloodlines with Dawson Stride, but they wanted to test him first, they wanted to see what they were going to get from breeding to him. These fox hunters also often drove in from long distances, and, while such visits often came into conflict with his attempts to operate a family farm, Hinkel felt sympathy for these men and tried to oblige them with a race with Dawson Stride. Furthermore, he enjoyed showing these Doubting Thomases the foxhound True Grail—Dawson Stride in all his glory. Hound men had a saying, referring to foxhounds but typically expressed in the first person, "If you beat me, I want your blood." After a night of running their dogs with Dawson Stride, such men always wanted his blood.

Eventually, Hinkel Shillings paid the price for all this night running of Dawson Stride, just as Editor Everett had feared that he might. After every night hunt Hinkel's wife Modie and fox-hunting daughter Rosel always asked him, "Are all the dogs okay?" and one morning in 1939 he had to reply, "No. Dawson Stride's got his head busted up." His beautiful foxhound was beautiful no more and, in fact, was lucky to be alive. What happened to Dawson Stride in the night woods around Boles Field was so painful to Hinkel that he did not mention it in three interviews with me or in any of his frequent historical writings for *Chase* and *Hunter's Horn*, except for one report in 1978. He wrote in this unusually-detailed version of his oft-told Dawson Stride story: "He got his head busted up close to Boles Field in 1939. We heard him holler. His jaw bone was broken, neck fractured, skull fractured, and he lost an eye."[8]

At that point Hinkel's 1978 story of Dawson Stride stopped dead and leaped ahead to Dawson's forced confinement, escape from his kennel after two years, participation in a fox chase, and death from exhaustion in 1941. But what had happened to Dawson Stride in the dark woods back in 1939? Readers of *Hunter's Horn* must have been left searching around in adjacent articles for the mislaid and missing paragraph, but it was not there. Hinkel stopped with reporting Dawson Stride's terrible injury, refusing to speculate, to lie, or to tell what subsequently happened. Hinkel was a nice old man when I got to know him in the 1990s, but he was not an old man in 1939—he was a proud young hunter with a sharp temper who loved Dawson Stride as only a red fox chaser could love his champion stud hound. Nor were the few friends of Hinkel in 2007 whose memories went back that far able (or perhaps willing) to shed any light on what happened to the champion foxhound. All said they knew nothing, and they showed a curious reluctance to speculate. If something happened after Dawson Stride's dreadful head injury—it might have been a clubbing—the historical account is closed and probably will stay that way. That something could have happened is obvious. In another context

Hinkle tersely summarized in 1994, unwilling to comment further but obviously knowing many things he could have talked about, "Been lots of killings over dogs."

Hinkel Shillings' foxhound breeding career did not end with the Dawson Stride story; it began with it. He continued with his hound business until his health broke around 1991—fifty years later. He usually kept ten or twelve "brood gyps" and sold each year's puppy crop, and he made money from his studs, whose fees began at $15 and rose to ten times that. Hinkel kept about twenty adult hounds in his kennels at most times—no more than that. Every other day he cooked up a batch of his own dog food in a big black yard pot. He put in twelve to fifteen free dead pullets from the local poultry house, boiled them in the pot to near fragmentation, vigorously stirred the pot with a stick to "break em up," then added a bucket of cornmeal and stirred the whole mess into a gruel and let it "set up." Hinkel's well-nourished foxhounds got the whole chicken—heads, feet, feathers, guts, and bones.

He chose not to become too large with his successful hound business, and he went on farming his rent farm until he got too old. Most men took up the frustrating and difficult task of hound making and labored for decades until they got an outstanding family line of red fox dogs, Walkers, Julys, Triggs or some other strain, and then hung out their shingle in a proud stud dog ad in one of the magazines. Many others never attained the stud-dog stage. Breeder Ottis King of Groveton, Texas, a man doubtless very well known to Hinkel, once wrote in *Red Ranger* in measured understatement that "Breeding hounds, good foxhounds that is, is an experiment and speculation." King's usual rule was "breed the best to the best" and then to hope for the best, also knowing full well that such a cross might result in, as he said, "a litter of quitters."[9]

Hinkel must have had a few quitters along the way, but he began with champions and then fought hard all the rest of his hound-breeding career not to fall too far off this early high-water mark. He safe-guarded what he called his "Dawson Stride family of hounds" and did rather well in this, judging from the exploits of many of his champion stud dogs—Mark S, Bone Hill Billy, Old Scott Crow, Trademark, Singing Sam, and others. Some of these hounds also lie in well-marked graves in the National Foxhound Hall of Fame Cemetery at Boles Field. Hinkel's successes even continued into the coyote era, as coyotes moved into deep East Texas after around 1950 and somewhat—and unfortunately, Hinkel thought—replaced the red fox. Unlike any fox, coyotes (invariably called "wolves" by hunters) often challenged foxhounds to a fight to the finish at the end of the chase, and many foxhounds were not ready for that. Hinkel's White Scott, however, "would go right into a bunch of wolves and fight em like a tiger." Coyotes sometimes bunched up and refused to run, and if some hound like White Scott did not have the fortitude to charge right into them there might not even be a race.

Hinkel's Mark S was given the most honored position on the back side of Dawson Stride's tombstone, and he probably deserved it. After winning various field trials and bench shows in his career, Mark S won the coveted "*Chase* Count of Field Sires" award in 1960, awarded annually to the hound whose get, offspring, had done best in all United States field trials over the two previous years. Foxhounds lived short, strenuous lives, but their blood held and carried down across the generations, and the blood of some of them had powerful effects on the breed. Mark S and Dawson Stride were that kind of foxhound.

Hinkel Shillings died in 2000 and lies with his wife Modie just inside the church-side gate of the Sardis Cemetery in Shelby County, only a few miles away from the graves of his famous Walkers. A blowing horn is engraved on his tombstone and Hinkel's grandfather's blowing horn, his own famous horn across ninety years, reputedly is interred with him, there being no real fox hunter in his family to inherit it. It is a small horn with a clear, piercing tenor sound—almost a spooky sound. On various occasions at night hunts people heard this horn from over five miles away. Once, during Governor Preston Smith's years in office, Hinkel sounded it in the capital rotunda in Austin, a fine cavernous place to hear a blowing horn. Every state meet included a blowing horn contest, and Hinkel won seven or eight of them and any number of smaller horn contests with this ancient horn. Some fox hunter friend sounded it the traditional three long blows at Hinkel's funeral, just as Hinkle had done at the burials of many other fox hunters. In the old hunter's language, three long blows means "the race is over, come to me."

Song leader at his rural Shelby County church for three quarters of a century, Hinkel saw no serious conflicts between the theologies of red fox hunting and Protestant Christianity, although—after a bad experience or two—he did learn to scale back his hunting activities on Saturday nights before Sunday mornings. Hinkel and others were inclined to believe in the heresy of the immortal animal soul. He speculated to me more than once about the possibility of the Good Lord arranging for him to meet Dawson Stride again in the afterlife, and in a biographical note for *Chase* in 1978 he wrote, "I know what I want to find in Heaven . . . I would like to wake up with all my friends and hear Dawson Stride leading the pack running a red fox at Boles Field." Hinkel did not comment, but this of course would require that there be red rangers in Heaven, too.[10]

Fox hunters like Hinkel Shillings and his brothers always had trouble explaining themselves to others not part of their mystic band. They felt that they knew something remarkable that other sorts of hunters and the general public did not know, but they found it hard to define. In 1974, fox man Richard Rochowiak of Wisconsin typically observed that the only ones who could appreciate and understand the fox chase were "those who are blessed with an inborn trait—it is impossible to tell or attempt to explain to someone who does not have this given quality! To most, our sport makes but little sense." Even the most eloquent defense of hilltopping ever made only pointed at a mysterious core experience known only to the brotherhood of fox hunters. Those not "blessed with an inborn trait" would not understand—in fact, *could* not understand. Bob Lee Maddux of Cookville, Tennessee, read these

words at the conclusion of his eulogy for Woods Walker, a famous
Kentucky fox hunter and hound breeder who had been his friend.

> Some men think unkindly of men who waste their
> time out in the night listening to a pack of hounds.
> But the men who know are closer to one of the
> great mysterious secrets and their ritual is like the
> ancient ritual of a lodge bound of oath and cause.
> They know when they are out on a cold night or
> morning and the bugle mouths of the hounds are
> riding the winds, that they are close to something
> lost and never to be found, just as one can feel
> something in a great poem or a dream.[11]

ENDNOTES

1. Francis E. Abernethy. "Running the Fox." In *The Sunny Slopes of Long Ago*, edited by Wilson Hudson and Alan Maxwell, 146–150 (Dallas: Southern Methodist Press, 1966), 146. Besides Abernethy, the scholars of American folk fox hunting form a very short list, and most of the history of the sport resides in the rare and largely un-archived back issues of three monthly hunting magazines, *Red Ranger* (est. 1911), *Chase* (est. 1920), and *Hunter's Horn* (est. 1921). The first is defunct; the latter two still publish, although what is left of the sport has moved into fenced hunting clubs. Two recent studies of hilltopping in the good old days are Mary T. Hufford's *Chaseworld: Foxhunting and Storytelling in New Jersey's Pine Barrens* (Philadelphia: University of Pennsylvania Press, 1992), and my own *Gray Ghosts and Red Rangers: American Hilltop Fox Chasing* (Austin: University of Texas Press, 2010).

2. Hinkel Shillings. "Texas Notes." *Hunter's Horn*, December 1978, 61–62. This was one of his more detailed re-tellings of the Dawson Stride story, but see also Hinkel's comments in the following: "Texas Notes." *Chase*. November 1953, 3-4; "Texas Notes." *Chase*. May 1984, 60–64; "Foxhunters of Note, Background of My Heritage." *Chase*. February 1976, 7–8. See also E. E. Everett. "Dawson Stride." *Hunter's Horn*. May 1941, 4. I conducted three lengthy oral history interviews of Hinkel on July 21, 1992, and on February 18 and March 12, 1994, and the tapes are still in my possession.

3. Benjamin H. Hardaway III. *Never Outfoxed: The Hunting Life of Benjamin H. Hardaway III By Himself.* (Columbus, Georgia: Privately Published, 1997), 17. While Hardaway's hunting had hilltopper beginnings as indicated in the quote, for most of his life he rode to hounds in the British manner and, in fact, operated a private equestrian hunt club headquartered at his family estate in Georgia.

4. O. M. Johnson, quoted in H. E. C. Bryant. "More Honest Sellers Needed." *Hunter's Horn.* March 1967, 18; Glen Hayden. "Calm Hunter." *Red Ranger*, October 1979. 43.

5. Bob Lee Maddux. "History of the Walker Hound; Part One." *Hunter's Horn*, September 1978, 55–74. See also his "History of the Walker Hound; Part Two." *Hunter's Horn,* October 1978, 52–76. These are the best things ever written on the Walker family and their creation, the predominant strain of American Foxhound.

6. Joe T. Stevens. "Crafty Import." *Texas Parks and Wildlife*, December 1969, 21–23. 21.

7. Hinkel Shillings. "Texas Notes." *Chase,* November 1953, 3–4. 4.

8. Hinkel Shillings. "Texas Notes." *Hunter's Horn,* December 1978, 61–62. 62.

9. Ottis King. "Hunting and Trailing." *Red Ranger,* June 1978. 33–34.

10. Hinkel Shillings. "Foxhunters of Note, Background of My Heritage." *Chase*, February 1976, 7–8. 8.

11. Bob Lee Maddux. "Woods Walker." *Hunter's Horn*, March 1956. 9.

West Texas hog hunters

THE LORE OF WILD HOG HUNTING IN WEST TEXAS

by Kenneth W. Davis

In many parts of West Texas on Friday and Saturday nights when there are neither football nor basketball games, chronological or psychological adolescents and others—male and female, from ages about fourteen through sixty or way beyond—delight in roaring around farm and ranch lands after dusk in high-powered all-wheel drive vehicles—mostly pickups equipped with strong spot lights. These vigorous people are armed with 30.06s and similar weapons. In a single four-wheel-drive pickup there is usually enough ammunition to quell a moderate-sized insurrection or flying saucer invasion. The presence of intrepid hunters is welcomed by owners of the land over which these Nimrods ramble frantically in search of what is considered a dangerous creature found almost everywhere in Texas: the wild hog. These hogs are a nuisance, a pestilence, threats to man and beast, and, of course, they smell bad, have ticks, and are ugly. In most species the very young are at least somewhat cute. Not so with wild hogs I have seen up close in West Texas. The wild pigs I saw were so totally ugly not even their mothers could have affection for them.

The origins of wild hogs are debated in spirited folk fashion. Some hog savants believe that these now primarily nocturnal ravagers of maize, corn, and vegetable crops are descendents of domestic hogs who escaped their pens and met up with other escapees and mated, the outcome of which couplings are hogs in a great variety of sizes, shapes, and looks. Other porcine authorities argue with equal vigor that present day wild hogs are the result of the heroic amorous propensities of the peccary with domestic hogs. Still others, impressed perhaps by the long tusks on wild boars, argue that the wild hog is a distinct breed going back to the days of the mastodons that had long tusks, too. And others argue that the wild hogs' looks and personalities are the result of their industrial strength libidos that prompt them to mate compulsively with their blood kin. Wild hogs not only mate with their relatives, but they will, if hungry, eat brothers, sisters, parents, and their own children. Some in West Texas like some in East Texas kill these gross creatures and cure out the hams, grind up sections of them for sausage, and will even desecrate a food sacred to most good Texans, i.e., barbequed pork, by using meat from cannibalistic wild hogs.

I enjoy a good wild hog hunt. Although an old man, I am not a bad shot with a 30.06. But just as I am loathe to eat cornbread made with flour, or to eat turnips at all—anything that draws flies when it is cooking isn't fit for human consumption!—I will not knowingly eat wild hog meat. One has to have *some* standards.

My experiences with wild hog hunting all took place in West and north central Texas. I have not yet been on a hog hunt in dankest East Texas. My first hunt or sort of was on the 101 section Nail Ranch near Albany, Texas, managed then by George Peacock. He took Lawrence Clayton and me to a 640-acre wheatfield the day after Thanksgiving in the late 1980s. There we saw hundreds of wild hogs of all colors, shapes, sizes, and dispositions. Many of the boars had long tusks that show the influence of their ancestors, reportedly imported from Russia to make Texas wild hogs have longer tusks and therefore be more prized as trophies by the pale skinned city folk who pay big money to roam about the countryside in high-topped hunting boots like primitive cave dwellers in search of food. The owner or manager who can lease property to deer, bird, or wild hog hunters can sometimes make more money from such fees than from sales of cattle or horses. On the cold, clear November day when I first saw a huge herd of wild hogs, we did no hunting. We were just observers, or an advance scouting party for the L. L. Bean-clad mighty hunters of these bizarre creatures about whom much lore exists.

Several years after that day, I went on a wild hog hunt that differed from ones I'd experienced in the Lubbock-Idalou-Floydada area, or on the Nail Ranch near Albany. On this hunt, we had pickups, but they were extended cab, air-conditioned marvels complete with CD players, containers of liquid refreshments, and so on. I remember hearing Willie Nelson sing plaintively on a CD "You are always on my mind." There were handsomely groomed hunting dogs in spotless cages in the beds of the trucks. Each truck was driven by a knowledgeable driver who was the personal guide for four hunters. Our hostess for this guided hunt was Mrs. Darlene Bellinghausen, former president of the West Texas Historical Association and an active Texas Folklore Society member. The head guide was a member of a prominent West Texas ranching family.

Our party of hunters was somewhat typical for a guided hunt. There were two state judges, a high dollar stock broker, the teenaged daughter of one of the judges, an administrative assistant in a district attorney's office, me, three polite young men, and the head guide.

A truck, a guide, and a dog

We assembled at 7:00 a.m. in Knox City and were soon comfortably ensconced in the air-conditioned and quite luxurious four-wheel-drive pickups. We left the city in a great flurry of barking. Town dogs free to wander the streets in search of food or fun barked fiercely at the dogs in the clean cages. Those highly trained dogs barked back in haughty fashion as if to say, "You town dogs run around knocking over garbage cans; we HUNTING dogs get to ride in fancy trucks and chase hogs and be out in the fresh country air!" A few small children ran to the edges of their front yards to wave at us. In small towns, a hunting party of four trucks, two of which had horse trailers with sleek horses in them, is a wondrous diversion, one to be admired and envied by children eager to be old enough to hunt the wild hog.

After a pleasant thirty minutes, we arrived at a farm near Rochester where the previous night a small, hungry herd of hogs had decimated a forty-acre maize field. When we would-be great hunters were out of the pickup with our guns and more than enough ammunition to defend the Alamo successfully, the guide gave us the ritualistic talk. We were admonished not to shoot each other. We were warned that if we shot at a hog we were to shoot to kill. The guide said that a wounded hog is a mean expletive deleted and [quote] "not to be messed with." We were also told to take water with us, for despite the almost freezing temperature we could in the heat of the hunt become [quote] "all dried out real quick." This part of the hunt ritual completed, we set out to search for hogs.

We had no luck. The West Texas wild hog is a genuinely intelligent and cunning beast. Those who had recently feasted on maize probably heard the trucks from three or four miles away and had quickly absquatulated to the relative safety of small gullies in the nearby shinnery. Our guide told us lore about the cleverness of the wild hog, a trait that has allowed the ugly creatures to flourish in alarming numbers. Supposedly, wild hogs have extraordinary hearing but weak eyesight. When we regrouped at the pickups to drive to a semi-wooded area near Weinert, the guide told us more lore about the hogs. Hunters from the Metroplex, he said, delighted in killing these vicious creatures just to get the tusks to have them cleaned, cured or whatever, and then put in shadow boxes to festoon the walls of law, medical, or high finance offices where presumably these parts of boar hogs have great symbolic value. Our guide put it this way: "Having those big tusks in boxes on the wall makes a man feel really macho." So, from being throwbacks to the cave men who hunted to survive, some of today's hunters have come to be ones who beef up their images as alpha wolves or whatever.

We drove on to Weinert, where the horses were unloaded. Our trusty assistant guides mounted them and the search for hogs for the party to kill began all over. In about fifteen minutes with great shouts and loud whooping, three riders came roaring out of the woods to the edge of the large winter wheat field where we hunters waited. The men and horses were in hot hell-for-leather pursuit of a single hog, a rather large one that looked suspiciously to me like the Poland-China boar I had when I raised hogs as a 4-H project in old Bell County. (That was in those days free of wild hogs; we had plenty of opossums there, but no wild hogs.) But this black boar was moving on at a rapid clip and looked wild enough. When the lady assistant district attorney was in good position for a clean shot, she downed that big hog. The young men leaped from their horses to tie it up just in case the wound might not have been fatal. And when the hog was pronounced really dead, another folkloric ritual was observed. The hog was immediately skinned. The backstraps were removed, the hams cut from the carcass, and the ribs cut out. All were put quickly in a waiting ice chest. The Diana of the group was to take this meat home for several feasts. The remainder of the carcass was left for various scavengers: coyotes, wolves, or perhaps some of the deceased's close kin. All I could think of at this point was of seeing pig cannibalism earlier in a cage of hogs caught in traps.

After some four hours we were back at the guide's ranch headquarters and just about to return to Knox City, when from a nearby motte of mesquites came the frenzied shouts of the three assistants who had left us to put the horses in pens. "Hog! Hog! Hog! Godamighty, a BIG Hog!" So, we jumped in the four-wheel-drive pickups and sped recklessly toward the young men who had a gray/orange/black boar cornered. Here we witnessed another bit of hog hunting lore: the polite, literate, and shy young men changed before our very eyes into savages as they wrestled with the hog, which was now either so scared or so hot it stank heroically. Then eight of the nine dogs began to do what they were so well trained to do. (The ninth dog, an amiably goofy creature, was far more interested in playing genial host to all of us who got out of the pickups.) The dogs circled the hog and at just the right moment, the leader of the pack grabbed the frantic animal by an ear and brought it to the ground. The young men quickly tied it up with a pigging string. The chase was over. Now came the big moment. The guide asked who wanted to shoot the hog. There was one of those loud silences that say much. Then the guide asked, "Does anyone want to cut its throat?" Again silence. To our credit, we would-be Great White Hunters declined to shoot a tied up wild animal *or* cut its throat. I think I was rather pleased at our reluctance to kill a helpless animal. For my part, I'd have shot the hog out in the wheat field, but somehow for me, there is no thrill of the hunt in killing a captured animal. I saw quite enough of that done in slaughtering pens when I worked during my college years as a meat cutter in a packing house.

I conclude with a few random observations about the lore of wild hog hunting in my part of the state. Traps are used in West Texas, of course, but my impression is that this practice is more common in East Texas than it is elsewhere. There is lore about the edibility of wild hog meat. Rumor has it that the very best smoked bacon sold at Klempe's Meat Market in Slaton is made from wild hogs. A friend who owns a successful apple orchard near Idalou insists that meat from apple-fed wild hogs makes sausage than which there is none better. Other lore holds that teenagers who are successful hunters tan hog skins to make belts and wallets. I have never seen such items myself, but as a folklorist I know that most rumors have some basis in fact, or to paraphrase the patron saint of Texas folklore, J. Frank Dobie: "Such rumors SHOULD be true."

Hunting the wild hog may seem to be a savage atavistic activity. I cannot argue with that view. But I have seen examples of what damage these perhaps to be pitied creatures do the fields, pastures, and even small calves and sheep. I have also seen the damage done when a pickup going full tilt boogie across a pasture comes in contact with a 300-pound wild boar. Not a pretty sight. But the pickup was there by choice; the hog's reasons for being there, aside from foraging for food, are known only to hogs. Finally, to tie hog lore to antiquity, I remind you that we know from the Biblical account that Jesus cast demons into swine. Perhaps some survived the jump from the cliff and became the progenitors of today's mean-tempered beasts that folks like to hunt . . . and even eat.

As a coda let me say that despite the long history of hunting wild hogs, there is indeed a real need for contemporary historians to record as many details as possible about this communal activity. Too much history in the making is lost because few contemporary observers have time or inclination to record lore about events. I hope that there will be encouragement given to public school and university students and to others to record details of activities such as hunting the wild boar—even if this communal ritualistic behavior does occur with all the comforts of modern vehicles and the use of high-powered rifles. There are a few in West Texas who hunt the wild boar with bow and arrow. But such preferences are grist for another milling.

And, if you happen to like the meat of the wild hog, Bon Appetit! As the Roman poet Horace said, "There is no quarrelling with tastes."

Javelinas roaming the wild

HUNTING JAVELINA
HOGS IN SOUTH TEXAS

by James B. Kelly

I learned to hunt with my father. My dad, Franklin F. Kelly, was born the grandson of Irish immigrants in 1892, and raised in Ft. Smith, Arkansas. At that time Ft. Smith was just across the Arkansas River from what was then Indian Territory, later to become Oklahoma. Ft. Smith was the last Army outpost, the "jumping off place" for the Army—and for adventurers heading into the Indian Territory. Even in the late 1890s it was a pretty wild and woolly place.

Dad's grandfather, Tobias Kelly, had arrived in America from County Wexford Ireland through the Port of New Orleans in September of 1850, and made his way up the Mississippi and eventually the Arkansas Rivers to the town of Ft. Smith, which in itself was pretty wild in those early days. Tobias worked hard and made his way quite successfully in the cattle business and wholesale and retail meat sales. Dad's father, James N. Kelly, joined the family business and they lived fairly comfortable lives. Dad always had a shotgun and small caliber rifles, and I have numerous photos of him with some rather good-looking bird dogs of various English pointer and setter breeds. He started hunting at a very early age.

With the outbreak of World War I, Dad joined the U.S. Army and served with the A.E.F. in the European theater of operations. During that time he met a number of men and became good friends with soldiers from Texas. When he returned from military service he decided that, rather than join the family business, he would head to Texas to seek his fortune. At the time Texas was in the middle of the early oil boom and for those that wanted to work hard, there was lots of opportunity. Through a number of jobs he learned the oil business and especially the specialty of being an "oil landman," the person who negotiates the lease on behalf of the oil company with the land/mineral interest owner. Some are company employees and others are independents who act as brokers of the lease.

In the late 1920s, he got a job as the "head landman" for the Texon and Big Lake Oil Companies that ultimately became the Plymouth Oil Company, and Dad was transferred from Texon, Texas to the company's Texas headquarters near Sinton, Texas, the county seat of San Patricio County. I arrived there at age six and was raised in the Plymouth Oil Camp, which was two miles north of Sinton in the heart of the Welder Ranch. In those days the Welder Ranch was a huge place that ran from the Chiltipin Creek on the south to the Aransas River on the north, and from just west of US Highway 77 on the west to Copano Bay on the east. It was many thousands of acres. As young boys, I and my fellow Plymouth Campers spent a lot of time playing and watching wildlife in the pastures around the camp. While we were not allowed to hunt on the ranch as young boys, we had the run of the place and learned a lot about game birds, white tail deer, and javelina hogs.

As the company landman, Dad knew a lot of local farmers and ranchers, and we always had places to hunt dove and quail. My early days of hunting White Tail deer were on a deer lease that Dad and several other company men had on the Rex Quinn Ranch in McMullen County, just a little northeast of Tilden. Dad started taking me along on weekend hunts during the season when I was nine or ten years old, and I got to go nearly every year until I finished high school and headed for college.

I can tell you it was not easy to get from Sinton to Tilden back then. From Sinton you took the old West Sinton Road to Mathis, up to George West and Three Rivers. From Three Rivers to Calliham. Now, to there the roads were paved, somewhat. But from Calliham to Tilden it was nothing but a fifteen-mile dirt track, which wasn't bad when it was dry, but deer season was usually rainy and it seemed like it was always like driving through a long giant mud hole. We always seemed to get stuck and had to get out and push or get someone to pull us out. It was exciting to me but the men always complained about it, even when it was dry.

The Rex Quinn Ranch covered about 10,000 acres along the Frio River and was owned by Rex Quinn, who at the time was the sheriff of McMullen County in addition to being a prominent rancher in that part of South Texas. Mrs. Quinn had grown up next door to the Quinn property and owned a ranch of similar proportions. I remember that Dad and Sheriff Quinn were very good friends and had met while Dad was doing lease work in the county for Plymouth Oil.

It was always a highlight of my year when Dad would let me go along with him and his hunting partners for a weekend of hunting on the Quinn Ranch. Sheriff Quinn had let them build a camp on the Frio River almost in the middle of the ranch, and the place was a young hunter's dream. The camp was right on the river and consisted of two old G.I. 16-by-16 pyramid tents that probably dated in style from WWI. The season being in November and December, there was always a campfire going. As I got older I was assigned a lot of wood gathering details. Looking back on it, it may not have been the world's greatest camp, but to a young boy it was paradise.

The hunting day started before daylight, and after a light breakfast we were off into the brush "lookin for 'em." The first year I had to follow Dad, me with a borrowed 32-20 lever action Winchester and Dad with his 351 Remington auto-loader. I was not a real quiet walker and Dad had a severe hearing problem acquired during his days in France with the army. We seemed to see deer, but mostly as they were running off in the distance. As we walked through the brush Dad was forever stepping on a stick and making noise that he thought was me and he would turn and admonish me to try and be quieter. I didn't try to place the blame but would just smile and shrug my shoulders. Needless to say, neither of us ever killed a deer while hunting together.

I loved to sit around the campfire in the evening and listen to the stories the men would tell. I remember hearing a lot of stories about javelina hogs and how dangerous they could be. Several would tell stories of how they had heard of hunters or ranchers being attacked by a bunch of javelinas, and someone always knew of old "so and so" over in another county who had actually been killed by javelinas. I heard these stories all the time while growing up in hunting camps, but must say in my life I have encountered many, many groups of these wild hogs and have never ever had one even offer to charge me. I have killed quite a number of them and their main interest was always to get away from me as soon as possible. I should tell you that a javelina is not a hog or a pig as I called them using slang terms, but they are a peccary, which is a species all its own. In South America they are called a collared peccary.

I do recall the first javelina I ever killed, and it was on the Quinn Ranch. After the second year Dad had stopped taking me with him to hunt; I think he finally decided that with the two of us walking together, neither of us would ever be able to get a deer. I think he thought I was old enough to hunt by myself, so he would find a place for me to sit and watch for deer and he would go off on his own. He would usually find a low limb of an oak tree along a good trail and put me up in it. I was given a lot of instructions. Number one was not to leave the place he had put me until he came to get me, and if I did shoot a javelina I was not to touch it or pick it up. I didn't quite understand this because he had shown me how to field dress a deer. Although I had never done it by myself, I thought I could. I still didn't question his instructions, but must admit I didn't always follow them.

It was the third year I was hunting on the Quinn Ranch, when I must have been about twelve. Dad and I left camp just at daybreak one morning and headed to one of my favorite places to hunt. It was a fairly large oak tree with a couple of low limbs, and I had put a couple of boards over these two lower limbs where I could sit and watch for deer. This tree was right on a fence line and I could climb up the fence and get in the tree.

I had been sitting in the tree for a couple of hours and had seen nothing but a doe and a fawn and was getting a little bored. I may have dozed off or was very drowsy when I heard something below and looked down, and a real nice buck had gone over the fence just a few feet down the fence line from my tree. I got pretty excited and was trying as quickly as possible to turn myself and get in a position to get a shot. I guess in my excitement I got too anxious, and in turning around fell out of the tree. Well, I landed sort of on my feet and rear end and was not seriously hurt. When I fully realized what had happened I began to whimper a little, not from the fall from the tree particularly, but because I had foolishly let the buck get away without a shot. Man, I was so mad at myself, and out of disappointment I had a hard time not outright bawling. After a few moments I regained my composure and quietly sat down against the trunk of the tree and remained silent. I guess I hoped the buck would come back by (oh, sure!).

I guess I sat there quietly for twenty or thirty minutes and, of course, heard or saw nothing. I can't describe my disappointment in what had happened. Finally, I was tired of thinking about it and decided I would walk back to camp. It seemed like a long way but realistically was probably no more than a quarter of a mile. I got my gun and headed for camp. I had gone no more than fifty yards from my tree when I looked out in front of me to see a small group of javelinas coming directly toward me. My excitement peaked again. I was both excited and frightened. I stepped a few feet off the trail and got behind a large tree and watched and waited. I was very quiet and the wind was blowing pretty good from them to me, so they did not smell or hear me. I waited until they all passed. The last one was the largest of the group and, not really giving the situation a second thought, I aimed at him and pulled the trigger. I hit him solid and he went down without a squeal. The rest all started squealing and grunting and looked at him. Then they saw me and all turned and ran as fast as they could to get away.

After I was sure the rest of the group had left the area, I cautiously walked over to where my trophy was lying. When I poked him with the barrel of my rifle, he didn't move and was obviously dead as a door nail! Now what do I do, I thought. Well, I wanted everyone in camp to know about my great success—and as soon as possible. The pig probably weighed about thirty or thirty-five pounds and I probably weighed about sixty-five or seventy. That didn't matter. I wrestled him around and got him over my shoulder and headed for camp. I was so happy walking along with this wild beast over my shoulder I can't describe my feelings accurately. As I got closer to camp, however, I began to think about the total picture and began to realize several things.

First and foremost, I had deserted the tree where Dad had left me; secondly, I was carrying game with a loaded rifle. The third violation of Dad's instructions was that I had picked up the javelina. I understood why I was to follow the first two instructions but didn't know at the time why I couldn't pick up the dead javelina. I soon learned.

As I continued down the trail I got within sight of camp and saw Dad coming toward me, and when he saw me he did not look happy. As he got closer he said, "What have you got over your shoulder?"

I proudly dropped it to the ground and said, "I got me a javelina boar!"

He said, "So I see. Good for you," with a smile that made me feel a lot better. "Here, I'll carry your gun and you get the pig and we will go to camp." It was only a few minutes to camp, and as I arrived and dropped the pig the men all came over to have a look. They all congratulated me and said I had made a good shot. Dad told me to wash up and we all sat down for a light lunch.

All through lunch I was awfully proud of what I had done but was beginning to worry that Dad was going to be mad about violating his rules and give me a stern lecture, and maybe even severely chastise me with threats that he would not let me hunt anymore if I couldn't follow his rules. Nothing was said between us during lunch.

As we finished lunch and I was helping with the cleanup, all of a sudden I began to have some itching in my hair. It didn't worry me at first, but in a few minutes it got much more intense and soon I couldn't stand it. I found Dad and told him about it. He said, "Let me have a look. Well, now you know why I told you to never pick up a javelina! Your head is covered with LICE!"

He made me take off all of my clothes and jump in the Frio River. I can tell you that river was appropriately named, especially in December. Dad pitched me some soap and told me to wash my whole body real good. I can tell you that didn't take long in that water, and I got out and toweled off the best I could and stood close to the fire. All of the men thought it was pretty funny but were not too hard on me. They thought it was pretty good that I had got the javelina. Finally, one of Dad's pals came out to the fire where I was standing and took my towel and dried my hair as best he could, and then he dusted my hair with a sulfur powder that was used in those days to treat cuts and scratches when in the field. It gave me a little relief but didn't kill them all. A little while later, one of the men was going to drive in to Tilden (I think they were low on bourbon) and told Dad he would pick something up at the drugstore to further deal with my lice.

After a while the men all went back out for the afternoon hunt. Dad and I were left in camp. He sat me down and much to my surprise and delight, he gave me a pretty stern lecture, not in an angry way but more in a correcting way. He reminded me that I had broken his rules and disobeyed his orders. He said he was more disappointed in me than he was mad at me. By now I was feeling about six inches tall and felt really bad about my actions. He told me he felt sure I would never do that again.

He then told me he was also proud of the way I had cautiously handled the javelina encounter and made a good shot. By now he had me almost in tears, and he grabbed me and gave me a big hug. He then gave me a swift swat on the butt and said, "Okay, let's go hunting!"

I can tell you that for rest of my life until Dad died at age seventy-five, I don't recall ever disobeying his orders again. I thought about this a lot, and especially now that I am over seventy-five myself. The thing I realize the most is that he never gave me an order that didn't make good sense.

Kelly's javelina trophy

Skunks, coons, and coyotes

JESS'S FIRST COON HUNT

by Lee Haile

When I was in high school in Hondo, Texas, I hunted for varmints all winter long. Furs were bringing good prices, and I could make some good spending money from selling them. Even though I was after anything with fur that I could sell, we always just called it "coon hunting." There were three ways that we hunted back then.

First, and my favorite, was walking the creeks at night with my dogs and letting them tree the varmints. My dogs were not noisy hounds, but rather quiet Border Collies that would only bark if they had something treed, and even then, they did not bark a lot. I trained them to be quiet so as not to scare off the rest of the critters along the creek. Also, I didn't always have permission to hunt on all the places along the creeks where I walked. Back then, nobody really cared about me hunting for coons along the creeks. That changed a few years later when fur prices got really high. I did this type of hunting by myself, and when I was most serious about the hunt.

Second, was when we went onto the farms of the area and "shined the fields." This had to be done with a group of at least two people. We would drive along the edge of the corn fields with some of us in the back of a pickup and a "Q-beam" spotlight that plugged into a cigarette lighter. It was very bright. The coons would be out in these bare ground fields eating the ears of corn that the combine missed. These fields were big and we couldn't drive in them because they were already bedded up for next year's crop. When we spotted the shining eyes of the coons, and if they were close enough that we could catch them, the person manning the "Q-beam" would keep the light on them while the rest of us would jump out with baseball bats and take off running across the fields after them. A lot of the time there were several coons in a field, so it was important for the person holding the light to keep up with the multiple targets and guide us to them. I was always a runner. We had headlamps on our heads, and we needed them to see where we were running, but they usually didn't shine out far enough across the fields to see the distant coons.

Now, it was difficult to run in a plowed field at any time, but when you were trying to run across beds that were over twelve inches high and didn't match your step or stride—at night—and at the same time trying to look up to see where the light was shining and where your coon was going, it was quite a bit more difficult! I learned to count steps and create a pattern—two short steps, one long or three long steps, two short, etc. It was humorous for the one with the light in the truck watching us fall, get up and get excited, and fall again trying to get back in a pattern. I learned that if the situation was right, I could determine the right angle across the beds to fit my stride while running full out. This was seldom directly at the coon but at least I could cover some ground. So, I would "tack" back and forth across the field like a sailboat!

This "shining the fields" type of coon hunting was usually the most productive. Sometimes there would be over twenty-five coons in a field. If we were good, each of us runners would get one. Then, on to the next field down the road. We would check back on the good fields about three times a night. The disadvantage from the money standpoint was that you had to split the take among the participants. The "shining the fields" type of hunting was a semi-social type of hunting. You could be really serious with a good team, or more relaxed with a party attitude.

We would sometimes take the girls (which may or may not be girlfriends) with us, and they would be in charge of holding the Q-beam light. They would sometimes forget to keep the light on the coons and would shine on us runners to see how we were doing. It would blind us and make us fall, and then we wouldn't know which way to run after the coons. Sometimes we would get mad and exchange a few heated words with the light holder. The last thing you wanted to do after running and falling across a quarter to a half-mile of field was lose track of the coon and it get away because they did not keep the light on it.

The third type of hunting we did was what we called "road hunting." This was more of a social event than any real serious hunting. We would usually get some critters, but that was not the main focus. It was more for visiting or hanging out with a friend or friends. Or, if you were the drinking type, you got some beer and drove the back roads with your friends drinking and shining a light out the window. This was the most common way we took the girls hunting with us when they asked to go. It was like a double date— one guy driving the truck, the other guy by the passenger side door, and the girls between us. You had to have one pair of really good insulated gloves. The driver had on the left glove and held a light out his window. The other guy had on the right glove and held a light out his window. You had to hold the lights outside the windows so you could see; otherwise, it would just reflect back in your eyes and blind you. It would get really cold in those trucks even with the heaters on full blast, and the girls would have to snuggle up close to keep warm. It was great! It was on this type of hunt that the tale begins.

My family moved out from the northwest side of San Antonio to a small farm near Hondo the summer before I started high school. Hondo is a tight little farming community, and it is not easy being the new person in town. You are usually the new person for the first twenty years that you live there. We lived on the Verde Creek, and all through high school hunting and fishing was my thing. My senior year started and I found out that a guy I knew from junior high school in San Antonio had moved out that summer and was living a couple of miles down the road on another farm. Jess Culpepper was not very "country," and was having an extra-hard time adjusting to Hondo.

I felt sorry for him because I had been the "new guy" not long before, and I started asking him to hang out. Well, that winter, sometime in December I think, I called up Jess to see if he wanted to go "coon hunting." He had never been before, so I decided we would just hunt the roads for his first time, kinda break him in easy. I told him to wear warm clothes, and I picked him up in my truck. The truck I was driving was a 3/4-ton Ford with a flatbed on it. We both lived about twelve miles east of Hondo. We started out south. We made about a hundred-mile circle around Hondo, never getting closer than eight miles to town, and almost always on gravel county roads. I knew all the back roads by then. We mostly just visited and got to know each other again. We had killed a coon and three ringtails, and had almost completed the circle back to my house.

We were crossing the Verde Creek about three miles upstream from our place. The creeks all run about thirty feet below the surrounding prairie and fields, so when you were next to the creek, you could see only from high bank to high bank, like a little canyon. I stopped on the cement slab crossing so we could shine along the creek. It had been cleared of brush and planted to coastal Bermuda grass. The creek was just a trickle there. About a quarter-mile south, downstream on the passenger side was a grove of big native pecan trees. When I shined those trees, they looked like a Christmas tree. "Let's go!" I yelled. I turned off the truck, turned on my headlamp, grabbed my .22 single-shot rifle off the rack, and ran around the back of the truck, calling the dogs off the truck as I went by. This happened fast. Jess only had a flashlight, and I heard him opening the door as I was just starting into the pasture.

It is important to get under the trees as fast as you can to keep the coons from climbing down and running off. With this many coons, I had gotten serious really fast. I saw some real money. I had my light and my concentration focused on those trees. I hadn't gone far off the road when I felt something tightening across my belly. Just as I was starting to form the mental question, "What?"—ZAAPP!! I got shocked. It was a single-strand, slick wire of an electric fence. What a shock (pun intended!). I yelped and dropped to the ground to get under it, and was back up and running without losing a second. As I was running I yelled out to Jess, "WATCH OUT FOR THE ELECTRIC FENCE." Not more than a few seconds later I heard, "OOWW!" He had found the fence.

I was about half-way to the trees and running fast, the dogs all excited and running with me. As I got closer, my light was focused higher and higher up in the trees because they were so tall. Just the edge of the light was hitting the ground, but I could make out a few bushes and weeds as I was running. I was coming up on a bigger bush that was about seven feet long but only about two-and-a-half feet high. I was going to jump it and keep going straight for the trees. Then it stood up. It wasn't a bush—it was a big Charolais bull! I yelled in surprise and went around it, never slowing down. I yelled back to Jess, "WATCH OUT FOR THE BULL." Just a little while later I heard, "AAAAHHHHGGG!" He had found the bull.

Now I was at the trees. As best as I could tell there were about six coons in those trees. When Jess got there I laughed about the bull and the fence. I don't remember if he laughed, too. We got organized and the dogs settled down. Coons will hide their eyes, so it's not always easy to see them. I worked around and finally got one spotted. I shot the coon, and when it hit the ground I ran in to get it away from the dogs before they chewed it up too much. This is not necessarily a quiet process.

As things settled down I heard a truck start up in the distance. It was very late by then and very quiet. I asked Jess to walk to the top of the bank and see what was up. He walked up to the top of the bank where he could see. "It's a pickup coming across the field real fast," he said. There was a house about 3/4 of a mile away.

"Which way is it going?" I asked.

"Toward us," he said.

"LET'S GO, WE GOTTA GET OUT OF HERE!" I yelled. "Quick, turn off your light. LET'S GOOO!" I turned off my light, grabbed the coon, called the dogs, and was on my way running back up the creek toward the truck in no time flat. I don't know what Jess was doing, but I was out of there.

As I was running for all I was worth, I perceived something looming up in the dark. "OOHH!" I cried out. "HEY JESS, WATCH OUT FOR THE BULL," I yelled as I swerved around it.

Five seconds later I heard, "AAAHHHGG!" He found the bull . . . again!

I was building up a good lead on Jess. I am sure he was not as experienced as me at running in the dark. As I was coming up on the truck I lobbed the dead coon towards the back of the truck. My momentum carried me to the middle of the road before I felt the tension across my belly. Oh No! Too late! ZZAAPP! The electric fence! Down I went and the wire sprang back.

"DON'T FORGET THE ELECTRIC FENCE!" I yelled. I called the dogs up on the flat bed and jumped in and started the truck. "Come on Jess, HURRY!" Jess was about five feet from the door to the truck when he slowed down, looked down, yelled, and did this funny little dance. "You forgot the fence," I said as he got in.

I popped the clutch and we were moving before he ever got the door shut. We went up the far side of the creek picking up speed fast. A hundred yards from the creek the road forked three ways. I never slowed down and took the middle one shifting into high gear, running with no lights on. Jess's eyes were so big I could see them in the dark. He had both hands spread on the dash with his arms stiff, but his head was leaning forward, looking out the windshield. I guess he couldn't see in the dark as good as me.

A few miles down the gravel road I slowed down and started laughing. I got to thinking that there were still at least five coons left in that tree. That was a lot of money. Jess wasn't too keen on going back for them, so we just cruised around some more, calming down. It had been over thirty minutes by now. "Well," I thought philosophically, "at least we got one of them."

"How many do we have now I wonder?" I said as I shined the light onto the back bed to see. "What?" I slammed on the brakes and we got out to see better. No coons, ringtails, or dogs! The bed was clean. I guess they fell off somewhere. Well, now we *had* to go back.

So, we eased around and went back down to the creek crossing from a different direction. We came over the bank on the road, and when the headlights shined down on the cement slab, there were the three dogs laying there beside the pile of dead coons and ring-tails! When I left out so fast, everything slid off the back and stayed right there.

I stopped on the slab and got out. The dogs were okay and very glad to see me. We put the dead critters back on the truck bed. It had been about forty-five minutes since we had left there. I could just feel those coons calling me to come get them in those trees just a quarter mile away.

"Hey Jess," I said, "we're already here; let's go for them." He wasn't too sure about it. We sat there in the dark listening. It was dead quiet. I chanced a quick shine with my not-too-bright headlamp. There were still eyes up there! "There's at least five more coons there," I ventured. "They will bring about $15 apiece—that's $75!" That did it. I said, "This time we will sneak up there in the dark and just shine a little light real quick so I can shoot them. We'll be real quiet; it'll be okay." That seemed to satisfy him.

So, we snuck back really quietly, listening for anything. Man, it was really quiet that late at night. We got up under those big pecan trees and moved slowly and quietly in the dark. I covered my head-lamp with one hand and turned it on, and I let out just a little beam of light. I would see some eyes shine just for a second, and then they would look away or hide their eyes. I couldn't get a shot.

Well, we kept this up for a while. Then I noticed a possum on a lower limb not more than eight feet off the ground. I called Jess over and showed it to him. I said it wasn't worth taking a shot, but I would knock it out with a stick. I leaned my rifle up against a tree and was looking and feeling around in the dark for a good stick. Then I heard, "KA-POW." My rifle went off! I looked at Jess about fifteen feet away and he was looking at me. I could still see the rifle leaning where I had left it. "How did that rifle go off?" I asked Jess. Before he could answer, off to the side we heard loud and clear, "REACH FOR THE SKY."

"Oh sh—," I thought. I could see Jess's eyes in the dark again. I bet he could see mine, too. Jess was looking at me and I was looking at him. After some hesitation, I slowly lifted my arms above my head! Jess did the same. A light came on about thirty feet away, shining in my face, and up came this guy from down by the creek. "What's going on?" he asked.

"Oh," I said fast, "we're just kids hunting coons. My name is Lee Haile and we live just a few miles down the creek on the old Franklin Muennink place where the old cotton gin used to be. My folks are Alton and Betty Haile, and this is Jess Culpepper and his folks just moved in down at Quihi just a few more miles down the road." I spilled my guts! Jess was looking at me like I was crazy. I was just hoping this guy was *not* crazy and would let us go. Besides, his rifle was pointing at *me*. He was standing about five feet down the bank from me and Jess was to his right, on my left about eight feet from him.

"How many coons you got?" he asked.

"We got three ringtails and one coon that we got somewhere else and the one coon we shot here earlier, but there are more coons up here in these trees." I pointed one of my fingers in my up-stretched hands, hopefully at the trees above us. He cocked his rifle!

"Oh no," I thought. "He *is* crazy and he's going to kill us and take our coons!" I could see a hole of water in the creek off a little four-foot ledge about three feet behind him. I thought, "I'll push him in and we'll run for our lives! How can I get Jess's attention to let him know what I'm fixin' to do?" I glanced toward Jess. The light was still in my eyes so I couldn't really see, just silhouettes.

All this was rushing through my head and I was just starting to lower my arms and get my courage up when he pointed his gun and light up in the trees and said, "Well let's get the rest of them." He called out and here came his buddy from farther down the creek. It took me a few minutes work all this out in my head. I still stood there with my hands above my head, dumbstruck. I think Jess moved first and broke the spell. I turned on my headlight and grabbed a stick and killed the possum.

It took about thirty more minutes to finally get all those coons out of those trees. We ended up with a total of six coons and one possum. Then the first guy said, "You take these to the fur buyer on Tuesday at the DQ and sell them and send me half the money. I will be in the crowd so I will know how much you get." He gave me a piece of paper and made me write down "C Mumme, Rt 4 Bx 66 Hondo, Tx." The whole time I never got a look at either of those two guys, but I figured out who the Mumme guy was.

I sold the furs, sent him half, and Jess never went hunting with me again.

The author and his kill

FISHING LORE

IN TEXAS

Joe boat tied to a snag

SKILLS OF THE RIVERMEN: WAYS AND MEANS OF MARKET FISHERMEN

by Wildwood Dean Price

Traveling down the path from our past is the only way into the future. With that in mind, let us look back down the path from whence we came.

If you are a native American—not an immigrant—and were born west of the Rockies, you more than likely descended from "River People." The purchase of the Louisiana Territory from France began a great migration into the American West. The Red River and other rivers, such as the Missouri, the Mississippi, and the Arkansas, provided the highways into the interior, and settlers took up residence along their banks.

The people that settled along the rivers made a living farming and ranching in the fertile bottomlands. With the taming of the Wild Frontier came other occupations: clearing timber, punching cattle, market hunting, and commercial fishing to name a few.

Throughout our history, ways of making a living have changed with the needs of a growing nation. Every so often there comes along an occupation that seems to be the panacea: offering a get-rich-quick scheme, high adventure, or a glorified way of life. The market fishing that had its start during the Depression offered none of those things; it lasted only a few short years, was more adaptable to the lazy rather than the hard-working, and, like the occupations before it, gave only temporary riches. The one thing market fishing did offer was dependable work in the face of starvation.

Sometimes varying forces come together in history and make the moment, then are gone, forever lost. That is the case with the fishing that began during the Depression era. The Depression was a time of great prosperity for river fishermen who fished the rivers of the Mississippi drainage. During the Depression there was a ready market for fish caught from our rivers. River fishermen developed the fyke net (of Scandinavian origin) into highly successful traps for taking catfish; and the crude riverboats, of an earlier time, evolved into dependable craft for tending nets.

What is the difference between a Commercial Fisherman and a Market Fisherman, you might ask.

In 1866, the first salmon cannery opened at Eagle Cliff, Washington, and marked the start of a salmon canning industry that flourished along the lower Columbia River for the rest of the 1800s. More than fifty canneries sprang up, using immigrants from Scandinavian countries and the Balkans to catch most of the fish processed in the canneries. They were true commercial fishermen and they brought with them—from their motherlands—net-tying and -making skills.

By 1880, the salmon runs were already declining as the net fleets, along with shore-based fishing methods, sharply reduced the salmon population. The spawning runs continued to decline, and canneries began to close. By the 1920s, there were only a handful of canneries still in operation. The "Great Depression" wreaked havoc, and brought more closures to the salmon canneries on the Columbia River. Some of the displaced salmon fishermen moved to rivers east of the Rockies and established themselves as commercial fishermen. It was one of those displaced salmon fishermen who migrated to the Red River and taught my dad, a riverbottom farmer by the name of Joe Price, net-tying and boat-building skills.

Up until the Depression, *fishing* was only a favorite "pastime" for farmers who lived in the river bottoms. Fishing with hook and line was a sport practiced by many of them, but rarely produced large enough catches to more than provide for the families' needs, or maybe an occasional fish fry for the community or Sunday School class. During the Depression some of the riverbottom farmers started to rely on the rivers for all or part of their living. Fishing, hunting, and gathering wild food supplemented the diet and income of many rural families. In a short time almost every fishing hole on the Red River and other major rivers east of the Rockies harbored a fisherman.

This new breed of fishermen who made their living from freshwater rivers were not commercial fishermen in the true sense of the word. The term "commercial fisherman" implies that a fisherman followed rules and ethics designed to provide fish to a commercial industry. A more accurate term for the Depression-era fisherman who made all or part of his living from fishing is "market fisherman." Most of the market fishermen made their own rules and they created their own market. They bartered fish for doctors' services, groceries, or supplies to make a crop, sometimes even trading a catfish to the country peddler for a block of ice. When there was a market for fish, they fished; when there wasn't a market, they did something else.

The cast nets and seine nets used by the commercial fishermen of the oceans and seas were of little benefit in the sandbar-and-snag-infested, log-and-rock-strewn rivers between the Rocky Mountains and the Mississippi River. The Fyke net, originally designed to catch eel, was the forerunner of what we know as the barrel, or hoop net. It was too small to catch big fish and its round shape made it difficult to anchor in swift water. Its design quickly evolved to meet the requirements posed upon it by the very nature of the rivers, and the need to catch great quantities of big fish.

Fyke net

Those newly designed hybrid nets were highly successful for catching bottom-feeding catfish and buffalo fish, and the Red River held a plentiful bounty. However, just as the salmon population declined, the plentiful supply of catfish and buffalo fish proved short lived.

Some market fishermen made their own tools: pushing-poles, oars, paddles, live boxes and trotlines; fewer of them hand-tied their own hoop nets, or made their own boats. The few fishermen that learned the skills needed to tie nets, hoop them and rig them (make them ready to fish), and build good riverboats enjoyed extra income selling their wares to other fishermen. Sometimes the money made from those crafts amounted to more than they made fishing.

Net tying requires special tools. Dad and I carved shuttles, or "needles" to hold the twine we used to tie the meshes. We carved them from narrow pieces of wood split from big ash logs. There are several sizes of mesh used in the webbing of a net, and we carved gauges or "net blocks" from bois d'arc to keep the meshes uniform in size.

Net fishing also required a special kind of boat, one that enabled a fisherman, singlehandedly, to raise hoop nets filled with heavy fish from swift waters. By the early 1900s small handmade, no-name boats showed up on the Missouri, Arkansas, and Red rivers. Some of

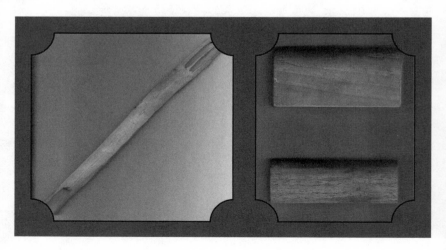

Net shuttle and mesh gauge

the handmade fishing boats that existed on the Red River during the 1930s resembled horse watering troughs, and there were as many designs of boats on the rivers as there were boats. They were made from the materials that were available, and they were made by fishermen, not carpenters. They were not graceful and trim—nor pretty. They were built to use, not to show. Those boats, mostly constructed out of green lumber with a pocketknife, handsaw, hammer and nails, were anything but leak-proof. The joinery at best was crude, not tight. In an attempt to keep the boats from leaking at the seams, the fishermen caulked them with various things, coal-tar the most common. Usually a combination of coal-tar and soaking the boat in water kept this type of boat more or less leak-proof.

The design of one such beautiful and serviceable boat known as the "Joe Boat" is worthy of being saved from extinction. It was a marvel in design, developed not from the accepted principles of engineering, but from the nature of the demands placed upon it. The slender design was simple in construction. One-piece sides cut from 1 by 12 pine boards twenty feet long gave the boat its rake. Empty, the boat sat high on the water and wasn't tipsy. It was bottom-heavy because of the heavy flooring used, like in a house. The shape of the end and middle boards gave the boat its flare. The ends were 2 by 4 pine, three feet long, and the middle 2 by 12, six feet long. When a fisherman, standing in one end of the boat, dragged a net full of big fish over the side, not only did the boat displace more water, but a lot more of it came in contact with the water. With the shallow end of a Joe Boat resting on the water, it was easy to drag a net filled with heavy fish over the side.

The profession of catching fish to sell from our streams and rivers was an honorable one, and remained so until the late 1950s. The flathead catfish, channel catfish, and buffalo fish populations declined to the point that they were nearing extinction in the Red River. With the ending of the '50s came regulations to protect the fisheries of the Red River and other rivers, and none too soon.

The market fishermen along our rivers—hard pressed to catch enough fish for the dinner table, much less enough to sell—gave up fishing and moved on to other occupations. Some of them

moved on to raising minnows and channel catfish in ponds specifically designed and constructed for the purpose of providing fish to
commercial markets, and they created a whole new industry.

A few years thence, it is unlawful to sell fish caught from our
rivers. Where are the hoop nets? Show me a hand-made riverboat.
Join me, as I re-live a day in the life of a market fisherman. I
remember clearly now, as if it were yesterday . . .

* * *

The morning's chores are done up. Breakfast is on the table: a
goblet of sweet milk filled with cornbread. I drink the milk off and
save the mushy cornbread for noon-time, known by us as "bean
time." The moon is setting in the west. The Morning Star invites
the sun to rise.

The day's chores lay ahead. In my mind's eye, I see Mother sitting on the porch in her squeaky rocker.

I'm not her "Little Sailor Man," anymore.

Dad is sitting in his straight chair, the one with the net twine
bottom. He cocks it back against the wall on its hind legs, and
frowns as the ragged screen door slams behind me.

I'm his "Little Fisherman" now!

It is full daylight by the time Dad finishes his pot of "hard-boiled
coffee." I don my brogans and start rolling my syrup bucket lid,
with a forked stick, across the hard beaten path in front of the porch.

"Get your good shoes off, Dean. We gotta go run the nets and
make some new sets."

Dad leads the way down the trail to Red River. I admire his
going-fishing gait—almost a trot—each pace, timed by a whistle,
ends in a drag-foot motion designed to dislodge sandburs from his
bare feet.

Dad sure whistles pretty.

My tender feet require more drag-foot motion. I trot along to
keep up. My lips pucker but whistles fail to come. Our milk cow,
"Gerty," climbs from the murky water up the worn cut in the river
bank to meet us. Dad's hand-built "Joe Boat," tied to a snag just
downstream from the edge of a sandbar, floats high and dry. The

sandbar indicates we're in the upper end of the fishing hole. Dad unties the boat, and points at it with his finger.

"Dean, I need you to help me. Set in the other end of the boat in case I have to land a big'un . . . I may need your weight to balance the boat."

Nothing I ever heard Dad say stirs my heart more than "I need you to help me." The rippling water, murky-brown with dislodged sand, rushes by the boat. Dad shoves the boat hard and jumps on the front end. The boat rocks under his weight and sends a wake splashing up on the sandy bank, as if to say . . . we'll be back after while.

"Daddy, to me, right here where the boat is tied looks like the best place in the whole river to set a net. I want to set one here."

"The upper end of a fishin' hole ain't a place for a net, Dean. Too much boiling sand, leaves and grass in the water. Flathead catfish don't have any eyelids, and they won't put up with sand in their eyeballs. Be a better place down yonder in the calm deep water."

Farther downstream the water turns dark blue with reflections of puffy white clouds—the water is calm, and slow. Slick water on the surface tells of a deep channel a few feet from the steep bank.

"I need your help Dean. You pole the boat. Put me downstream right in there to that big ol' log." Dad points, "See the net's lead rope tied to it? Put me there!"

Two shoves on the cedar pushin'-pole put Dad on a collision course with the log. We whiz past the log . . . Dad bends down, grabs the net's lead rope, and holds on. The boat changes ends! Dad keeps his balance; a deep frown wrinkles his brow, but he doesn't say a word. Silence is not golden.

His, "Put me there!" didn't mean as fast as I could; he's afraid there won't be anything in the net.

Dad interrupts my thoughts.

"Down on the bottom is a catfish trail that runs off toward that raft of logs yonder. The trail's hard. A lot of swimming flatheads are using it. The water's deeper than my pole—dark, deepest there under that slick water. There's apt to be something big in this net. Yes sirree."

My patience runs out.

"Well raise him up!"

Dad pulls the lead rope, hand-over-hand. I watch the first hoop of the net come to the surface. The water explodes! Dad grabs the net hoop, and takes the drenching whatever is in the net dishes out. In one powerful backward roll Dad goes down in the bottom of the boat, fish and net on top of him.

I watch through a spray of splashing water. Dad and the flouncing fish tangle with the net. Dad flails his arms, freeing himself from the net, and then in one sweeping motion dumps the fish out of the net, into the boat. I can't help laughing—behind cupped hands, though.

"I think that's the biggest flathead catfish I ever caught, Dean!"

After Dad let the net back down to do some more fishing we float off downstream. Dad stands on the front seat of the boat and jabs his pushin'-pole up and down, looking for another hard catfish trail, a place to set another net. Finally he finds a trail that suits him and gives me a bit of advice.

"Dean, you don't want to put your net down on top of a log. Don't ever set a net without knowing exactly what's on the riverbottom." "W-h-e-w—w-e-e!" Dad screams, and dives off of the boat seat

52 lb. catfish

into the icy water! His whew-w-e-e, turns to bubbles as he makes his way down to the bottom of the river. The splash and his voice reverberating between the river banks send me diving in after him. After our swim we take time to eat: A big slab of cornbread and boiled eggs, chased down with water caught in cupped hands from the river.

We work the rest of the day running nets, taking fish to the live box and making new sets. Our live box is made from hog wire and split cedar saplings with a hinged lid. We keep it at the boat landing, handy for customers wanting fish.

The live box overflows after we empty the last net of our catch and dump the fish into it, so we take the flathead catfish home to eat. The setting sun shimmers off the water behind us as Dad shoulders the big catfish and climbs the riverbank.

Dad leads the way down the trail to the house. His "going-fishing gait" disappears under the weight of the heavy catfish. The rising full moon casts eerie shadows. The, who-who-hooting stands my hair on end. I stay right on Dad's heels.

Dad hangs the catfish on the cotton scales. "W-h-e-w—w-e-e! fifty-two pound. Yes sirree, Dean. That's the biggest catfish I ever caught! I'll take care of Mr. Catfish. You go on to the barn and take care of the night-chores."

I shut the door and let the windows down on the chicken house on my way to the pig pen. I slop Squiggles "our super sow" a bucket of fermenting grain and then head to the barn. Gerty is waiting at the corn crib window. I shuck her some little nubbins of corn to eat, and then milk her out in front of the barn, by the light of the full moon. With one hand in my suspenders and a pail of milk in the other, I stroll toward the house. The smell of fish frying wafts across my face.

We'll have a pot of red beans too!

"W-h-e-w—w-e-e! The day's work is done!"

ENDNOTE

Salmon canning information taken from Washington State Department of Archaeology and Historic Preservation: http://www.historylink.org, Article #8036.

Nina Marshall Garrett

THE BIG FISH THAT DIDN'T GET AWAY

by Nina Marshall Garrett

In 1938, when I was eleven years old, my family moved from Arizona back to Oklahoma to Lake West, a community about ten miles south of Boswell and three miles north of the Red River. While we were in Arizona for three-and-a-half years, my brothers and father used the irrigation system on the farm where they worked. They were impressed with how one could water the crops at a time when the weather was dry and thus have a sure way of having a successful harvest. After share cropping one of the large farms at Lake West for two years, the Government placed the former plantation land up for sale in 1940, and my dad and brothers were some of the first to buy their farms. It seems they chose just the right land, for the creeks that flowed through their farms would feed a lake to water the land with a gravity flow system, which was what was used in Arizona and California. In 1954, they purchased a bulldozer and, with their mule teams and tractors, built a large fourteen-acre lake, making the proper dam and outlets to irrigate about 100 acres of my father's land. My two older brothers were partners with much more land. Between 1959 and 1960, they began moving dirt in order to make somewhat the same setup just across the road from Dad's property, and their seventy-acre lake was much larger, with a bigger creek that flowed into it.

Because my brothers and I had married and each of us had four children, we often planned outings near and far where we could relax and visit for a day or two. My mother and dad had a large house, and after a good meal we spent many hours sitting, visiting, and playing games at their home. Each of us continued that same pattern once our own children left home and returned for a weekend of laughter and visitation.

In 1961, my brother Julius heard about a farmer near Bonham who had a lake similar to theirs, but he had also stocked his lake with catfish fingerlings and planned to market the fish by letting citizens come to his farm to fish, paying for the fish as they caught them, thus providing the pleasure and amusement of catching the fish and the satisfaction of taking them home for consumption and enjoyment of a great meal.

My brothers soon visited the Hodge Fish Farm near Bonham. They telephoned us telling us what fun it was and that they wanted to take us on Saturday morning to visit the fish farm to fish. Julius, being an innovative thinker, and with the desire, was really thinking about stocking a pond with fish and utilizing some of the water from his big lake. All of our family were excited about something we had never done and spent a lot of time preparing to fish as well as making things clean and pretty around our place.

Finally, Saturday morning came, and we arose with gusto. Everyone was taking care of their chores and happy we were going to all get to be together. My brothers and their families soon arrived. There was Julius and Eva Mae with two of their four boys, Major and Martha with their two girls and two boys, and William and I had three of our four girls. After a lot of hugging and laughter we each got into our own vehicles and started north. We turned west on the Ravenna road, and it wasn't too far to the fish farm. We looked around and seemed to be the only ones out to fish. After making arrangements with the owner, out of three lakes we chose the one the farthest to the east. The sign with the rules said, "You Pay For What You Catch. We Will Dress Your Fish If You Choose."

We busied ourselves with rigging our lines and baiting the hooks. Eva Mae had brought her favorite cane pole. Of course, we had to fix them for our children, but weren't too anxious for them to get started until we saw just what we were getting into. Soon we were scattered all around the pool and we threw our lines into the water. Before I could get my line out, William started reeling his line in, saying, "Boy, do I have a big one." I stopped to watch him and saw the big fish break the water. As he continued reeling, I saw someone else reeling, saying, "I've got a big fish, too." Others were shouting and hollering and laughing. What fun to have a big fish on one's line.

About that time, my line started running out halfway across the pool. "William, what should I do?"

"Reel it in toward you," he said.

I could hardly move the reel, and started walking backward while the line was backlashing. I had never caught a fish that big. Everyone was getting big fish. I said, "William, come help me."

He laughingly said, "I can't, because I've got a big fish on my line."

I looked over at my sister-in-law Eva Mae with her cane pole, and she had such a big fish she could not even think about lifting it out of the pool, so she just put that pole over her shoulder and started walking down the bank. After about two steps, her foot slipped, and she went rolling down the pool bank. We all laughed and some went over to help her. The whole group was laughing and yelling and catching big fish.

I was sitting next to my younger brother Major and his wife and overheard him say to her, "Martha, you need to take your line out and quit fishing. It's going to cost us too much." She just kept baiting her hook and threw it back into the water. He repeated, "Martha, did you hear me?"

She said, "Now Nub (his nickname), I like to fish as well as you, so as long as you fish, I am going to fish." Soon they both caught two more very large fish.

I can't remember how many fish we caught or how many pounds they weighed, but we were forced to quit, thinking about how much money we were spending. We went up to the shed where the owner and a friend were working. The friend weighed the fish and an agreement was made for them to clean and dress the fish. We drank a cold drink and couldn't quit talking and laughing about our experiences with the big fish. We agreed this was the most fun we had had in a long time.

Soon, they had everything dressed and wrapped in nice freezer paper, as we had much too much fish for our fish fry later in the day. I heard the man tell my husband William, "That will be $189, please." Well, we had not quite expected it to be that much, so they laughingly passed the hat again.

We each helped to put our gear and fish in the autos and pick-ups and looked at the new people who had taken our places. As we drove away William said one of the men mentioned how much fun we were having, and if it had not been so early in the morning, he would have thought some of us had been drinking.

After we were home awhile, cleaning up and relaxing, we relived all over again every fish we caught, the education we all received in such a short time about catching large fish, and the conversation and fun we had. We had a picnic table in our back yard and a cooker made from an empty barrel by the FFA boys at school. The women prepared the fish to be fried, and made coleslaw, hush puppies, and iced tea to drink, and the men took care of the cooking. I will always remember those good times we had over thirty-eight years ago.

Oh, yes. My older brother Julius and his wife Eva Mae built a nice catfish pool with a cabin near their house. They stocked the pool with fingerling catfish, and when the fish grew large enough to sell, they advertised and sold catfish much the same way that Mr. Hodge had done near Bonham. They were happy doing that on weekends and other times while interspersing pleasure with farming, for they were successful farmers, also.

In ending, I want to tell you that the news of the Vansickle Fish Farm spread all throughout southeastern Oklahoma. A *Denison Herald* reporter traveled the sixty miles to find the fish farm and took pictures of the operation, and wrote a story about the public's response for his newspaper. *The Daily Oklahoman* also picked up the story. Because the fishing process was under the jurisdiction of the game warden, after reading the story the state game warden telephoned Durant to see if my brother had bought a license to sell fish. Of course, he didn't know about a license because his fish farm was on private land. When the local game warden came from Durant and told Julius about the state game warden calling him, Julius was pleasant. When he paid his $5 for a license he thought about how far the man had driven for $5, but he supposed he really had just wanted to see what kind of setup Julius had. My brother kept the fish farm for seven years and then closed it.

When William and I traveled several southern states in 1990, we encountered lots of fish farms across Alabama, Mississippi, and Georgia. It's too bad the Chinese got into exporting their catfish to the U. S. and because their product was priced less than that of our growers, the demand for our catfish became less and less. Today there are very few fish farms in our United States—and probably many fewer enjoyable family outings such as the one we shared.

Checking the seine

OUR FAMILY FISHING TRIPS

by L. R. McCormack

One of my fondest memories of my Coney family is the fishing trips. Fishing was one of the activities the Coney boys loved. The "boys" were the four sons of Leon Josephus Coney and Ida Augusta Hawkins Coney. Their farm was located about five miles southeast of Ladonia, Texas. Not only was fishing their favorite sport, but it also provided some good meals. Their fishing was not done with a rod and reel. They used seines, and "grabbled" for the fish. My dad, Lowell (Sheep), and his brother Roy Leon (Buster) were the only two of the boys who could swim. Being the two youngest boys, they had developed a close bond through the years. Dad could hold his breath under water so very long that they sometimes wondered if he had drowned. Buster could dive deeper than Dad. between the two of them, they checked out each fishing hole for suitable fish—as well as for water moccasins that were living in those holes—and selected the holes they would fish. They had several places that they visited regularly.

One place was on the South Sulphur River. When they chose to go, it was really only a creek instead of a river; by the time the early spring rains had ceased, the water had run on down, so the water was not extremely deep. During such times, the catfish would choose places for their nests and would not be as active as when the water was running swiftly.

The boys took two seines along. One was placed below the fishing hole, and another was placed at the entry to it; then Sheep and Buster got side by side behind the entry seine. Holding the bottom edge of the seine as close to the bottom of the creek as they could with their feet, and with their arms swinging back and forth in front of the seine, they slowly edged forward, pushing the entry seine toward the bottom seine and "herding" the fish in front of them. Edgar and Dave, the two older boys, who were positioned behind the bottom seine, used their feet to keep it positioned on the bottom of the creek so the fish could not get out underneath it. As the fish tried to get through the seine, the boys caught them in their hands and tossed them up onto the creek bank. Of course, they never caught all of the fish. They left some of them to grow and produce more fish for the next year. The location of these "fishing holes" was kept a family secret, since they did not want others to completely "fish-out" their well-searched out holes.

In later years, they would go fishing several times a year and bring back loads of fish to fry at home. These fish were always a welcome change to our diets. Once or twice a year they took all of their families along for a day on the creek, and we had a "fish-fry" out in the open. This was an event we all loved.

Since these trips were planned in advance, the anticipation of that excursion had we children all agog! Our mothers had a lot of planning to do. There were no paper plates nor plastic utensils, so the family dishes and silverware were packed, as well as the needed pots, pans, pot-holders, plenty of water, and even some first-aid supplies. Basically, we had a chuck-wagon, with meal, flour, coffee, lard, sugar, potatoes, and catsup. Although our mothers always seemed happy to go on those fishing trips, I'm sure that sometimes they were not as happy as they appeared to be. They had to cook over open fires, and since it was always warm weather when we went on those jaunts, their faces would be red as beets and streaked with perspiration. They took a big cast iron wash pot in which to cook the French fries and then the fish. One or two coffee pots were also placed over the fire. Desserts were made at home and carried with us. One luxury food was the loaves of bread bought at the store. And that was all we had: Fried fish, "light" bread, French fries, coffee, and desserts! Oh, boy, what a feast. But the pots and pans they carried along were blackened with smoke at the end of the day and had to be scrubbed clean when they got home.

We kids would travel along the banks of the creek finding all sorts of treasures, playing hide-and-go-seek, tag, Red-Rover, Cowboys and Indians, or swinging on tree branches over the creek, Tarzan-fashion. We played baseball using a rock for a ball and tree branches for bats. We manufactured our games. Our imaginations knew no bounds, and the area rang with our laughter.

Once, the older (not necessarily wiser) boys devised a new game. They noticed that my sister Gwen was tiny and red-haired. They decided that if they pulled a sapling over until it almost touched the ground, put Gwen on the top branches and then turned the sapling loose, she would go sailing through the air looking just like a red-headed woodpecker. So, they proceeded with their plans. The sapling was pulled over, and Gwen was placed on the top branches. Almost too late, I saw what was happening and yelled, "Hang on tight, Gwennie!" Just then the boys let the top of the sapling go—had she NOT been "hanging on tight," she could have been hurt badly. Gwen said she remembers being scared to death. The sapling sprung forward, then snapped back to its original position, and continued whipping back and forth several times before it finally stopped. Hearing our screaming, the adults turned their attention to us. Dad came running from the creek bank. In no uncertain terms he told the boys to pull the sapling over again, and to hold it firmly. He then tenderly removed Gwen from the sapling, threatening the boy's lives if they ever tried anything like that again. Mom and Dad both got very mad about that stunt.

Of course, we kids always wanted to go swimming. The girls brought their swim-suits, if they had any. Otherwise, they just wore old shorts and blouses. The boys wore cut-off blue jeans. The dads let us swim after they had "fished out" the swimming hole. While the men dressed the fish, and our Moms cooked them, we dog-paddled to our hearts' contents. Our dads sat on the creek bank watching us, so we felt very safe. We never worried about snakes or drowning; we just had the times of our lives. We would head for home late in the afternoon, sunburned, mud-caked, covered with chigger-bites, full of fresh-caught catfish—and quite sure that NO ONE had as much fun as we had. Those were the days!

One of these outings had quite a different turn of events. When we arrived at the creek, the women began unloading the cars, while the men went to the creek with their seines. Dad and Buster waded into the creek to begin checking it out. They ducked beneath the water's surface to check the holes in the sides and bottom of the creek where fish stayed. The murky water in the creek made it difficult to see very far. They had seen several nice fish in the water, when all of a sudden Buster disturbed a water moccasin. It bit him on his leg just a few inches above his ankle. He shot to the top of the water and yelled, "Snake bite." Dad had seen the action under the water and came up right behind Buster. Hurriedly they got on the bank. Dad had Buster lie down with his head higher than his feet so that his blood would flow slower to his heart. Dad grabbed his sharpened pocket-knife, cut two deep X's over the fang marks, and began sucking out the blood and poison, then spitting it on the ground. The women and children were horrified. We cried, prayed, wrung our hands, and paced back and forth while this was taking place.

All the while, Grandpa Coney was begging Dad not to do it. "Lowell, if you've got an open cut in your mouth, that poison will go right to your brain and kill you. Let's take Buster to the doctor." Dad didn't even pause to answer; he just continued sucking out that poison and spitting it out. He knew that the snake was very large with a lot of venom. He also knew it would take at least half an hour to get to the nearest hospital. By that time, Buster could be dead. Dad continued the treatment for about fifteen minutes until he was satisfied that he had removed all of the poison that he could. Then Buster's leg was bandaged. Everyone began loading the cars with whatever they had brought, and we all returned home, emotionally exhausted. We caught no fish that day! But the main thing was that Buster was alive, thanks to an old-time folk remedy.

Mom, Gwen, and I cried all the way home, thinking daddy was going to die from the snake poison—thinking he had given his life for his brother. We were so glad to see him alive the next morning, but still worried that the poison might just be slow-working and he would die at any time. It was several weeks later when we finally realized that Daddy was truly going to be all right. The horror of that day still lingers in my memory and in my heart.

Although the Coney men continued to fish for several more years, that was the last of the family fishing trips.

FISHERMAN'S LUCK

Dean Price—age 12

Caught no fish, tell you why:
Water too low, wind too high,

Left dark glasses, brought wrong bait,
Boots sprang leaks, started too late,

Too many people—drat those boys!—
Too many dogs, too much noise,

Flies wouldn't float, lost best hooks,
Owner of stream gave dirty looks.

Could tell more—talk two seasons.
Got no fish, plenty of reasons.

Dewey Granberry fishing, 1959

FISHING FROM INDIANOLA TO BOCA CHICA AND WATERS IN BETWEEN

by Jean Granberry Schnitz

In the early 1900s, on the banks of the San Antonio River near the little town of Choate in Karnes County, Texas, Dewey Lafayette Granberry discovered that it was fun to catch fish. Not only that, but fish added variety to the diet of a large family experiencing hard times. After his father died at the age of twenty-eight, when Dewey was only two years old, his mother and two brothers went to live with his grandparents in Karnes County. Dewey, my father, joined the United States Navy in 1917, when he was eighteen years old. He did a pretty good job of seeing the world during World War I, but that love of fishing endured throughout his lifetime, providing my family with many exciting adventures.

Dad's fishing trips spelled something different for each member of my family, but for me they spelled "fun." My brother, Billy Granberry, actually fished with Dad, but Mama used the time for beachcombing or what we now call "birding." Grandpapa was an avid fishing buddy for Dad, but Grandmama spent the time writing letters or joining Mama and me in exploring the area near where the fishing was going on. The rule for me was to "stay in sight," but that left plenty of opportunity to explore. I could swim, climb trees, dig in the sand, pick up shells, or any of dozens of other activities—so long as I could be seen by the fishermen or by Mama.

When we lived in Victoria from 1936 to 1944, there were many interesting places to catch fish, including in the Guadalupe River just a few blocks from our home. Dad took me with him as we walked down the hill to the river. Our job was to catch grasshoppers, lizards, and/or frogs to be used as bait. We soon learned not to approach the river bank without carefully surveying the bank for water moccasins. There was a sunken barge near where we reached the river, and I still cringe when I remember seeing dozens of fat, black moccasins soaking up sun on the deck of that barge. Usually, they slithered into the river when we approached. We always threw some well-placed rocks to be sure they had all gone swimming before stepping down onto the deck. No way would I have put one toe into the water of the Guadalupe River at that location! We kept a careful watch to be sure the barge was not visited by another moccasin while Dad caught enough fish for several meals.

Dad was careful to catch only as many fish as our family could eat or share with the neighbors for a few days. We had no room in our freezer for anything but a few ice cubes, and we didn't have enough money to rent a freezer locker. When I say we ate fish, I mean we ate FRIED fish. Once in a great while, Mama baked some fish (usually flounder), but almost always it was fried. She salted and peppered it and dipped it into corn meal before frying it in bacon fat. Even though we had plenty of eggs, I don't remember ever seeing her dip the fish into beaten eggs before coating it with corn meal. We fried *everything* in bacon fat, which made things taste much better than it does fried in more healthful oils.

One summer we went back to Choate and camped on the San Antonio River where Dad had fished as a boy. He was able to identify several large trees he had accidentally planted when he went fishing there so long ago. He had stuck his fishing poles into the ground at his favorite locations along the river bank. Amazingly, some of them took root and grew! He showed my brother and me how he had cut fishing poles from small tree limbs that were as long and strong as he could find. Fish hooks were made from wire found on the farm. He showed us how they baited hooks for trot lines with pieces cut from suet or sometimes homemade lye soap deemed useful for that purpose. It didn't surprise me at the time that fish found lye soap tasty, since I had helped my grandmother make soap from bacon grease in a big kettle in the yard at home. The lye probably wasn't as tasty, but it made the grease congeal into a form of soap that would stay on a fish hook for awhile.

Dad and I had different criteria for judging a fishing spot. For Dad, priority-one was finding a good place where the fish would be biting and bait was easy to obtain. For me, positive factors included a shady place to park the car and a sandy beach or smooth bank. I didn't like to go to Rockport and Aransas Pass or other places along the various bays near Victoria because there were too many sticker burrs on the bank, too many jelly fish in the water, and too few trees for shade or climbing. I didn't like to tromp through tall weeds or poison ivy to get to the water. Beach locations with a good fishing pier or jetty were among my preferences. However, it was not *my* decision to pick the spots for Dad's fishing adventures. I learned that it was not good to complain, but it was easy to find something to enjoy everywhere we went.

One of our family's favorite spots to fish was at old Indianola, which had been destroyed in a series of hurricanes. When we were going there in the late 1930s, Dad could sit on the rock walls at the edge of the water where he caught plenty of fish. We children could walk around the walls of the buildings that were not completely under water. There were some old cisterns we could explore. Linda Wolff knows a lot about Indianola, having researched the area for her book, *Indianola and Matagorda Island 1837–1887*. She was amazed when I told her how we could walk and fish along some of the walls of the buildings. She described how the only way to see the walls of the old city now is to fly overhead in an airplane or helicopter on a quiet day when the water is clear.[1] The walls have been completely submerged in sea water because of the changes in the shoreline.

When Dad was fishing, Mama would walk or drive the car some distance down the beach to what I thought was quite a magnificent statue of the explorer credited with finding Indianola. There was a base on the platform about three or four feet high on which I could go round and round the statue, chanting his full name that was etched in the stone: Rene Robert Cavalier Sieur de la Salle. I still have no idea how to pronounce some of the French names, but it seemed melodic to me!

In seeking to find a picture of the monument I remember, I found Henry Wolff, Jr.'s column in the *Victoria Advocate* of

January 17, 1999, which showed a picture of the ruins of a statue of LaSalle with only the boots remaining.[2] I was dismayed when I thought that the magnificent statue was destroyed in an unspecified hurricane. The Indianola Cemetery web site (http:// www.indianolatx.com/LaSalle_Boots.html) shows a picture of the broken statue of LaSalle's boots. During a visit with Henry Wolff, Jr. at the 2010 Texas Folklore Society meeting in Abilene, Henry clarified that there were originally TWO statues of LaSalle at Indianola. The one near the old cemetery was the one that was destroyed except for the boots. I was happy to learn that the "magnificent" statue of LaSalle remains.[3] Pictures of it may be found on the Internet on several web sites about Indianola.

On one memorable fishing trip to Indianola, Dad was fishing at the town site and I was wading near the point of the peninsula not far from the old town when I cut my foot on a broken bottle. When I lifted my foot out of the water, all I could see was blood. Some Boy Scouts were swimming nearby and they came running to administer first aid. That fishing trip ended with a trip to the Emergency Room in Victoria to sew my foot back together. That was the day I learned to wear old shoes when swimming in unknown waters.

When Dad wanted to go on a "serious" fishing trip, he and Grandpapa (and sometimes Billy) left home about 3:00 a.m. in order to arrive and have time to do some fishing before dawn. Sometimes he had other fishing companions, none of whom had a boat. They fished from the bank or from piers, but also did "wade fishing" in summer. They went "floundering" often, since waters were shallow and flounders were plentiful. Fishing for flounder involved carrying a gasoline lantern in one hand and a gig in the other. No poles were involved. At certain times of the year, flounder was the usual catch.

On one trip Dad was floundering and accidentally gigged a stingaree (sting ray) instead of a flounder. He climbed as high as he could on his gig until he managed to get the stingaree loose without his being stung by its dangerous barb. Dad's fishing buddies included our doctor, Dr. Roy Lander, a friend by the name of C. B. Fallis, and another man from Goliad, Victor Albrecht. Dad had other fishing buddies in just about every little town on the coast near Victoria. Cold weather was not a deterrent to their fishing expeditions, nor was hot weather. In fact, Dad always declared that fishing for red fish was best after the third norther of the winter. The colder the weather, the bigger the red fish!

Not all fish were considered by Dad as "fit to eat," so he rarely brought home anything but catfish, trout, redfish, flounder, and sharks. I didn't notice until many years later that Dad would not eat the fish himself. He blamed that on having to be the one who always cleaned the fish. He gutted them, cut off their heads, and scraped off the scales. When he came home with a huge stringer of fish, as in the picture, he got help from my brother and me to help scrape off the scales. If the fish was very large, it may have been too difficult for us, and Dad had to do it, but we could usually do a pretty job of scaling fish. It was always a mess to clean up—no matter how hard we tried to keep scales from flying everywhere. Also, since there was no garbage pickup in those days, it was difficult to dispose of the inedible parts of the fish, and whatever area was used to clean the fish remained "fragrant" for a long time.

In cleaning fish, I don't remember Dad ever "filleting" fish with the possible exception of cutting fillets from very large fish. He always cut the fish into pieces that had meat on both sides of the bone—and there were always plenty of bones! We had to be very careful when we ate the fish lest we swallow a bone. There were many dire stories that served to warn us of the consequences of not being careful. In the event we accidentally swallowed a fish bone, the remedy was to eat a few pieces of bread in hopes of keeping the bone from piercing something vital. It must have worked!

Having our doctor as a fishing buddy paid off when Dad got very sick during the early 1940s. After numerous hospital stays, home visits and office visits, Dad was dreading the huge doctor bill he expected to receive. Instead, when the statement came in the mail, it declared the amount due: "fishing trips on demand." The doctor got his payments!

Sometimes Grandpapa and Dad took me and Billy, and Nippie, Grandpapa's dog, when they went to Garcitas Creek fishing. On one trip, somebody caught an electric eel, which was on the bank. Nippie appointed himself to catch it, but soon gave up on that project when he was shocked nearly senseless by the eel. Nippie would bark a minute or two, then attack. As he grabbed the eel with his teeth, he would yelp and fall trembling on the ground. Then the cycle was repeated until the eel found its way back into the water. We thought it was really funny! On another trip, Nippie caught a skunk, which did what skunks do. We didn't want to leave Nippie at the creek, so we tried to bathe him in the water. That ended with all of us smelling like a skunk—and having to bury all the clothes that came in contact with Nippie. Happily, the clothes we went fishing in were old and ragged, so it was worth it for the laughs we have had for years about Nippie's misadventure.

On one fishing trip to Palacios or Matagorda, Dad caught a nice middle-sized fish. I begged him to tie it on a string and let me hold the end of it instead of putting it on a stringer to go back into the water. After awhile, I got tired of holding the string, so I tied it to one of my fingers and dangled the fish down into the water as I lay on my tummy and watched it swimming around. Suddenly, I saw a BIG shadow coming toward my fish. Dad barely caught me by the heel as I was being pulled into the water when the big

A good catch

shadow caught my fish. I was already off the edge of the pier when he grabbed me. I almost became bait! Mama declared she had a life-sized mental picture of me on the bottom of the bay on my way out to sea. After that, I was banned from tying a fish to a finger or anywhere else that could cause me to get pulled into the water.

We sometimes went camping at Goose Island, which had nice camp sites. We never had a tent, but slept outside on cots. That was a good way for Dad to start fishing without having to load up and drive somewhere very early in the morning. At Goose Island, we liked to go climb around on the famous "Biggest Tree in Texas." In those days, we could climb on it, but today, people are asked not to do that. It was a wonderful treasure of a tree! The biggest problem with camping without a tent was mosquitoes, but we managed. Rain during the night posed a separate problem, which we solved by sleeping under a big tarp that Dad spread over our cots.

Dad had better equipment for salt water fishing than he did for bank fishing in a river. He had several big reels that he was constantly taking apart and putting back together. There was one table in the house that was used solely for the purpose of keeping parts of reels until he could get them well lubricated and put back together. He bought an old boat motor from someone and set it up in our garage in a big barrel of water. He spent lots of time "playing with" his motor and getting it ready for the time when someone had a boat they could use. Rarely, they were able to use Dad's motor and get farther away from the bank to do their fishing.

Billy told a story about how he and Dad once rented a small boat and, using the small motor, made their way toward what Dad thought would be a good location to fish. On the way, the water got too shallow, and the propeller of the motor hit something that made it almost break off. Dad knew that it needed something to hold the propeller in place. Billy worried about the situation as they drifted farther and farther out while Daddy tried to find something to use. He finally was able to find a makeshift pin for the propeller so they could get back to shore.

Special vacations found us in Port Aransas. You wouldn't believe what the road from the mainland to the ferry landing was like back in those days! Between small islands there were parallel boards just a bit wider than car tires, with a board nailed to the outside forming a small barrier to running off into the water. There were pull-outs every few miles so that cars could pull over and wait for another to pass. One time Dad didn't see a car coming soon enough, and we had to back up. Scary! I helped by covering my eyes. It never scared me when we got to the ferry. That part of the trip was fun. I found backup for my memories of the wooden plank structure:

> A toll road was opened in 1931 between the town of Aransas Pass and the Ferry Landing of Port Aransas. Before the toll road, one was required to buy a ticket, load their vehicle onto a flatbed or train, and use the wooden planks inside the rails when the train was not on a scheduled run. With the advent of the toll road, drivers could simply pay a toll and drive on a wooden plank structure built next to the rail tracks. After the railroad closed in 1947, it was used only to transport automobiles until 1960, when the state built a modern road to Harbor Island from Corpus Christi and the ferry landing.[4]

The causeway I remember was "next to the rail tracks" because I remember seeing the tracks "over there." I also remember that it was a toll road. A similar plank causeway also existed between Port-land and Corpus Christi across the Bay. It was removed long ago, but one can still see the pilings which were not totally removed when the new causeway was built.

We stayed in Port Aransas in some little cabins for the grand sum of $6 per day, which Mama thought was exorbitant. Those little cabins still exist, but you sure wouldn't want to stay in them now. Back in the early 1940s, they were fairly new and nice. They were screened in with bunk beds and cotton mattresses, and a bathroom and kitchen. We brought our own pillows and linens. The shower was more or less outside the cabin so that the water drained onto the ground, but it was enclosed and provided privacy.

Dad liked to fish as far out on the jetty as he was able to go. That depended on the wind and tide. We were able to get all the way to the end of the jetty if the waves were not riding high. I remember seeing lots of huge boulders of granite stacked at one end of the ferry on Port Aransas, and there were railroad tracks that extended far out on the jetties over the water at that time. Research revealed that work began on the jetties in 1888. The existing jetties were built by the U. S. Army Corps of Engineers beginning in 1907, with construction initially completed by 1919, but maintenance work continued into the late 1930s (and probably is sometimes necessary even today). Two jetties were eventually built—one on either side of the channel.[5] We enjoyed seeing large ships go by on their way from the harbor to the Gulf of Mexico.

Since all of us had red or blonde hair and fair skin, we were allowed to swim only until about 9 a.m. After that, we had to stay inside until about 6:30 in the afternoon when we could walk back to the beach for more swimming and digging in the sand. During our time out of the sun we played lots of games, took naps, and had a great time! Dad slathered on a thick layer of white goo (I think it was some kind of zinc ointment) and went fishing anyway while covered in a long-sleeved shirt, long pants, gloves, a kerchief around his neck, and a big floppy hat. He also got sunburned every day despite his precautions. Since there was no other sunscreen and we didn't want to wear the white ointment on our faces, we simply stayed out of the sun.

Of course, we ate fish every day while we were there. One day someone caught some jack fish bigger than my brother and me and we went outside in the sun to take pictures. Another time, while we were at the beach our dog, "Rascal," followed us into the water. He headed out to sea and never looked back. We yelled and screamed at him, and then as he disappeared into the distance, we cried and mourned that he probably would drown. We could see his ears over the tops of the waves before he disappeared in the distance. The next morning, Dad was down by the pier and someone came by in a boat with our lucky dog on board. The fisherman had found him many miles out in the Gulf of Mexico and pulled him into the boat. What a joyous occasion that was when Dad brought our beloved lost dog back to the cabin!

It was not as easy back in the 1930s and 1940s to find suitable bait as it is now. There were no "bait stands," and even if there were, Dad found his own bait. Near fresh water rivers and lakes, we usually caught plenty of grasshoppers or frogs, and Dad might use his shovel to look for nice wiggly worms to put on the hook. We might use the minnow seine to try to get some small fish. When Dad fished in salt water, he caught his own bait with a large cast net. Dad's net was about six feet in diameter with lead weights all around it. It took some skill to throw the net so that it deployed to its full size, catching a maximum amount of bait. He usually had plenty of bait for a day (or night) of fishing after two or three casts of the net. With luck there might be small shad or other fish and lots of small shrimp. Dad's bait bucket was filled with water from the bay or whatever body of water we were fishing near. We caught the small fish and shrimp with our hands and put them in the bucket.

Most of the shrimp Dad used for bait was pretty small and didn't smell very appetizing. It was many years before I discovered that we could actually eat shrimp. At our dinner table when fried shrimp was served, Billy and I routinely requested, "Please pass the bait."

When we moved to Alice, Texas, in 1944, Dad's fishing habits changed because there wasn't much salt water close to Alice where he could fish. He liked to go to Mathis Lake and upstream of Mathis Lake on the Nueces River near the little town of Lagarto. He still managed to catch enough fish for us to enjoy. Occasionally, he and some friends went to Corpus Christi, where they could fish in salt water, but usually we children were not able to accompany him on those "serious" fishing trips. Still, we always enjoyed our trips to Mathis Lake and always took picnic lunches. Sometimes we took cots and friends, and camped on the bank of the lake. Dad fished from the bank. There were places where tall bluffs provided access to good fishing spots.

In 1946, when we moved to the Rio Grande Valley of Texas, to Raymondville, Dad's fishing trips continued to be a part of our activities. There was a fresh water lake west of Raymondville near

Monte Alto called Delta Lake. Dad liked to fish there, but he never caught much. It was probably the closest place to fish, though some people actually fished in irrigation canals. Not Dad. He preferred other locations. There was a swimming area and a pavilion at Delta Lake, with shade and picnic tables. The banks had tall eucalyptus trees and other tropical varieties of vegetation. They also provided places for rattlesnakes to lurk, so we children went swimming while Dad fished. Mama, who could not swim, served as life guard. The water was nice when the wind wasn't blowing, but it was choppy and muddy on windy days.

In Raymondville, Dad finally found a fishing companion with a boat. Frederick Humphrey, father of one of my classmates in the Class of 1948, had a little-bitty flat-bottom boat. They made many trips to Red Fish Bay (now called Port Mansfield), where they brought home plenty of fish. Later, Fred got a bigger boat, and they decided to go to Boca Chica, near Port Isabel, where the Rio Grande runs into the Gulf of Mexico. My family went along, as did Fred's wife and two daughters, as well as his daughter's boyfriend. Dad and Fred spent a good day fishing offshore in Fred's boat while the rest of us enjoyed the beach. That night Fred simply pulled his boat up on the sand, and the girls and ladies slept on cots in the back of his empty cotton truck that was covered with a big tarp. The men and boys slept on cots on the beach. During the night a Gulf storm moved in. Dad stepped off his cot into ankle deep water. We had to push the two cars and Fred's cotton truck into the dunes. Dad and Fred set out to save the boat. During flashes of lightning, we could see them having great fun pulling the boat through the wind and rain high up into the dunes so it wouldn't wash away. We had to stay there a couple of days until the tide went out enough for us to drive on the beach again. In those days there were no hurricane or storm warnings, but even if there were, we never listened to a radio. No fishing took place after the storm, but it certainly was exciting. We walked up and down the beach retrieving our cooking equipment, which had washed away.

On one fishing expedition to Red Fish Bay, Fred and Dad came back to the Humphreys' beach house after fishing all morning.

After cleaning the fish, Dad decided to take a nap. It was a beautiful sunny summer day, so Jane Humphrey and I begged her father to take us swimming in the bay. We had a wonderful time diving into the water and climbing back on the boat with ladders Fred had rigged for the purpose. We stayed too long. I was blistered by the sun from head to feet, and had to stay in bed for more than a week until the blisters got better. I couldn't wear clothes or shoes for the blisters! That was a hard lesson. Thank goodness we now have sunscreen—and maybe even a bit more sense.

One summer we went to camp along the Nueces River on Mr. Lawl Reagan's property near Oakville, Texas. We set up camp in the trees and slept under the stars. Every day Dad went fishing somewhere near our camp site while Billy and I enjoyed swimming in the river. One day the river suddenly got muddy and began to rise. Though it had not rained at our camp site, sticks and logs began to float by. Dad watched it awhile and announced that a flood was coming, so we packed up everything. As we were leaving, Mr. Reagan came to warn us about the coming flood. It was a good thing we were vigilant because by that time the river covered the spot where we had camped.

After my family moved to Beeville in 1950, Dad was able to find several large stock tanks on ranches where he could fish. Occasionally, he went to Bayside or some destination along the coast, but stock tanks were pretty good places to catch fish since the fish were "planted" there by the landowner and/or by Texas Parks and Wildlife personnel. They grew quite large with time. Before then, Dad's bait was usually something he put onto a hook, but at this time he learned to make and use lures. Stock tank fish loved that! He even made successful lures from the colorful tags that he got off sacks of Bull Durham tobacco, which was frequently used in the 1940s and 1950s to "roll your own" cigarettes.

Dad's cousin, Jack Tidwell, lived just a few houses down Tyler Street in Beeville, so he and Dad had lots of fun together fishing out of Jack's boat. The picture at the beginning of my story is the last one we have of Dad before he got sick in September of 1959. He died of lung cancer in November of that year at the age of sixty-one.

Unfortunately, I didn't inherit Dad's love of fishing. I did inherit the love of camping and visiting seashores, lakes, rivers, and other good fishing places. Most of all, I still enjoy eating fish—even baked fish! Nothing can compare with the fresh fish that Dad caught and brought home. Freezing may preserve fish, but it loses some flavor in the process. Besides, it isn't much fun shopping for fish at a supermarket. Fishing provided a lifetime of enjoyment to Dad and our entire family.

Endnotes

1. Wolff, Linda. Personal Interviews by the author at several Texas Folklore Society meetings between 2005 and 2010.
2. Wolff, Henry, Jr. "Henry's Journal." *Victoria Advocate.* January 17, 1999.
3. Wolff, Henry, Jr. Personal interview by the author at the Texas Folklore Society annual meeting. April 2, 2010.
4. Port Aransas, Texas. "Transportation to and from Port Aransas." *Wikipedia, the Free Encyclopedia,* http://en.wikipedia.org/wiki/Port_Aransas,_TX#Transportation_to_and_from_Port_Aransas, Accessed 26 March, 2010.
5. "Tourists Followed Karankawas to Island." *Visitors' Guide* (to Port Aransas), http://visitorsguide.portasouthjetty.com/news/2010-08-20/History/Tourists_followed_Karankawas_to_island.html. Accessed 15 April, 2010.

Fishing on the jetty

THE JETTY

by Randy Cameron

Port Aransas, that island town off the Texas mainland, is, of course, surrounded by water. But even that is not enough for some people. They want to go farther than the edge. They want to go to the very end. And to those who do, the jetty is their route, a mile-long, twelve-foot wide stretch of old cement first constructed in 1940, and more recently widened, patched, and finally strengthened with Volkswagen-sized blocks of Texas granite. The whole scene is a marvelous mixture of jumbled and jagged rocks, moss, kelp, wheeling gulls, and sea spray.

And fishermen. What an eclectic lot the jetty lures out upon it—especially, I think, on a mild December day of streaky, high cirrus clouds and little wind such as this. We see people of all ages and genders, some serious anglers, some semi-so, and some not at all. Those are the ones content to watch and listen to the sea, catch some sun, check their bird books and just be a part of the relaxed, communal scene. Still others, like myself, and my wife and seven-year-old son, try a little bit of it all.

The array of tackle scattered across the jetty is truly vast— formidable in some cases, very simple in others. Suffice it to say, on this Sunday before Christmas with the temperature in the 70s, the jetty is littered with rods, reels, nets, gaffs, buckets, tackle boxes, coolers, and discarded jackets.

We start out on the walk with two rods and a very small tackle box. Fishing, for those who know what they are doing, is very good. We see several good fish taken in the first 100 yards of our walk before we stop and turn to the Gulf side, our back to the channel, and fish for a while ourselves.

The tide and breeze have dictated that the Gulf side is the calm side today. Some fifteen feet behind us across the rocks is the mile-wide ship channel, choppy this afternoon with the bulging wakes of passing boats of all sizes and styles. After a while, Will and I leave Mary casting a Spec-Rig (a lure set-up we did not know existed until yesterday) and explore farther out on the jetty. Free of his mother's hand and admonishments, Will bounds goat-like from rock to rock, sailing over the gaps.

We come upon an older man, fast to what is obviously a good fish. After a strong and determined fight, the prize is netted deftly by a neighboring lady angler. "You are having a ball," she says as she fumbles in the net to retrieve a six- or eight-pound fish. "Man," he says grinning broadly, "this is the best fishing I've had in years."

Back at our home, still in Texas but way up by the Red River, fishing is often poor when the weather is as glorious as it is today. But the jetty fish seem to like the conditions just as much as the anglers. The bait fishermen are catching large Sheephead from the dark green waters, and other good-sized species that I can't identify.

On we go, farther out still, easing along among the gulls and an occasional Great Blue Heron. A giant freighter, *The Florida Express*, slices through the channel towards the yawning gulf. Will and I stand silently and watch, feeling the ancient, magnetic pull of the romance and adventure of the open seas.

We turn to watch a Hispanic teen confidently—no, arrogantly—wear down a big fish on a ridiculously light rod and push-button reel, a cigarette fixed firmly in one corner of his mouth. After several minutes, he lands a fish of some ten pounds without benefit of net or gaff.

Farther out still, Will strikes up a conversation with an old timer who has just landed a nice Sheephead. He shows Will his bait, Fiddler Crabs swarming in a plastic jug. He tells us his wife catches them for him. "I can't hardly see them anymore," he says.

Out almost to the end, a man heads past us for the mainland with a handsome pair of speckled trout. An L. L. Bean-attired couple watches a pair of Curlews and consults their Roger Tory Peterson *Field Guide to the Birds of Texas*.

Will and I start back. Mary is sitting on a rock, lulled by sun and sea. The Spec-Rig has been claimed by the deep. We walk back to the beach, meeting other people just starting out. A big, rusted orange tanker comes down the channel heading in, eerily silent as it ghosts by. When we are almost to land, we pass a couple of guys burdened with tackle, heading out.

"Do any good?" one asks in the traditional fishermen's greeting.

"No," I say, "but we don't really know what we are doing."

Which is not exactly true. Later that evening as I drifted towards sleep, replaying the day, I realized what we had been doing on the jetty that day. We had participated in a timeless Texas coastal tradition, a cultural experience that is pure in its shared simplicity, one that is heedless of age, gender, origin, and even ability.

YOU HUNT WHAT?!

UNUSUAL PREY AND OTHER THINGS WE CHASE

Black-tailed jackrabbit

JACKRABBIT DRIVES (AND OTHER TYPES OF RABBIT HUNTING) IN THE PLEASANT VALLEY COMMUNITY, FISHER COUNTY, TEXAS

by Ruth Cleveland Riddels

Jackrabbit drives were conducted in Fisher County as early as 1920 and continued until after World War II. In *The Picture Book of Fisher County*, compiled by The Fisher County Historical Commission, page 192, there are two pictures of groups of men with guns that were labeled "Rabbit Drive, 1920" and "Rabbit Drive, 1941." During those years the jackrabbit population had increased to plague proportions, "eating everything in sight." Rabbits will not only eat plants above the ground but will then dig up the roots. Rabbits also will eat the bark off young trees, and large jackrabbits standing on their hind legs can eat a lot of bark. I don't know what the conditions were that caused the increase of the jackrabbit population to the extent that the jackrabbits were a menace to all edible plants and the livelihood of rural families, nor do I know why the jackrabbit population has never increased to the point of being such a menace again. They certainly were not hunted to extinction, as plenty of them can still be found in west Texas.

I have relied on the memories of my brothers, William and John Cleveland, for my information regarding jackrabbit drives in Pleasant Valley Community, Fisher County, Texas, where we grew up. Rural communities were common and were very loosely designated as to boundaries. Pleasant Valley had two churches, one Methodist and one Baptist, and a two-room school. There were a number of small farms in the area, and those who were considered Pleasant Valley community neighbors numbered approximately fifteen to twenty families. Other communities were similarly formed, some with only a rural one- or two-room school, and some with only a church.

The jackrabbit drives would be casually organized by the men, usually after a church service as they stood outside visiting while the women inside the church were also getting in their weekly visit. A day would be decided upon and a location for the drive would be chosen. The place would be some "pasture"—uncleared land of scrubby mesquites and cactus. Some of the neighboring communities would hold a drive on Sunday, but I grew up in Pleasant Valley and I am very sure that would have never been the case in our community. The jackrabbit drives were held in the spring and sometimes in the fall of the year. The chosen day would be passed on by word of mouth to the neighbors and the neighboring communities.

Likely, the women folk would be informed of the day during the ride home from church. The women would then know what was expected of them, and since very few, if any, had telephones they would handle the "dinner on the ground" without a lot of formal organizational talk.

Other men from neighboring communities would join the jackrabbit drive. In turn, some of the Pleasant Valley men would join in the neighboring community jackrabbit drives. Before the day of the drive, one man from the group would make a trip into town (Rotan) to purchase cases of shotgun shells of various gauges. Only shotguns were used. On the day of the drive, men could purchase as many shells as each could afford or thought he needed. The unsold, unopened boxes of shells would be returned to the store.

The drive would be held in one day in two phases. On the morning of the drive, the men and older boys would be divided in two teams. The older men along with other men with shotguns would form the stand. The men would line up side by side approximately ten feet apart. The other men and boys, some with guns, and some without, would then be designated to be the drivers. The drivers would then go approximately a mile away from the stand and they, too, would be approximately ten feet apart. The drivers would proceed to walk towards the stand making noise and shooting as they went, driving jackrabbits in front of them towards the stand. Remember that rabbits, even large jackrabbits, are low to the ground and so all shooting was aimed downward. The shooters could swing their guns in a small arc to the left and right but, of course, never turn their bodies so that they were in danger of shooting another man. When someone determined that the drivers were close enough to the stand to be in danger or cause the men in the line to be in danger, a halt would be called and they would turn rabbits back towards the stand until it was decided that all rabbits that had not escaped had been killed. The rabbits killed were deemed inedible because it was believed that the jackrabbits were infected with a parasite.

After the morning drive, the hunters went to the church where "dinner on the ground" had been laid out by the women folk. In the Baptist church, the pews had been home-made and had flat seats, unlike the Methodist church which had store-bought pews and thus the seat part was curved. Some of the Baptist pews, or "benches" as they were called, were taken from the church and placed face to face and end to end, with the seat part touching. This provided a flat surface for the ladies to place their table cloths and food. A drawback to this arrangement, especially from the viewpoint of small children, was that one had to reach over the back of the bench to reach the food and the younger ones were way too short to do so. Small children not only had to wait for the men folk to eat first and then the women second, but they were also subject to being served whatever their mother or older sister decided they could have and in the quantity those servers thought was enough. After the dinner on the ground, the men then went to another location and proceeded to stage another jackrabbit drive for the afternoon.

Neither William nor John could recall how often the drives were held or when they quit having them. William remembered the last drive he went on was in Claytonville. He was fifteen or sixteen years old at the time. It is also the time he was shot. As stated above, all shooting was more or less downward, so the danger of being shot in the torso was remote. William caught the edge of a buckshot scatter in the lower part of his leg. The buckshot made holes in his britches, and some lodged in his leg. To quote him, "I wasn't hurt much but it did sting quite a bit." The buckshot lodged in his leg was "picked out" with the sharp point of someone's pocket knife. No medical care was considered necessary.

John was not old enough to participate in any of the drives until after the end of World War II, and he only recalls participating in one. In his description of the stand and drivers, the hunters formed a slightly curved line so that the ends of each line would reach each other sooner. This made sense, as this created less of an area to each side for the jackrabbits to escape.

My youngest sister-in-law, Lora (who did not grow up in our community but in our county), remembers her granny going rabbit hunting for food. However, when I mentioned that we did not eat the rabbits killed in the drives because of the parasite, she recalled that some time later, even though her granny went rabbit hunting, she no longer brought them home for food. Lora recalled stories of jackrabbit drives in the part of the county where she grew up and said that those jackrabbit drives involved the women and small children being the drivers and banging on pots and pans to make noise.

Another jackrabbit hunting method for William and John and their friends was at night in the winter wheat fields using a vehicle, preferably a pickup. After the farmers harvested the cotton and cleared the fields of cotton stalks, they would plant winter wheat in their fields. It was planted in part to hold the soil in place and in part to provide grazing for their livestock during the winter. The jackrabbits would begin eating the winter wheat sprouts before the wheat had grown enough to let the livestock graze, so when the young men wanted to hunt in the winter wheat field the farmer was very glad for them to do so, as long as the ground was not wet and they drove their vehicles carefully so as not to make ruts. Today, wheat is still planted for those reasons, although the threat to the crops is not jackrabbits but deer and wild hogs.

Jackrabbit drive wagon

Someone would borrow a vehicle, preferably a pickup, although a car might sometimes be used. Two boys with their shotguns would ride one on each fender (vehicles had fenders in those days) with their legs wrapped around the headlight (not in front of the light), and if it was a pickup sometimes two or three boys would ride in the bed of the pickup, steadying their shotguns on top of the cab. They were able to kill "quite a number" of jackrabbits in one evening. Occasionally, they would hunt in this manner in a pasture. This was much more exciting, because the rocks and rough terrain increased the chances of being tossed off the fender or out of the bed of the truck.

Sometimes the boys would go hunting along the county roads at night, shooting from the windows of a car or pickup. A nephew remarked that this is still done, and he said he and a friend worked especially well together because my nephew shoots left handed and his friend shoots right handed. (I'm sure this type of hunting is highly illegal.)

John recalled how he and his friends frequently went hunting for jackrabbits in the "shinnery" (an area of extremely sandy soil that will only grow "shin" oaks). Shin oaks are small bushes that only grow approximately shin high, although now they appear to be somewhat taller. When they went hunting in the shinnery they used .22 rifles. There truly was not much activity or amusement for young boys in those days. There was no TV, and certainly no computers; in our case there was not even electricity. There were no organized baseball little leagues, nor any way to get to town even if there were. They had to make their own fun. The boys would be allowed to do this type of hunting when they were as young as ten or twelve years old.

I found on the Internet two accounts of rabbit drives in western Kansas and Nebraska during the Great Depression and Dust Bowl days. The jackrabbits were "eating everything." One account was on YouTube and is a short news movie made by Pathe News. Pathe News and Movietone News produced these short news reports, which were then played between features in the movie theaters. The pictures were silent and an announcer intoned what the action was and where it occurred. I remember these features especially during World War II when battlefield action was recorded.

A Kansas jackrabbit drive, 1914

The other account is posted in the Kansas State Historical Society web site.

The rabbit drives in these states were conducted differently. They didn't use guns. The drivers included everyone—women, children and men. Prior to the drive large, eight-sided pens furnished by the U.S. government were erected with one side open. The rabbits were herded into these pens and subsequently clubbed to death or taken to other areas of the state.

ENDNOTE

The following web sites contain news articles related to jackrabbit hunts. http://www.youtube.com/watch?v+YDxvc-BuS5A and http://www.kshs.org/kansapedia/jackrabbit-drives/12097

Gracie

RATTLESNAKE AT THE ANTS IN THE PANTS

by Clyde (Chip) Morgan

In his book *Rattlesnakes*, J. Frank Dobie discusses with his good friend, Texas naturalist Roy Bedichek, the diamondback rattlesnake's profound attraction to birds. I have come to the conclusion they were correct in their assessment, since most of my rattlesnake encounters have occurred in close proximity to wounded birds.

I will admit I feel no compunction and make no apologies for the elimination of those rattlesnakes that choose to make a habit of being where human foot traffic is likely. Gracie's snake, when compared to those of Texas lore, wasn't large, only measuring a tad over four feet after I blew off the first six inches. She and I found it in open pasture. Normally, I let those go. But this one saw me before I saw it, which is frightening no matter the size.

The Ants in the Pants tank is a narrow spit of water approximately one hundred-fifty foot long by fifty foot wide. A clay gravel-laced dam on the east and thick mesquites on the west surround its bare, dirt perimeter. Shooting there is like the scene where Luke Skywalker flies his Starfighter down into the valley of the Death Star. The birds first appear high out of the treetops, then dip down low over the water into the narrow open, giving only microseconds to draw a bead and pop a round. It's all a green and gray blur.

"Here Gracie. Here," I said, positioning the two of us opposite the dam in the shade of a large mesquite. We stood on the tree-lined side looking east across the water and waited. The action was slow and the September afternoon hot.

Gracie panted, staring at the water. Then a single dove topped one of the mesquites and plunged toward the tank. I shot. It fell with a splat into the soft bank. Gracie quivered in anticipation, dripping great drops of saliva upon the sand. "Stay! Mark," I barked, holding her, forcing her to become more affixed upon the downed dove. "Okay!" Released, she leapt, splashing through the shallow water the length of the tank until she reached the bird lying in a muddy hoof print left by a thirsty cow. Snatching it, she turned and crashed back. "Gracie, you could have just run down the side and avoided the water all together," I said, taking the bird from her. Gracie responded by shaking her head, sending small flecks of discolored water flying through the air.

Toward dusk the wind began to blow hard, about twenty miles per hour from the south. It was from that direction the birds arrived, blitzing the length of the tank. I watched, hoping they would flare over the water, allowing me to blast them. They did turn, but waited, cupping their wings at the far end to flutter into the safety of the mesquites. I was forced to either move our position into the thick trees or stay and shoot as they zipped by.

Now at my feet lay an additional fifteen empty shells and only three birds in my bag to show for the effort. Gracie, bored with so little to retrieve, resorted to chasing down my hulls.

As sunset approached, two birds, followed by a third, flashed into the opening above the tank. I shot, missed the first, fired again and tumbled the second hard into the opposite bank. The third made a sharp turn. I popped a late round and watched a puff of feathers float across the water. The bird dove over the top of the dam.

It is moments like these I understand why the purest of wing shooters frown upon the use of anything but double bore shotguns. My third round was a gasp of a chance. One pellet, maybe two, pierced the bird. It now lay out of my and Gracie's view in the shadows on the far side of the dam. Gracie was yet to be efficient in blind retrieves. The one squarely hit bird lay in a pile of feathers at the end of pond. Gracie sat waiting for me to release her.

"Okay," I said. Gracie lunged into the shallow water again, crashing the length of the tank to retrieve the dove. "Here, here." I met her halfway back. "Dead bird, dead bird," I said, picking up a rock. "Dead, dead," I said again, throwing the rock over the top of the dam in the general direction of my last shot. I don't know if throwing rocks is proper training for blind retrieves, but Labradors are genetically hardwired for "chunk it, and I will chase it." Gracie watched the rock sail, dropped the bird she was carrying, and scrambled up the clay face of the bank. I followed.

I topped the dam. The last piece of sun dipped below the horizon in the west. Gracie shuffled among the broom-weed that grew upon the crest. The backside of the dam, which sloped to the east, was steep. Its bare aggregate gravel lay exposed from erosion. "Dead, dead," I repeated looking down the incline, attempting to adjust my eyes to the deep shadows.

The ground at the bottom was flat and exposed. "Here, here," I said, waving my hand toward a gray clump I could see on a patch of sand.

Time itself seems to slow to a crawl during episodes of this nature. Gracie spied the bird and with one bound was at the bottom. I don't know where the snake came from. It seemed to melt out of the sand. I looked at the bird. I looked at the bare ground. There was nothing! Then in an instant, directly below me, appeared a five-foot coil of buzzing rattlesnake.

Labs are also hardwired for another attribute: lip and mouth dexterity. Most of my friends look at me cross-eyed when I tell them such, but it's true. Research the history of the Labrador Retriever. You will find they were originally bred to help fishermen gather loose fish and nets from the frigid waters off the coast of Newfoundland.

Gracie stopped short of the snake. It struck. With the deftness of a Spanish matador she moved to one side and plucked the bird. All I could seem to do was yell, "No Gracie No!" In my haste to rescue her, I stepped too quickly and slipped off the embankment. Feet first, legs spraddled, crotch exposed, I slid downward toward the snake.

I thank the United States Marine Corps every day now for instilling the discipline of having a clean, dependable weapon. I don't remember flipping the safety. I don't remember pulling the trigger. But I do remember my little Franchi jumping in my hands, firing point blank, and the head of the snake flying off into the underbrush. I sat motionless, blinking, catching my breath. The headless snake lay between my feet twitching, continuing to buzz lightly. Gracie walked up and placed the dove gently upon my lap.

THE POINTER

by Ruth Cleveland Riddels

My cousin Bunk had a fine hunting dog that couldn't be distracted off point. One day when Bunk went hunting with the dog, she disappeared from Bunk's sight and he went looking and calling for her. He searched tirelessly, but he did not find the dog, and he subsequently looked for her each time he went hunting that season. The following year during hunting season he kept looking for his dog. Eventually, he finally found her skeleton and she was still standing on point, as were the skeletons of her four pups. That was some fine hunting dog.

Dog sergeant I. R. "Nig" Hoskins, 1930s

MAN HOUNDS AND DOG SERGEANTS

by Thad Sitton

In 2007, retired Texas Department of Criminal Justice dog sergeant Paul Whitmire tried to console himself with Beagles chasing rabbits, but the thrill was not the same. The little hounds made fine dog music in the hunt, but Whitmire missed running people, the ultimate quarry that he had pursued professionally for over twenty years. As Whitmire told me, when you hunted a man with hounds you moved into an entirely new dimension of the chase, "because you're running something that thinks."[1] Foxes, coyotes, and deer also thought in their own limited ways, but they played most of their tricks by instinct. What they did often could be predicted—unlike what a man might do.

Like most older TDCJ dog sergeants, Whitmire had grown up steeped in East Texas dog culture. His family at San Jacinto County often ran trailing hounds after foxes and coyotes, and Paul had spent many weekend nights in his early years standing near a fire listening to the hounds run their game across the thousands of acres of national forest land around the county seat of Coldspring. Whitmire and his family and friends had practiced classic American "hilltopping," a hunting sport played entirely by ear. Hunters contributed their chosen dogs to the group pack, launched them into the night, then listened to them run for hours.[2]

Casual visitors to the hunt might see only a group of silent men listening in the dark, but as one hunter explained to folklorist Mary Hufford, the hound men in a way were not really in the camp at all, "you were there [with the hounds] in your mind."[3] Listening to the faint hound music coming from the night, hunters' educated ears told them what game had been jumped, where it had gone, what tricks it had played, and—most important—how each man's dogs were responding to the challenges of the chase. "Something happens to a man inside when he hears his dog bark," an old hunter once told me, and hunters listened first and foremost to the performances of their personal hounds. Little remained hidden from the hunters with really good ears, who had the mental ability to turn sound into sight. All might hear a man's hound at the front of the pack, "carrying the mail," but if a man's dog could not keep up and fell behind, or trashed on deer, or entirely quit the chase (the worst of all hound sins), some men had ears good enough to visualize what had happened. And, rather often, the embarrassed dog owner knew that they knew.

"Don't brag on your dog," some men advised, since you were never sure what it would do in the next race, and this cautionary admonition was one of many cultural elements that carried over into the professional lives of hunters operating man-hound packs for the TDCJ. Former dog sergeant Victor Graham had grown up with stock dogs and coon dogs, and he told me, "That's nice, but it does not fit you to train man dogs. But the love of dogs, I guess, was what got me into the man-dog part."[4] A TDCJ officer at the Ellis Unit, Graham began by going out with the Ellis dog sergeant every chance he got. Then, after this man's promotion in 1969, Graham took over the dog sergeant's job and held it for fourteen years.

He found it a fascinating, exhausting, and all-consuming business. Breeding and training hounds to do what came naturally and to effectively pursue such game as deer and coyotes seemed child's play by comparison. Consequently, while other TDCJ officers worked by the clock, dog sergeants did not. With the help of inmate volunteers called "dog boys," Graham trained his hounds to track people on a daily basis. Exciting real pursuits occasionally punctuated the dog sergeant's weekly round. Graham very occasionally sent his man hounds after prisoners who ran for freedom on the multi-thousand-acre state prison farm of Ellis Unit #1 and #2. Rather more often, he loaded his horse and his hounds in a trailer and went somewhere to chase someone at the behest of a county sheriff, municipal police chief, or federal agency.

Dog sergeants called these excursions (which had to be approved by their wardens) "free world chases." Free world chases offered the ultimate excitement for a dog sergeant like Graham, but they also put the professional man-pack unit entirely on the spot and in front of witnesses. Dogs had to be very well trained, because, as Graham said, "a man will try everything in the world to beat you. That first mile or two, he's just going to be running to get away. But after he gets that mile or two on you, then he's going to start throwing figures, wading water, walking fences, throwing back tracks, everything possible—getting in a blacktop highway. He's going to be doing it all."

Hunter and hounds were running "something that thinks," the human super-fox or perhaps even the fox from hell, and the mounted dog sergeant and his pack of hounds always ended up on their own out in the woods and fields, chasing a desperate human quarry, who might be armed. Called in to Jackson County at the request of the sheriff and Texas Rangers, dog sergeant I. R. "Nig" Hoskins spent all one long and memorable night on the trail of a murderer with a pistol. Two sheriffs, eleven deputies, and a Texas Ranger were on the case, but none of them assisted Hoskins and his hounds in the dark woods. He recalled:

> There was eleven deputies there and two sheriffs, they just had one horse for me to ride. Wasn't none of them on horse with me. I was by myself. I picked up his trail with my number-one pack of six dogs and run him through a big old bottom in the moonlight. They'd be a big black shadow here, and over between these two trees just light as it could be. Well, you went right out of a shadow into a light, and you couldn't look back in that shadow and see nothing. But I run him, anyhow, until just at daylight the next morning where I found where he'd went into a house.[5]

No wonder that Hoskins recalled the big black shadows he could not see into. He did not pursue a normal animal, but a man. Dog sergeants all worried about the possibility of a desperate fugitive that swung around in a big loop, got behind the hounds, ambushed the lawman coming up on his back trail, then rode to freedom on the captured horse. But not this man. Jumped from the house at first light and pursued by the hounds, Hoskins' fugitive soon turned his pistol on himself.

Nig Hoskins' story comes from the 1930s, but it could just as well have happened in 2011. Modern legalities require that a TDCJ dog sergeant in a free world chase be initially accompanied by a certified law officer, and the dog sergeant always brings along an extra horse for whatever sheriff's deputy, DEA agent, Border Patrol or other officer is ordered to accompany him, but the professional companion rarely lasts very long in the chase. Typically, the dog sergeant's pack of fast man hounds picks up the trail and goes baying on their way, the dog sergeant relentlessly begins to bust brush on his trained mount to stay within hearing, and the accompanying officer gives up and goes back. That is understood and expected. Formalities have been observed, and few lawmen today are able or willing to ride like Civil War cavalry. Rather soon it is Nig Hoskins once again, riding alone behind his pack "through a big old bottom in the moonlight."

In 2007, on my way to interview a retired dog sergeant, I passed through part of a TDCJ prison farm unit near Navasota and stopped my car to observe a timeless scene. Two crews of twenty or so white-clothed prisoners swung long-handled hoes down a cotton field under the watchful gaze of two uniformed field officers on horseback. Across the field under a tree, a trustee dog boy kept charge of a pack of man hounds. The scene might have come from 1907 or even 1887, and it could have been anywhere in the cotton South where state prison systems operated work farms. Prison work farms made good economic sense, at least in the old days, but you could not cultivate cotton, harvest sugar cane, make charcoal, dig lignite coal, or gather pine sap to distill for turpentine without setting up somewhat low-surveillance work situations. Armed guards—willing to shoot—discouraged prisoners from running, but there was often some point in the long workday where a desperate man might take a chance—for example, when his plow team reached the far end of its passage down the field and the tempting woods or tall corn lay just beyond the fence.

That was where the man hounds came in: they strongly deterred prisoners from running, and if some still chose to run they quickly hunted them down. Woods and brush hid runaways from guards' sight, but not from their man hounds' fine noses. Probably none of the white-clad prisoners I saw that day in 2007 gave even a thought to escape, but that had not always been the case. When Nig Hoskins first went to work at Harlem #1 near Raymondville, Texas, in 1928, prisoners rather often ran for the woods, and they had their reasons. State work camps of that time were places of harsh discipline, poor living conditions, indifferent food, and exceedingly hard work. Corporal punishment was common, and most prison officials did not

Nacogdoches County Sheriff A. J. Spradley with man hound

feel they could keep control without it. "Spare the rod and spoil the inmate" was the rule of the day, except that in Texas they did not use the rod but an implement known as the "bat" (supposedly abolished by Governor W. Lee O'Daniel in 1941). The huge Parchman State Farm in Mississippi used a similar tool, also with a notorious name, "Black Betty." This was a three-foot by six-inch strip of heavy leather with a handle on it, normally applied to the back, legs, and buttocks of the erring prisoner as he lay on the ground. It was claimed that the Mississippi version of the bat spread the damage around so prisoners would not be incapacitated for work the next day, but that might not apply to attempted escapees, who by rule were subject to unlimited whipping at the warden's whim.

Mississippi prisoners on Parchman and the other state cotton farms *could* run for the woods, but they had to be very motivated to try it. First, perhaps, came the shotgun blasts of disabling bird-shot from trustee guards, then came the exhausting man-hound pursuit, which normally ended when the treed prisoner climbed down to "fight the dogs" for a brief period that must have seemed much longer to him. Then, back at headquarters, last but not least, came formal whipping with the Mississippi bat.[6]

Texas was—perhaps—not quite as harsh as Mississippi, but what with man hounds and the bat (which continued to be used in some quarters after 1941), it hardly seemed sensible for Texas prison farm inmates to try to escape, but into the 1940s many of them still did. Local law enforcement officials took a critical view of all these desperate inmates coming across their territories and castigated the then Texas Department of Corrections both for its drastic treatment of prisoners and its failure to keep them behind the fences. The magazine of the Texas Sheriffs Association reported that 151 men had escaped from the state's eleven prison farms in 1943, 110 had been recaptured, seven had been killed, and 34 remained at large. The editor of the magazine, citing "unofficial sources," claimed that no less than 482 prison farm prisoners had escaped the farms between 1938 and 1943. (And these were, at least for a time, the *successful* escapees, the rare individuals who had outwitted and outrun the man-hound packs. With little doubt, many hundreds more had been caught by the dogs while still on the prison farms during those years and never made it into the statistic.)[7]

Sheriff I. R. "Nig" Hoskins did not talk much about bats and disciplinary measures in my 1988 interview with him at the Bastrop County Court House, though he did readily admit that Harlem #1 in the late 1920s "was penitentiary—it wasn't a recreation center like it is now, it was penitentiary." Hoskins' warden gave him the dog sergeant job around 1930 with only one admonition, "I don't want you to lose nary a man, if one runs, I want him caught," and the young Hoskins did his best.

In some ways his job much resembled the circumstances of modern dog sergeants. Assisted by several volunteer trustees, the dog boys, he had charge of a kennel of forty or so mixed-breed hounds divided into several packs. Hoskins' dogs were mixtures of old-line hound breeds that proponents of the speedy American Foxhound might disparage as coon hounds or "potlickers"—Black and Tans, Blueticks, or Redbones—with a leavening of the ancient Bloodhound breed thrown into the mix. As Hoskins quickly found out, dogs pursued human beings reluctantly and with difficulty, and the hound dog man's belief that whatever works, works emphatically applied to man dogs. A hunter from childhood, Hoskins quickly launched into a breeding program to make better hounds.

As did modern TDCJ dog sergeants, Hoskins much depended on his dog boys. They laid training trail for the hounds, kept the kennel clean, fed the dogs, and took care of Hoskins' horses. Describing procedures that varied little from the present, Hoskins explained:

> One of them would stay at the dog pen all through the day and do the cleaning up, and I'd have two or three that would go with the hoe squads and plow squads. All they'd do is just go out there and sit in the shade with the dogs and wait. Each of them would have part of the pack. See, some of those fields is a mile and a half from the camp. And maybe they'd be cutting wood down in the woods three,

Claude Davenport and Hardin County Sheriff's
Department bloodhounds

four, five miles from the building. There were thousands and thousands of acres in those 21 farms, and 1,700 men. Over here there's a bunch of them working on this side of the farm; well, you'd have a pack of dogs with them. And if there's a bunch of working over here, you'd have a pack with them, too. So, if one would run or something other, all you had to do, then is get there on your horse. A pack of dogs was already close. They would shoot a gun twice when something happened, and I'd go to it. The dog boy wouldn't go when I run a man, he'd go to the water wagon. Lots of times two or three would run at once. A plow squad team might drive up to a corn patch right over the fence on a free labor farm, and when they turned around—maybe they stopped the mules or maybe they didn't—but over that fence they'd go into that corn. The guard didn't have much chance to stop them. We'd average about three runs a week. Yes sir, I was on the road pretty muchly. Course, if nary didn't run today, I'd just sit up under a shade tree and wait.

From time to time during Hoskins' weekly round, a dog boy laid a trail and the dog sergeant took a pack on a training run, but he did far less training and many more live chases than modern dog sergeants. Three live on-farm runs a week is unheard of these days, where weeks and months go by on a given state prison farm without an inmate runaway. Presumably this is because of improved living conditions on the farms. What with air conditioning, adequate food, TV, and other modern comforts, there is less "penitentiary" to escape from. Presumably also, no modern prison chase concludes as Hoskins' chases always did, with an inmate required to fight the dogs. Fighting the dogs had several purposes. It punished the prisoner for running, and it trained the naturally friendly, mixed-breed hounds to be more aggressive toward their human quarry. For his own safety and for the safety of his hounds, the dog sergeant needed dogs aggressive enough to put the dangerous human quarry up a tree. Reticent about other Gothic details of Texas prison life, ca. 1930, Nig Hoskins had no problem describing his treatment of a prison farm runaway. "When I got to him, he had to come down," Hoskins told me. He continued:

> He wasn't gonna stay up there and me chain them
> dogs up and not let them get to him. Naw, he had
> to come down from there and fight them. I'd cut
> some switches myself and give them to him and tell
> him what to do. I'd let him fight them for two or
> three minutes, then I'd pop my whip. And when I

popped that whip, he'd drop his switches and the dogs would just run up to him and that's all—they wouldn't bite him [then!].

Modern dog sergeants may not compel treed runaways to fight their hounds, but they have the same reasons to breed and train their man hounds for adequate aggression. For their own safety and for the safety of their handler, tracker-dog packs need to stop the quarry, threaten him, and compel him to take refuge in a tree, road culvert, or stock pond. If they needed to nip him a little to accomplish that, well, so be it. Paul Whitmire emphasized that his dogs were "react dogs," not attack dogs. If you stood very very still when they caught up to you, they would not bite you. (But don't twitch.) Nor does modern law enforcement elsewhere have any particular problem with biting dogs, as TV watchers of the popular *Cops* series may attest. K9 units or "air scenting dog teams" on urban patrol often use German Shepherds and Belgium Malamutes to locate evildoers hidden in dark backyards or house crawlspaces, and these dogs are trained to bite on command, which these "police" breeds do quite readily. Such dogs also work well as deterrents, and the handler's cry "I'm about to let the dog loose!" often brings the fugitive out with his hands up. (Paul Whitmire and other dog sergeants on free world chases also reported similar incidents. At the first sound of man hounds on their trail, some fugitives walked over to roads or the nearest houses to give themselves up.)

In truth, the use of dogs abounds in modern law enforcement. Officers use specially trained "sniffer dogs" to detect drugs, explosives, injured humans in collapsed buildings, cadavers, and a variety of other things. Some canines in medical applications can even smell previously undetected cancers or incipient epileptic attacks. Sometimes, often after other measures have been tried and failed, officers and search teams call in Bloodhounds and their handlers to track lost persons or pedestrian criminals who have successfully avoided immediate captures.

The Bloodhound is an ancient man-tracker breed, ancestral in complex ways to American Foxhounds, Black and Tans, Blueticks, Redbones and all the rest of the long-eared, cold-nosed, tracking dogs, but with scent-detection abilities far surpassing its descendants. The oldest track that Vincent Graham's TDCJ man hounds followed to successful conclusion began with a scent trail nine-and-one-half hours old, and that was an exceptional case with perfect scenting conditions. Generally speaking, any track more than eight hours old is beyond the capacities of the usual TDCJ man-hound pack in normal circumstances. Pure Bloodhounds, however, could go far beyond that, could follow scent trails several days old across landscapes where foot searchers and air scenting dog teams had tramped all about. As one Bloodhound handler noted to the 1994 conference of the National Association for Search and Rescue, "A Bloodhound team (dog and handler) routinely trains on aged trails 12, 24, 48, or 72 or more hours old in varied environments and weather conditions."[8] Stubborn, implacable, slow, unaggressive, and almost oblivious to its surroundings when on a scent (it might even bump into trees), the leashed Bloodhound and its handler nonetheless followed a trail that no other kind of hound could follow. As Panola County sheriff Corbett Akins noted, "The Bloodhounds follow the distinctive scent of the one person as readily as it were marked with a colored string." The colored strings of scent lasted uncannily long for a hound with sniffing power variously estimated as 300 to 3,000 times greater than that of human beings. In rare but well documented instances, Bloodhounds successfully followed scent trails over ten days old. They tracked trails buried under deep snow. They followed men in cars from scent traces blown out of open windows to the roadside ditch.[9]

Having been required to do so, a good many TDCJ dog sergeants now keep a couple of pure Bloodhounds alongside their kennels of traditional man hounds. In Texas, they use the nonaggressive dogs to locate lost children, wayward hunters, and old people who wander away from rest homes. They also use them to track wanted persons across municipalities, exurbs, or suburbs where swift but aggressive man hounds might stray from the criminal tracks and threaten the general public. Bloodhounds were just "another tool," according to Captain William "Bubba" Dalton, TDCJ "tracking dog coordinator" at the time of my 2007 interview. To his dog sergeants he was the "dog captain."[10] Bloodhounds were an old breed but also, perhaps, the wave of the future; for one thing, they did not bite and generate lawsuits. Although state prison bureaucracies are defensive about their dog programs and it was difficult to get a straight answer about such matters, Bloodhounds on leashes seem to have replaced traditional man-hound packs in prison systems all across the South and Middle West—this despite the slow Bloodhounds' dubious ability to run down escaped inmates or suspected criminals who knew dogs were after them and did not wish to be caught.

In part, the fast pack hounds are gone because prison farms are gone. By 2002, only Texas, Louisiana, and Arkansas still had appreciable portions of their prison populations in prison farms. Of 34,180 national prison farm inmates in that year, Texas alone accounted for 22,148 of the total. Arkansas had around 5,000, most of them in its legendary Cummings Farm. Louisiana housed 2,500 unfortunate souls in Angola, "The Farm." Changing agricultural economics and an exceedingly bad national press had driven most Southern prison farms out of existence. Mississippi's formerly famous—or infamous—prison farm system was down to only 125 inmates.[11]

In 2007, Texas bucked the trend, however. It had kept both prison farms and man hounds. In that year former dog sergeant and now administrator Captain Bubba Dalton loosely supervised forty-three dog sergeants, each with three or four packs of man hounds apiece, scattered all across the state. These tracker-dog packs pursued men like varmints at high speed, with the mounted dog sergeant riding along somewhere behind. In a way this sort of man hunting resembled hilltopping, with great attention paid to interpreting the sound of the chase heard from afar. In a way it also resembled equestrian hunt-club fox hunting, with black and red-coated huntsmen thundering after the pack and chasing the fleeing fox. In no manner was it like a Bloodhound pursuit, the implacable, slow, stealthy tracking of a leashed scent hound and handler on foot. Bloodhounds did not bay on the trail, and with good reason. A slow, noisy approach gave the felon plenty of time to prepare an ambush, and when the dog found the criminal his handler was only a twenty-foot leash away. Dalton's dog sergeants looked askance at certain applications of their newfangled Bloodhounds. Imagine, they said, a worst scenario—on a free world chase, walking with your leashed dog through thick brush in pursuit of a drug dealer armed with an Uzi machine pistol!

Each dog sergeant supervised by Dalton still ran his own operation, and bred and trained his own man hounds, but Dalton offered helpful advice and monitored performance. There was even a manual of how to do it, a secret document not open to public gaze. When the dog sergeant went out on a free world chase, Dalton tried to be on the scene to back him up if he could get there in time, which of course he often could not. Dalton was only the second man to hold the supervisory position of tracking dog coordinator. It had become necessary because the stock of pre-trained Texas hound-dog men had run thin, and the TDCJ now struggled with building dog sergeants from scratch. Would-be tracker-dog men from the towns and suburbs now apprenticed with established dog sergeants and struggled to learn skills of dog handling and dog interpretation that rural hunters like Bubba Dalton, Paul Whitmire, Victor Graham, and Nig Hoskins had shown up with.

Being a dog sergeant took a lot of "imagination," Dalton said—a statement he repeated to me more than once. Much was based on knowing your dogs so well you could interpret the little nuances of their behaviors. He talked about knowing their voices so perfectly he could project himself forward into the unseen pack and know just what was going on at that point in the chase. The man-hound pack and the dog handler were a team, a man-pack unit. Human foxes were smart and could often beat a pack of dogs, but they could not often beat the man-pack *team*, which included another thinking animal, a fellow *Homo sapiens*.

Bubba Dalton told of one chase where the dogs circled the area around the last sighting of the fugitive without picking up the three-hour old scent, but he had watched them closely while they tried to start the trail and so had noted a slight hesitation at one point from two of the dogs before they gave up and went on. Dalton brought them back to that point on the circle, directed them to search some more, then stood back from them and waited, just watching, until a dog or two showed more attention, another picked up the scent a few yards away, and Dalton got a line of direction. Other dogs began to join in, a slow tracking began, and they ultimately caught the culprit. This sort of slow, subtle begin-ning typified old and/or faint trails. Dogs needed time to work them out, and the dog sergeant needed to be able to read their subtle behaviors. Perhaps a little PSI also was involved, who could say? Bubba Dalton had stood beside sincere men trying to learn to be dog sergeants and pointed out some meaningful subtlety of canine voice or body language to them—said, "Do you hear that? Do you see that?"—and try as they would, they could not.

East Texan Paul Whitmire had grown up with trailing hounds, and he could listen to a dog or look at a dog and pretty much tell what was on its mind. No sooner did Whitmire begin work for the TDCJ than he knew he wanted to be a dog sergeant. Dog sergeant positions were few in number, especially in the days before rapid prison expansion, and the job was not that easy to come by. The men who wanted to be dog sergeants wanted that rather badly, but usually they had to wait until a position came open. And dog sergeants tended to stay in place for many years, often until they retired. Whitmire did the usual: he understudied for the job on his own time. From 1974 to 1978 he served as field officer at the Wynn Unit by day, accompanying work squads of inmates back and forth to the fields on horseback. After duty, Paul ate supper, changed clothes, and walked down to the kennels to help dog sergeant Gene Stokes train his pack. Young, fit, and fast on his feet, Paul often alternated with the dog boys in the role of human fox, laying down scent trail for the evening training run. Like most dog sergeants, Stokes trained incessantly. He might get to work before daylight to run his puppy pack, run the off-duty pack during the morning after the other packs had gone with dog boys to the field, then train one of the field packs in the cool of the evening after their return. Packs had to be able to run at any time of day or night and in any weather condition. You could not just train them 8 to 5.

Like many dog sergeants before him, Stokes was new on the job and on a hound-breeding mission, trying to reinvent the wheel once again and make a better pack of man dogs. The daily training focused first and foremost on weeding out the unsuitable and selecting breeding stock. Dog sergeants had time and resources that most avocational hound dog men only dreamed of. TDCJ professionals could breed a kennel of dogs to be exactly as they wished, perfectly adjusted—they hoped—to the local running conditions, but a new man rarely felt satisfied with his predecessor's bloodlines. Gene Stokes was no exception, and he and his volunteer apprentice were of one mind about man hounds. In something of an innovation, they were introducing the blood of speedy Walker foxhounds into the mixed-breed coon-hound stocks common in endless variation to all TDCJ kennels—the Black and Tans, Blueticks, Redbones, and every combination thereof.

Their breeding change had logic behind it. Man hounds had to be bred for un-hound-like aggression so they would tree and hold their dangerous human quarry, but this meant that they could not be used anywhere there were many people, and by the late 1970s a lot of people were moving into the Texas countryside. What was needed, Gene Stokes thought and Paul Whitmire agreed, were fast man dogs that could catch the runaway inmate before he reached the boundary of the prison farm or the free-world felon before he reached town or suburb. As Whitmire summed this up, they sought "a fast Walker-type dog, a quick-response dog that can rock and roll."

Paul Whitmire continued this quest after he finally got a dog sergeant job at a prison farm near Navasota in 1985. By that time, back at the Wynn Farm, Gene Stokes had his packs pretty much as he wanted them, fast and aggressive, but the kennel that Whitmire inherited was initially very different—slow on the trail and so docile that some of them "would not bite a biscuit." In a fever to get packs of man hounds that worked, that would not professionally embarrass him, Whitmire put his dogs through the wringer, quickly got rid of over eighty of them, imported much breeding stock from Gene Stokes' kennel, and filled his puppy pen with new blood.

As his new "fast Walker-type" dogs grew to adulthood, they encountered a problem to which Walkers and other American Foxhounds were especially vulnerable—the temptation to trash on deer. Deer had returned to the Navasota countryside, and Whitmire ruthlessly got rid of every dog that turned aside from its rightful man trail to follow them. Dog sergeants tore their clothing and whipped themselves and their horses bloody from brush and tree limbs on every for-real chase, and Paul could not tolerate trashing hounds leading him on false pursuits. Besides that, such wrongful pursuits could be humiliating. Pointedly leaving out names and details, Paul told a cautionary tale of a certain famous prison farm pursuit at the Ellis Unit that had been graced by the presence of the head of the TDCJ, several wardens, and five or six dog sergeants, but had ended with a white-tailed doe bounding out of the woods ahead of the local dog sergeant's pack of man hounds instead of the escaped prisoner. The dog sergeant's warden felt himself a laughing stock and later administered an epic "ass chewing."

All dog sergeants felt professionally on the spot and haunted by such stories. Probably they showed up in their bad dreams. Sometimes it seemed that the more notorious the fleeing felon, the more helicopters circling overhead and Texas Rangers and FBI agents on the scene, the worse your dogs performed. Another true and cautionary tale involved the escaped prisoner who was caught by two packs of dogs, petted them down, and was finally discovered cozily laired up in a hay barn with the whole bunch. "Don't brag on your dogs," the old-time fox hunters said, and handlers usually did not, but they were still responsible for what their man hounds did, and these dogs were, as Bubba Dalton admitted, "just a bunch of animals." They had their off days.

Texas fox and "wolf" (coyote) hunters of the informal hilltopper tradition also identified with their hounds, took their performances very personally, and were obsessed with breeding better ones, but they did not train them like the dog sergeants. It was all breeding for the traditional fox hunters, all a playing out of inborn tendencies and abilities; the training virtually took care of itself. The hunter only took his pack out often enough for it to remain fit and capable. He raised a young dog until it was a year or so old and he judged it could pretty much keep up with the adult hounds, carried it out on a fox or coyote chase, then launched it into the race. It soon got its nose full of the scent of proper game, learned what it was and what it was supposed to be doing, and committed itself to a lifelong quest for fox, coyote, deer, or whatever. (Occasionally, of course, it failed the test, but this was not a question of training but of inadequate inborn capacities.)

This simple and natural approach to training emphatically did not work for man hounds. As Nig Hoskins summed things up, "Running a man is not natural at all for a dog. You couldn't take a year or a year-and-a-half-old dog and make him run a man at all, because it just ain't in them to do it. They've got to be trained from a puppy up." Generally speaking, humans did not smell like anything a dog wanted to trail. Certainly, people had a weak scent compared to a deer or coyote, they did not smell like natural game, and perhaps their odor signaled an intimidating master species best avoided. Many dogs also did not like to track bears—at least after they found out what sort of beast lay at the end of the pungent scent trail. Bloodhounds, despite their long history of selection for use in human tracking, were much the same and also required training that began when they were young puppies. Man hounds, even those selected over many generations to run people like the hound stocks of the TDCJ, had to be trained continually, several times a week, from puppies up, and even then a certain percentage—often one or two from each litter—lost interest in the human scent trail at some point and had to be culled from the developing pack. Even when the man hounds were fully developed and part of a seasoned pack, that pack had to chase a person at least two times a week, or individual hounds began to lose their abilities. It was a strange and unnatural business, like pushing a rope.

Dog sergeants faced a daunting, continual task to get hounds to run a man at all, and running him was not enough. Each dog, or at least several individuals in each pack, needed to scent the quarry, run his trail (baying all the time), catch up to him, be aggressive enough toward him to put him up a tree and keep him there, and then bark treed. Not every dog had to do all these things individually (although that was the ideal), but every man-hound *pack* had to do them collectively.

The dog sergeant's Sisyphean task began very early. He or one of his dog boys gave a certain call and rattled the puppy chow in the pan to get the little puppies to follow him, then he fed them. This was their first taste of pursuing a human. Gradually, the pups grew larger and faster, and the dog boy went farther away with his pan.

At some point he ran from the pups while they chased him for their reward. Finally, a second person entered the training scene to hold the puppies while the feeder moved completely out of sight. Now the pups had to find the feeder by following his scent trail. Soon thereafter the food reward ceased. The dog boys playing the role of "rabbit" teased them and played with them with a towel, then ran away while a second person held them. Then they were loosed, and they began to trail the rabbit across the landscape. The rabbit might have marked his route with little bits of toilet paper dropped on the ground or tied to bushes so that the holder, who now followed the puppies, could see if they were on the rightful trail. When the pups reached the rabbit, he took refuge on a low limb of a tree, teased them once again with the towel, and encouraged them to bay at him. Sometimes he hit them a little hard with the towel to anger them and stimulate an aggressive attitude toward the human game.

At some point, often when the puppies were three or four months old, the dog sergeant took over the young hounds' training, culling them and selling them off as needed, until the remaining dogs were more or less finished products at age two or slightly beyond. It was a matter of practice and hard work—of running a man several times a week following older and older scent trails in increasingly varied and difficult conditions. By age three the new man hounds were as good as they were going to get, able to follow human tracks from thirty minutes to several hours old, and in a variety of conditions, though the dog sergeant and his dog boys had to train them continually to hold that high standard. Dog sergeants watched closely to identify the exemplary hounds, the dogs that did almost everything right, and they were the ones that got to breed, so—hopefully—the overall kennel continued to improve.

By around 1990, this breeding process had worked, and Paul Whitmire had his kennel of fast-response, rock-and-roll, foxhound-influenced man hounds—Walker-looking dogs that ran fast and showed their teeth. Besides the puppy pack, Paul had four adult packs, two all males and two all (or mostly) females. Packs had been brought up together, trained together, and operated as units, like the offensive squads of football teams. A female in heat tended to disrupt things, so Whitmire, Vincent Graham, and other dog sergeants thought it best to run single-sex packs. A female in heat did not bother other female pack members, but she did galvanize every male farm dog and household pet a free-world chase passed by, so Whitmire kept his two packs of females well-trained on hot trails in the prison farm. Paul trained his two male packs on scent trails from two to six hours old, simulating the usual age of man scent in a free-world chase. Free-world felons faced the "dogs," but if you jumped and ran on the prison farm, Paul's nippy gyps got after you.

Vincent Graham also operated single-sex packs. Graham (dog sergeant 1969–1983) and Paul Whitmire (dog sergeant 1985–2002) lay on each side of Gene Stokes' foxhound revolution at the Wynn Farm. As we have seen, Whitmire was part of the fox-hound breeding innovation. Previously, dog sergeants had gener-ally believed that American Foxhound strains like the Walker were too fast, too wild, and perhaps too disinclined to threaten human beings to be used as the predominant blood line in man hounds. Also, men like Graham regarded Walkers as "deer hounds," and the tempting deer were making a statewide comeback. Suiting himself in breeding, as did every dog sergeant, Graham began with the usual mixed-hound packs, but over time he gravitated toward an intelligent, smallish breed of general purpose trailing dog, the Redbone. His packs became mostly Redbone in appearance, just as at a later date Paul Whitmire's became mostly Walker.

Beyond those significant differences in breeding preferences, Vincent Graham and Paul Whitmire worked and trained very much alike. They both demonstrated much "imagination," to use Bubba Dalton's term for the qualities that made dog sergeants a success. They trained incessantly, sometimes before daylight and again after dark. They trained because man-hound packs needed constant train-ing to remain efficient in pursuit of their unnatural quarry, because hounds required endless work on all the tricks that the human ani-mals might put on their scent trails, and—just as important as the above—so that the dog sergeants could observe how their dogs did in every conceivable scenting condition and circumstance.

According to both Graham and Whitmire, some unidentified dog sergeants somewhat went through the motions with their train-ing, running the same sorts of tracks every morning then going back to their air conditioning. This not only did not work, it set up the possibility of a humiliation before one's peers and supervisors, or an injury inflicted by a desperate fugitive in a free world chase. A well-trained pack not only kept you from embarrassment, it could save your life. And a well-trained pack took effort far beyond the norm in bureaucratic law enforcement. As Graham summed things up, "Being a dog man, if you have good dogs, is the hardest job in TDC—if you have good dogs. If you don't have good dogs, it's the easiest job in the system." Consequently, Graham stated:

> I trained them on all the things a man might put on them in a real race. I had a little bit of everything on them. I ran a cold track, a warm track, and a hot track. And in between all this, I run dirt roads, plowed ground, woods, open fields, creeks, and sloughs. So, I tried in every pack of dogs I trained, I tried to put something that a man would do to me in every one of the tracks I laid out. I crossed dirt roads, run plowed ground . . . And nighttime, when the farm was put to bed and there wasn't any traffic, I'd come out on the blacktop and run about a hundred or so yards of it, and then duck off on the woods on the other side.

Fox hunters sometimes prided themselves on a certain ability to think like the fox in front of their hounds and so predict the course of the race. Dog sergeants like Graham and Whitmire had no problem at all thinking like the human quarry, and in fact had played that role in front of their man hounds and the packs of other men many times. Graham knew that the super fox might use a wire fence to trick the hounds off of his scent trail, and so he trained them on fences. He had a dog boy stand on the first wire of a barbed wire fence, hold on to the top wire, and go hand by hand down the fence for fifty yards or so. Then he watched his hounds work this problem and discovered (as did Paul Whitmire a decade later) that, while hounds often could not smell scent on the wire (at least in the absence of muddy feet), they picked it up on every post the man had touched. Following that experiment, Graham had his rabbit go hand-over-hand down a higher portion of a hog-wire fence, then, on a final and most extreme test, to walk down the top of the hog-wire fence, steadying himself with hand poles on each side long enough to reach the ground. His hounds successfully ran that, too, again picking up the scent from the upper part of the wooden posts that the rabbit stepped on as he walked down the top of the fence. Perhaps one or more of Graham's dog boys thought this a silly exercise, but not so. Later on, an escaped prisoner near Mason, Texas, walked the top of a hog wire fence for thirty yards in front of Graham and assorted Texas Rangers during a major free world chase, and Graham's well-schooled Redbones tracked the man down the fence until they found where he had jumped down, ran him, and later caught him.

Humans had no difficulty putting themselves in the mind of the human fox. Later on, Paul Whitmire taught his hounds to deal with fugitives that slid down forty-foot sloping banks to the Brazos River, catching themselves a time or two on brush on the way down, then traversed down the river bank for a hundred yards, then scrambled up the bank again. Paul could imagine a desperate human quarry doing that, and his dog boys were willing to lay the trail, so he trained his hounds on it. (In that circumstance the hounds did not throw themselves off the bank. They sought the track down the top of the river bank in both directions until they found the place where the man had climbed back up.)

As Whitmire and other dog sergeants attested, the volunteer trustees attached to the prison farm's kennel program, the dog boys, liked their work and they were usually more than willing to jump down banks, wade creeks, slog along the edge of river overflows, and even swim sloughs and rivers to test and train the hounds. Some of Paul's dog boys even willingly anointed themselves with heavy skunk scent to see if that would discourage his dogs. (It didn't, as Paul told me; the dogs "split the scent" and smelled man through skunk.) This was a fascinating business—at least when the likely alternative was swinging a long-handled hoe in a cotton field work gang. And things could get worse. Nig Hoskins described a ten-man crew in 1928, planting ten rows of corn at a time by hand. Each man had a sack of seed corn. The squad would bend as one man, plant a grain of corn, stand up, take one disciplined step forward down the rows, bend once again to plant, stand up, and do that all the long work day, can see to can't. Nig had no trouble getting dog boys.

Furthermore, in time dog boys often became a serious part of the kennel program. When he first assumed the position of dog sergeant, Vincent Graham had learned a great deal from certain ancient dog boys, who had been working with hounds on the farm for more than two decades. Graham sometimes had his veteran dog boys plan the daily training runs: where they would go, what sorts of "figures" they were going to put into the track (circles, successive right-angle turns, figure eights, etc.), and what sorts of scenting challenges they planned to test the dogs with. Dog boys had a curious relationship to the rest of the prison farm population, people who, especially in the harsh old days, might decide to risk the dogs and try to escape. Dog boys had some allegiance to their dog sergeant, but they had a foot in both camps and would probably tell mostly the truth about the performance level of the local man hounds. If the local dogs could not catch anything and would not bite a biscuit, the dog boys always knew it. Conversely, the dog boys of men like Vincent Graham, Gene Stokes, and Paul Whitmire probably advised, "Don't even think about it!" Dog boys were an integral part of their prison farm's system of escape deterrence—*if* the man hounds were efficient enough to deter.

Standard training track, the daily grind, was laid down in stages. Instead of a continuous even-age track, dog boys laid scent trail for a half hour or so, stayed put for about a half hour (taking a nap, going fishing in the Brazos), ran like a rabbit for another half hour, waited another period, then perhaps laid down the final section of scent trail. After a certain amount of time the dog sergeant put one of his packs on the track. Thus, the hounds experienced old faint trail, then warmer trail, then in the end hot trail with the scent virtually hanging in the air followed by a dog boy up a tree. This gave them training in track of varied age and more closely simulated real-world pursuits, with the fugitive running for a while, resting up, and so on.

Beyond that, dog sergeants used their human foxes to explore every aspect of scent trailing across the varied landscape and in every conceivable weather condition or time of day. Foxes and coyotes could leave tricky scent trails, but no hunter could train his dogs on such a trail. He had no cooperative foxes or coyotes. The dog sergeant could and did. He could tell his dog boy, "Lay a thirty minute track toward the creek bottom, wait twenty minutes, then go to the creek and jump back and forth from one bank to another ten times, then walk downstream in the creek ten minutes, then walk along that section of wooden board fence fifty yards, then come straight back here." He could do that, and what is more, he could position himself at key points along the training run to *watch* his hounds try to deal with all of these scenting problems. Scent as dogs knew it was undetectable to the feeble human nose, but dog sergeants had excellent human vision to read dog behaviors and so indirectly learned more about scent, and scent trails, and how dogs experienced scent than any other person. No fox or coyote hunter had even the merest fraction of their knowledge. Dog sergeants spent hours each day watching dogs work out known scent problems on prepared tracks—seeing which dog was fooled, which one figured the situation out first, and which one took the lead, reading all the nuances of scenting behavior of hounds they had known intimately, on a daily basis, from the puppy pen.

Dog sergeants continually used their imagination to set up circumstances to test what dogs could and could not do, and would and would not do. Bubba Dalton, for example, wondered if his hounds would bay a strange man in a tree after they had been sent out in an area to search for a trail. So, he tested it. The dogs wandered around, running their usual search patterns, until a couple of them passed downwind of the strange trustee in the tree and smelled him. They went to him and bayed treed, and so did the rest of the pack that came up. Vincent Graham knew that fugitives often got in water to try to throw hounds off their scent, so for days at a time he had his dog boys lay track in all sorts of water to see what hounds could do and also to train them to do it better. He discovered that if a man waded close to the bank along a flowing creek the hounds often could pick up his scent from the bank-side vegetation, and that if the man waded down the middle of a wider flowing creek, they usually could not. Dogs could not smell a trail across water, but if it was a stagnant pond with duckweed and floating scum and debris on the surface that the rabbit crossed, they some-times could track across that, swimming along, nose close to the surface. A decade later, Paul Whitmire trained his hounds in the Brazos backwaters of early spring and found that his dogs could fol-low a man across the backwater so long as he touched a branch or weed stem every few feet or so as he waded along. Paul's hounds swam from branch to branch, sniffing and baying.

Paul Whitmire wondered one day if his hounds would track a woman. In all their lives they had trailed only men. A female war-den volunteered to lay down some track, and Paul's man hounds ran her without a bobble. Paul also found that his hounds would successfully trail dog boys in sealed rubber boots, in airtight suits, with several plastic bags on their feet, naked, across freshly fallen sleet, during heavy rain, with socks full of black pepper, and reek-ing of skunk scent. Certain tracking circumstances always gave trailing hounds trouble, and dog sergeants sought them out both to discover the limits of the problem and to give dogs experience in trying to solve it. Freshly plowed fields, just-mown hay, bare sandy ground, recently burned pasture land, railroad tracks, blacktop roads, and pastures where herds of cattle had milled about gave hounds fits. Either there was little scent retained on the surface or the scent had been interfered with in such a way that the dogs could not follow it, but Graham and Whitmire made them try. After a while they both had some hounds that could painfully work out a trail across such horrors, although in real world circum-stances the hound handler often directed his dogs to circle the bad spot and pick up the scent on the other side.

Always, they tried to find out the limits of dogs' abilities. Little scent was retained on the surface of blacktop road, but Paul Whit-mire discovered that, while at three in the morning on dry windy nights hounds could not follow scent trails on blacktop, on moist still nights at three in the morning they could. (During the day, of course, forget it, and for more than one reason. Dogs virtually could not trail on daytime blacktop and the intensive effort to try to do so rendered them insensible to highway dangers. Whitmire had two hounds run over by cars during free world chases; Graham had five.)

Being a dog sergeant with *good* dogs was a wearing job, as Vincent Graham attested, and a sheriff's call for help with a free world chase came as an exciting relief from the constant training. Long, weary weeks might go by between every for-real race. As Graham recalled, "I had Friday night and Saturday night and Sunday night [only] that I didn't run. I drove myself to the point of exhaustion, just about, because I wanted to have the best dogs that I could possibly have. I didn't want mine to be embarrassed; *I* didn't want to be embarrassed." Free world chases were exhilarating but also the ultimate test; they could indeed be embarrassing. Hounds also tired of the relentless training and the all-too-familiar scent of certain dog boys, and they relished the prospect of chasing strangers in strange places. An intense psychic link of mysterious dimensions existed between the dog sergeant and his animals, but no such mystery was required to explain the hounds' excited response. When their handler loaded them in the dog trailer, they knew a real race was afoot.

By 1980, the Texas countryside was filling up with people, and it required fairly remote circumstances to call in the TDCJ man hounds. Sometimes after a long talk with the sheriff or whoever thought they needed the hounds, the dog sergeant had to reluctantly decline. If he accepted the assignment, then his warden still had to approve. Rather often, there had been a rural car chase, then the suspect had jumped from his car and hit the woods. The dog sergeant drove at speed to the PLS, the Point Last Seen, perhaps waiting for the necessary approval call from his warden to come in on his radio. When the call did come in, the dog sergeant knew that this approval meant, "Stay there until you get the job done." The modern warden still did not want to lose "nary a man." If Department of Public Safety Troopers or other officers were on the scene, the dog sergeant might put in a call to them requesting that they remain close to their cars. DPS Troopers and deputy sheriffs were notorious for walking around the PLS in explorations and vain foot pursuits and polluting the ground with false scent trails. TDCJ man hounds were trained to follow the first fresh human scent trail they came to, and the dog sergeant did not wish for it to lead to an officer in a patrol car. The dog sergeant hoped that DPS and sheriff's department officers would be out setting up a proper perimeter on roads closest to the chase area—this to confine the quarry and keep him from reaching places where too many people lived for TDCJ man hounds to safely go.

Finally, the dog sergeant arrived on the scene, hopefully well within the six-hour limit for effective man hound pursuits. (These were no Bloodhounds.) He talked to the officers at the PLS, listened with a large grain of salt to what they said about where they had gone and where the adult felon or suspected adult felon had run, and began to unload his dogs. He gave them a minute or so to mill around and "clean out," then began to "drag" them in a big circle around the PLS, staying well beyond where he thought the officers had been. When the dog hit a fresh human scent trail, that was it; the chase had begun. If the trail was hot enough, the hounds immediately began to run and give mouth, and the mounted dog sergeant began to ride hard in pursuit. At this point the second mounted officer normally fell behind and fell back. But the dog sergeant had to stay in good hearing of his dogs—had to. The dogs were his responsibility, they were not absolutely certain to stay on the right human trail, and they had been laboriously bred and trained to threaten humans. If the dog sergeant had to cut fences to stay with them, and he usually did, he cut fences.

As hard as he rode, he listened attentively to the sound of the dogs and watched the ground in front of him to pick up the shoe print of the fugitive. The dog sergeant had important things to worry about in any free world chase. Unlike Bloodhounds, who almost never departed the particular human scent trail, TDCJ man hound packs sometimes did. If a fresher human track happened to cross the felonious scent, dogs sometimes—very rarely—derailed on that one, and if the criminal scent merged in a footpath with other human scents, the dogs just might take the wrong one when all the various scent trails finally diverged. The dog sergeant listened to his pack for a change in the hound voices that might signal their shift to a wrongful track, usually a fresher one provoking different baying. And he watched the ground surface for the fugitive's known footprint—his shoe tread—to change disastrously to another one. If either of these things happened, he called the dogs back by "popping 'em off," by snapping his whip as loud as a gunshot.

Perhaps the dogs caught up to their quarry, harassed him, and made him climb a tree, awaiting an ignominious capture. Perhaps he rushed out to the nearest road before the dogs reached him and gave himself up. Both outcomes commonly occurred. Rather often, however, something happened to the scent trail, the dogs "made a lose," and it was not so simple. Perhaps the quarry passed through a herd of cattle or did something tricky in water that successfully put the hounds off the scent. Who could say? In any case the dog sergeant stopped with his hounds at that point, reported in, and did not move. He rested his dogs and waited. Officers still held the road perimeter around the search area, so the fugitive could not get away. Another dog sergeant and his dog pack might arrive at the original PLS, and if a "ghost" sighting came in for the fugitive this man might take his hounds there and check that out. But the first pack and its dog sergeant stayed put and chased no ghosts. Until information conclusively to the contrary came in, the first dog sergeant assumed his quarry was still close by and laying low. When the fugitive lost patience and ran and somebody saw him, the chase would take up again at that PLS. Alternately, the first dog sergeant might drag for the man's scent in a big circle around his last known position, and if no fresh trail was struck he would know he was in there, still "laying out." The mad chase through the woods had turned into a chess match and a waiting game, but in time the mad chase would resume. The TDCJ man hunters had more time and food and safe drinking water than the beleaguered felon did. The human fox was already caught. He was not actually in hand, but he would be.

During the late 1980s, Paul Whitmire took part in an eight-day pursuit of a nineteen-year-old murderer in Bastrop County, Nig

Hoskins' home territory. In a way, what happened in those eight days showed the TDCJ man-hound program at its professional best, but it also suggested why there was a Bloodhound or two in nearly every dog sergeant's kennel by 2007. The modern world was impinging on the way TDCJ dog men preferred to do things. The young man shotgunned his grandfather to death in Missouri, then fled to relatives in the town of Bastrop, where he exchanged gunfire with officers and took to his feet. Paul was called in, and that night he ran the young man with his dogs along the Colorado River bottoms out from the town of Bastrop. At some point he lost him, probably because the young outlaw took to the river, and the dog sergeant had to lay up and wait. There were far too many people living along the river to go dragging around with his aggressive man hounds looking for the scent trail.

Paul waited, and the next day somebody five or six miles downriver was taking in clothes from their line and noticed a pair of coveralls was missing. Paul went there, confirmed the scent trail, began running the fugitive, and once again lost him at the river after a prolonged chase. History had repeated itself. Five more runs of the fugitive occurred in subsequent days, most of them ending in escapes into areas too populated for Paul to follow. The young man escaped into the little community of Winchester, a church camp just outside of Giddings, a creek valley, then yet another church camp. Eight days later Paul ran the young man once again near Giddings and finally got so close that the man knew he could not get away again. So, he rushed to the highway and gave up, having had quite enough of drinking ditch water, running the blacktop roads at night, and missing meals. With considerable admiration, Paul recalled, "This boy was putting some foot to the ground!"

Paul Whitmire had changed out several packs of dog and several horses during this laborious week. At his various loses, he had waited with great patience at the PLS until the fugitive surfaced again somewhere else. It was a disciplined, impressive pursuit, but an experienced outside observer, perhaps one that liked Bloodhounds, might have suggested that the TDCJ man-hound instrument seemed not to fit the circumstances. Twenty years after Paul's pursuit, the population of Bastrop County has doubled, and the free-ranging packs of TDCJ man dogs probably could not be used at all in many areas. And a lot of rural Texas is like that. Perhaps it is all now Bloodhound country?

The TDCJ tracker-dog program yet persists, probably the only surviving program of its kind in the United States. Man-hound packs seem like an anachronism in a way, but they still do the job. No other instrument of law enforcement can hunt down a man in woods, brush, or broken country as swiftly as one of them can, even when he knows the pack is coming. Helicopters are next to useless. All a man has to do is step under a densely-leafed tree when one passes over.

Dog sergeants still exercise their strange profession, rather like ardent fox hunters chasing the ultimate game, something that thinks as it runs. Dog sergeants always played a curious role in the bureaucratic TDCJ. They put feathers in their hats and sported big boots. They labored all hours of the day and night, wild dog-man zealots among the shift workers and clock punchers. In the nature of their commitments and their identifications with their hounds, they resembled nothing so much as classic American hilltoppers, but with intensity levels raised as high as they would go. And no wonder; they hunted the super fox, they hunted man. They fought and intrigued to become dog sergeant, mastered their highly-skilled job, and then traditionally never were promoted. They remained until retirement. Some of their wardens regarded them as too valuable to promote.

Once upon a time there was a saying all across the rural South: "Fox hunters are crazy." Insiders reported that the TDCJ saying was, "Only way to be a dog sergeant is to be crazy." Insanity was an old outsiders' accusation for hound-dog men. Eighteenth-century English fox hunter Peter Beckford had heard that too, and in his *Thoughts on Hunting* (1781) he responded: "It is said, *there is a pleasure in being mad which only madmen know*; and it is the enthusiasm I believe of fox-hunting, that is its best support: strip it of that and you had better leave it quite alone."[12]

Endnotes

1. Paul Whitmire. Personal communication to Thad Sitton, March 7, 2007. All other references to Whitmire and information from him in this essay derive from notes taken during my lengthy conversation with him on this date.
2. For a detailed study of American hilltopping, see my book, *Grey Ghosts and Red Rangers: American Hilltop Fox Chasing*. Austin, University of Texas Press, 2011.
3. Mary Hufford. *Chaseworld: Foxhunting and Storytelling in New Jersey's Pine Barrens*, Philadelphia, University of Pennsylvania Press, 1992. 9. Besides *Grey Ghosts and Red Rangers*, mentioned above, Hufford's work is the only other book-length scholarly study of American "folk" fox hunting that I know about.
4. Vincent Graham. Taped interview with Thad Sitton, May 20, 1999. All other information from Graham and quotes from him in this essay come from this 1999 interview.
5. I. R. "Nig" Hoskins. Taped interviews with Thad Sitton, 1992. All other information from Hoskins and quotes from him in this essay come from these interviews. In an edited form, Hoskins' interviews form his autobiographical chapter in my book, *Texas High Sheriffs*, 1988.
6. For Parchman Farm, see William Banks Taylor's *Down on Parchman: The Great Prison in the Mississippi Delta*, Columbus, Ohio State University, 1999; and, David M. Oshinsky's *Worse Than Slavery: Parchman Farm and the Ordeal of Jim Crow Justice*, New York, New York Free Press, 1996. (On page 272, Oshinsky notes that specially trained fox hounds were the man dog of choice at Florida turpentine work camps, ca. 1900.)
7. An insider's view of the Arkansas prison system's famous Cummings Farm is offered in Bruce Jackson's *Killing Time: Life in the Arkansas Penitentiary*, Ithaca, New York, Cornell University Press, 1977. The best of all memoirs of Texas prison farm life is the fascinating autobiography of Race Sample, *Racehoss: Big Emma's Boy*. Austin, Eakin Press, 1984.
8. Ann Brooke Holt. "Bloodhounds: An Underutilized Resource." Paper presented at the National Association for Search and Rescue's annual conference, June 1994. http://www.cee.mtu.edu/~hssantef/sar/others/Hardy/Bloodhounds.html. Accessed 3/30/07.
9. Sheriff Corbett Akin's comment about the colored string comes from his "Sheriff's Column," *Panola Watchman*, February 8, 1951. Akins was interviewed by me and talked his way to a chapter in my *Texas High Sheriffs*, 1988. He was also interviewed on several occasions by

high school students from the journal *Loblolly* at Gary High School, Panola County. Although they otherwise go unmentioned, Akins was only one of the man-hound sheriffs who contributed to my understanding of tracker dogs deployed in this essay. Other sheriffs operating tracker-dog packs were Leon Jones, Angelina County, interviewed 1986, and John Lightfoot, Nacogdoches County, interviewed 1993. My information on the extraordinary scenting exploits of pure Bloodhounds comes from Catherine F. Brey and Lena F. Reed's *The Complete Bloodhound*, New York, Howell Book House, 1984, 48–119.

10. William "Bubba" Dalton. Personal communication to Thad Sitton, February 23, 2007. All other information from Dalton and references to him derive from my conversation with him on this date.

11. Criminal Justice Institute. *The Corrections Yearbook 2002.* http://www.cji-inc.com/cyb/cyb.html. Accessed July 7, 2009.

12. Peter Beckford. *Thoughts on Hunting.* New York, Alfred A Knopf, 1826 [1781]. 230.

Pelican near Lake Buchanan

THIS IS FOR THE BIRDS

by Charlie Oden

My wife Georgia and I were bird watchers, or "birders," as folks frequently called bird watchers. It is in this sense that we hunted wild birds. We also hunted for wildflowers, which led to hunting for arboretums and botanical gardens. Different species of trees also held our interests.

The government of the State of Texas had passed the laws making the mocking bird the State bird, all species of blue bonnets the State flower, and the pecan the State tree. Georgia and I saw wild birds just about any place we looked. We also had a fair amount of knowledge about the local birds in our part of Central Texas. Mourning doves, quail, and wild turkeys we knew as game birds. Other Central Texas birds included mocking birds, scissor tailed flycatchers, jays, wrens and sparrows, whip-poor-wills, owls, hawks, crows, cliff swallows, cardinals, and turkey vultures.

We found mocking birds just about everywhere, representing Texas as the State Bird. They were in the residential areas, warehouse areas, and commercial districts with banks, malls, small businesses and offices for professional people. Scissor-tailed flycatchers with bright salmon-pink sides and belly snapped up flying bugs out in the open country. Jays in populated areas scolded cats. Wrens and sparrows in barnyards hopped about and pecked for food. Whip-poor-wills in creek bottoms made their presence known by calling their "whip-poor-wills" where the stars at night were big and bright, deep in the heart of Texas. Owls of all sorts, those ghost riders in the sky, were also in all sorts of places—trees, barns, and vacant buildings where they called "Hoo, hoo-hoo, hoo, hoo" and scared little kids. Hawks sat on utility pole wires, sternly scrutinizing their surroundings for lizards and mice. Crows ate the farmers' corn and called "caw, caw, caw!" while they waved black wings like pirate's flags as they navigated over farm houses, yards, fields, streams and woodlands. Sparrow-sized cliff swallows were made happy by the building of freeways because there was always mud for building their nests.

We also found cardinals that flashed their red beauty through the shrubbery. Their mates were even more beautiful. And there were the turkey vultures that were material for Aggie jokes and road kill. Back then, there were no grackles yet to bomb our windshields. But the red, red Robins came bob, bob bobbing along each year in February and March in their frock tailed coats and red vests, cheerfully chirping, chattering, and splashing in what was the nastiest of cold drizzling rain to us, the local folks. They were singing in the rain. These little fellows were lessons in proper posture.

When my employer moved me to Houston in 1959, birding opportunities increased ten-fold. The moneymaking developers had not yet "developed" Galveston Island, destroying the habitat for wild creatures while in the process. When driving on the Gulf Freeway from Houston to Galveston, birders could pull over as they approached the Galveston Causeway and watch the roseate spoonbills (thirty+ inches from bill tip to tail tip) standing in wide, shallow ditches filled with water, frogs, bugs, and long stemmed grasses. These birds put their long, slender necks down in the ditches where their peculiar wide beaks seined the water for food. The color combination of their feathers reminded one of folks wearing white sweaters and pink skirts. In the same area with them, pink flamingoes (forty-eight inches from bill tip to tail tip) were doing much the same. In the same area, also, other bird life—white egrets (forty-one inches from bill tip to tail tip), variously hued herons (thirty such inches), and white storks (forty-four such inches) were busily living out their struggles through life and mating to produce the generations to follow.

On the island itself, birders could drive along the Stewart Ranch Road. If memory serves, portions of it were unpaved, just dirt road, generally speaking. As the car's wheels rolled slowly along, they flushed large flocks of red-winged blackbirds, briefly

Great Blue Heron

startling the birders riding in the car. There were feeder roads that were mere tire prints on grass where waiting birders could watch sandpipers and sandpiper-like birds—curlews, dowitchers, and occasional snipes. These birds bring chickens to mind as a comparison with their shapes and sizes.

Down the coast from Galveston Island was Surfside Beach. The best way to access this bird "hunting ground" was by driving to Freeport and driving back up to Surfside Beach. Along the highway nearing Freeport was a fast food place called The Sandpiper. Birdwatchers could refresh themselves there. On an inside wall toward the back, carved in pine that was lacquered in a clear varnish, and in Gothic lettering, was:

SEVILLE DERE DAGO
TOUSAND BUSSES IN ARO
NOJO DEMS TRUX
SOMEMIT COWSIN, SUMMIT DUX

It took a long time for me and, in this case, Paula, my daughter, to decipher this mysterious message. It means, "See Willie, there they go; Thousand busses in a row; No, Joe, them's trucks; some with cows in, some with ducks."

Georgia went with me to the Aransas Wildlife Refuge to see and learn more about the Whooping Cranes. The natural wariness of the big beauties and the guarding of them by Federal Game Wardens prevented our hunting them—even just to view. The way to see these big birds is to carry strong binoculars and take the boat at the Refuge. "Whoopers" are one of the more spectacular birds. Hunting and habitat destruction reduced the population of these birds to about fifteen in 1937.[1] Their numbers are increasing now. They are pure white with black wing tips. They breed in Canada and winter in the Aransas Wildlife Refuge. They stand forty-five to fifty inches tall, and their wings spread to about seven feet six inches. Their calls sound like trumpets.

Georgia Oden

However, it was hunting sandhill cranes that became favorites of both Georgia and me, and we watched for the "sandies" during the winter migrations time between Sealy, Texas, and somewhere north of Katy, Texas. They are very skittish. They are big birds, too, having a wing spread of about six feet eight inches and a height of thirty-four to thirty-eight inches. Their long necks and long legs are gray, and they sport red spots on their heads. The call of a Sandhill is a loud rattling "karooooo." They breed during the time they are in Siberia, Alaska, and arctic Canada. Their mating dance is spectacular: partners face one another, then leap into the air with feet extended and thrown forward, after which they bow to each other and repeat the performance. They also run about with their wings outstretched and toss tufts of grass into the air. One time we spotted a big flock of them about five miles north of Katy. They were in the second field away from the car, perhaps 200 yards away. The farmer had not plowed the land for the winter, and the leafless stalks of winter vegetation were still standing. The sandies were standing, too, their necks looking like so many dead corn stalks. Georgia said to me that we were lucky to have seen them.

One of those wonders of nature is the migration of wild birds each year from the cold North down to the Gulf Coast, where they spend a few months, and then fly back to the North in early spring. Rice production in the 1960s ranked a third of the State's entire grain production, yet it was concentrated in only twenty of the Gulf Coast counties out of Texas' total of 254 counties. Some of these counties include Wharton, Colorado, Matagorda, Brazoria, Jackson, and Jefferson. There is no telling how much rice was left in the fields, but it must have been a tasty incentive to cranes, geese, and ducks to come and stay longer. Snow geese and Canada geese come to the Houston area each year by the hundreds of thousands, perhaps millions. Some of these creatures are small, but those best known to the public are the Canada geese, thirty-five inches to forty-five inches from bill tip to tail tip, with a black head, long black neck, and conspicuous white cheek patch. The snow geese, somewhat smaller, are white with black wing tips.

Sealy, Texas, is on I-10 about fifty miles west of Houston. About three miles beyond Sealy is a dogleg on I-10. This dogleg is not on the flat coastal plain, but on a "flyover" where the car turns right and enters the flyover and, at the summit, turns left and descends down to the plain. When making the turn at the summit, a birder will suddenly see acres and acres of thousands and thousands of geese.

One day we were driving on U.S. 59 about forty miles from Houston toward Victoria. As the car approached a place where the Highway Department had made a cut through a hill, we could see goose activity on the tops of both sides of the hill. We stopped in the cut and parked in a place where both of us could watch the big birds. During the times that geese feed, they have their heads down in the grass. They would be vulnerable to attack, except that every split second a different goose head will pop up and take a gander to make sure the flock is safe. Suddenly, the geese that we "hunters" wanted to watch took flight. The air was filled with their big bodies no more than forty feet overhead. I was overwhelmed with a feeling somewhat like apprehension (it must have been awe) while the white masses passed over.

Georgia and I enjoyed visiting the Warren Ranch Lake that is just west of Hockley. About 2:00 p.m. was the best time. There might be five or six huge flocks of snow and Canada geese flying in the skies overhead, while great numbers of them remained upon the surface of the lake. And, all the while, a virtual swarm of geese were intermingling, as some settled on the lake and others ascended perpendicularly, yet amazingly there was never a goose "fender-bender."

Once when Georgia's brother and sister, Melvin and Jean, were visiting, we were having lunch at a nice place in Seabrook, not too far from Galveston. The conversation turned to bird hunting and geese. Georgia said to me something like, "Let's go to Warren Ranch Lake." Thinking that we couldn't drive the distance and get there in time, I answered to that effect. She insisted, and I found myself with promises to keep and miles to go, the geese to seek. We went. The geese were there, and they put on an exciting per-

Canada Goose and goslings

formance. Melvin turned in a performance, also. Just as the car pulled by the north end of the lake, I began a wide circling turn to park. Melvin was so excited that, before I stopped, he jumped out and began running toward the lake. There I was, trying to apply the brakes enough to avoid hitting Melvin, yet not braking so hard that the swinging front door would bend or break a hinge.

At times when Georgia and I were with others and the conversation turned to geese, one of Georgia's favorite jokes was to ask, "Do you know why there is a short side and a long side of a 'V' when geese are in flight?" When no one present could gave an answer other than a guess, she would say, "Because there are more geese on the long side than there are on the short."

One day about a half century ago, we were driving from Houston to Austin. The day was chilly, damp, misty, and gray. We were driving along old U.S. 290 and had the windshield wipers set on slow. The car was near Cypress when one or the other of us noticed a flight of geese. They were not in the usual flying Vs such as the field guides picture and describe. They were in flights of so many

Vs that the Vs themselves formed a half-mile-wide column of honking determination, flying from the southwest into the northeast. I pulled the car over at an extra wide area of the main street in Waller, and we two bird hunters watched. The front of the cloud of geese extended to the horizon ahead. Toward the southwest horizon as far as the eye could see, more geese kept coming, each goose in its own body-space. Together we watched this airborne flood and commented about it with the natives for about fifteen minutes. When we continued our way, we could see no end of the flight in sight.

Some of our bird identifications we made using the "three ifs and a then" method. For instance, when we saw a bird that looked like a duck, quacked like a duck, and swam like a duck, then chances were that it was a duck. So it was at our house. If it looked like a warbler, if it flew like a warbler, and if it sang like a warbler, then chances were it was a warbler. The house was the usual subdivision house, with trees and lawn in both front and back, with a chain link fence in back. Some of the trees in each back yard were hurricane-blasted tallow trees that had holes in them that made good nesting sites for birds. (Let it be noted here that a lot of bird watching is done with binoculars, but birders should be careful about using binoculars in residential neighborhoods because folks seeing a person using binoculars may call police and report them as peeping toms.)

During one nesting season, a ladder-backed woodpecker began building her nest in a hole in a tallow tree that was in the neighbor's yard and almost touching our fence. It was directly in the line of sight from Georgia's kitchen window. Georgia was excited—she was going to watch the ladder-backed woodpecker raise its family. This shy bird was busy realizing its life's calling when along came a black, bullet-bodied starling that bullied itself through life. The starling usurped the woodpecker's nest. The poor, shy, ladder-back was agonized over this change in her life. Georgia was shocked and enraged. Georgia was unable to climb ladders, but she mixed up a tin can of mud, leaned the family ladder against the chain link fence, stood on the top of the fence, and stuffed the nest with mud. Nature's ways might be Nature's ways, but right was right, by George! Her blitzkrieg attack on the starling forced it to nest elsewhere.

Cedar waxwings visited us once. It was in wintertime. These birds are smaller than robins. The National Audubon Society's *Field Guide to North American Birds (Eastern Region)* describes the bird as being 6½ to 8 inches . . . "A sleek, crested, brown bird with black mask, yellow tips (sometimes reddish) on tail feathers, and hard red wax-like tips on secondary wing feathers. Almost always seen in flocks." And in the same place it comments, "These social birds have the amusing habit of passing berries and even apple blossoms from one bird to the next down on a long row sitting on a branch, until one bird eats the food."

The stoop at our front entrance between the house and the garage was several steps in length. On the side of the stoop that was opposite the wall of the house, there was curly-cued ironwork. Out in our yard was a row of pyracanthas with red berries gleaming on every twig, and these little fellows were feasting on the fruit like honeybees swarming in honeysuckle vines. Neither Georgia nor I was aware that the stoop was swarming with these little visitors. When we opened the door, we startled them as much as they startled us, and with a loud whooshing sound of many wings in flight, they flew away.

Georgia's favorite birds were the Robins. Between the 1960s and the late 1980s, the birds arrived from more northern climes beginning in middle to late January, spent a couple of months, and went back toward whence they came about the first half of March. There were a number of locations where we birders could find Robins during their annual stay in Houston. One such place was along White Oak Bayou between Loop 610 North and I-10 on the two T. C. Jester Boulevards. Robins stand erectly and look like they are clad in red vests and black or gray frock tail coats. The sloppier the weather, the more the birds act like kids at morning recess on the school ground, chattering their "cheer-up, cheer-up" while dashing and flying about. During the 1980s, when Georgia was enduring her personal "Trail of Tears," I watched for Robins

Pair of Mallard ducks

and, on finding some, hurried home and drove her to the location where we two birders parked in a warm car and watched the fun.

Ducks come in colorful varieties. Georgia and I once went to Anahuac National Wildlife Refuge. There they were plentiful—Teal, Mallard, Merganser. Georgia drove the car while I walked about looking for and identifying the various species of ducks, and kept a wary eye out for the alligators. The alligators are not seemingly aggressive, luckily.

Hawks did not escape our bird hunting. To my soul mate, hawks were the guys in the black hats. I tried to identify those I saw. Texas does not have a great variety of hawks. I mention them only in order to tell of an experience we had that surprised me. Georgia and I were driving from Houston to Austin by way of Hempstead. As we were leaving Hempstead we saw over the golf course a large number of hawks circling around like what we call "buzzards" do. All of us have seen "buzzards" in numbers floating in the air, riding the air currents up and down while they looked for something to eat. This is called kettling. But hawks? Never before. There were all sorts of hawks kettling while waiting to migrate.

There are many folks who enjoy being bird watchers. *The Texas Almanac 2004–2005* has a section on birding in Texas. According to this reference, there are nine birding education and observation centers designed to protect wildlife habitat, and they offer visitors a view of more than 450 species of birds. The World Birding Center has partnered with the Texas Wildlife Department and the U.S. Fish and Wildlife Service to turn 10,000 acres back to nature. The places are along the border with Mexico. The Great Coastal Birding Trail winds through forty-three Texas Counties along the Texas Coast. It includes 308 wildlife-viewing sites with parking, boardwalks, and observation platforms as well as other amenities for those interested in hunting birds—but not wanting to kill any of them.

ENDNOTE

1. During the long dry spell of recent years, blue crabs, the whooper's main source of food, have not been reproducing. This has caused some sizeable die-offs of the whoopers, and they are losing habitat to housing developments. *Austin American-Statesman* Metro & State, Thursday Jan. 28, 2010.

The author during a treasure hunt in the Guadalupe
Mountains of West Texas

HUNTING THE ELUSIVE LOST MINES AND BURIED TREASURES OF TEXAS

by W. C. Jameson

~~

INTRODUCTION

The current and growing fascination with lost mines and buried treasures has been manifested in movies, television specials and reality shows, and has triggered the dramatic increase in the sales of metal detectors and expedition gear. In addition, books about lost mines and buried treasures have reached best-seller status and are in demand more than ever.

Though never more popular than today, "hunting" for lost mines and buried treasures has long occupied the thoughts and actions of adventurers and explorers. This kind of quest has oft been represented in tales such as *King Solomon's Mines*, *Treasure Island*, and *Treasure of the Sierra Madre*, as well as the numerous books and movies treating the search for the Golden Fleece by Jason and the Argonauts.

Many would argue that the notion such treasures might be attainable by the common man can be attributed to J. Frank Dobie and two of his books, *Apache Gold and Yaqui Silver* (1928) and *Coronado's Children* (1931). In these books, the famous Texas writer and folklorist recounted and recorded some of the most compelling treasure legends and lore of the day, thus introducing the populace to the existence of lost wealth—and the hunt for it. As a result of Dobie's tale-telling, hundreds of men and boys and not a few women entered the wild and rural lands of Texas and elsewhere in search of The Lost Sublette Mine, The Lost San Saba Mine, The Lost Seminole Mine of the Big Bend, the lost treasure of the pirate Jean Lafitte, and many more.

Most of these quests were failures—no treasures were ever officially located and recovered during those days, at least none that were reported. Some began to wonder if the lost treasures of which Dobie wrote ever actually existed. It has been suggested that the folklorist embellished some of these tales and perhaps concocted others out of whole cloth. Dobie himself once stated that it was his job to tell the story better than it really was. While *Apache Gold and Yaqui Silver* and *Coronodo's Children* were great reads that could fire the imagination and tempt a real or potential quest from nearly anyone who read them, it was bandied about that none of these treasures or mines ever existed, that the reality was quite different from the myth and legend, that they were only stories and nothing more. Or were they?

As a result of an increasing number of men and women undertaking the hunt for lost treasures, along with the often sophisticated planning and preparation for such quests, more and more are beginning with an examination of the existing history and lore.

Folklore versus Reality

Do such lost mines and buried treasures as described by Dobie and others exist? Like a lot of folklore, there is always room for debate. In recent years, however, a number of significant discoveries were made that verified, at least in part, that Dobie's tales, as well as those from other sources, were based in reality.

One of Dobie's most popular tales was the one involving the so-called Lost San Saba Mines. First seen by Spanish explorers in 1756, the allegedly rich silver veins were known to the area Indians for centuries. Reportedly, Comanches and Apaches visited these mines from time to time to harvest silver for the manufacture of jewelry and arm bands. Also known as the Lost Bowie Mines, they have allegedly been found and lost several times over the past two centuries.

In 1756, a contingent of Spanish soldiers led by Lieutenant General Don Bernardo de Miranda entered the San Saba region, stumbled onto the mines, and, according to the tale, encountered several veins of rich silver. He dug out numerous large chunks of the ore and shipped them to his commanding officer in Mexico City.

As Miranda tried to convince his military superiors to facilitate a mining operation in the San Saba area, a Mexican viceroy authorized the establishment of a mission in the region for the purpose of converting the local Indians to Christianity. In time, military officials agreed to Miranda's proposal, but before the authorization reached him, he was sent off on another assignment in East Texas. He was never heard from again.

In the meantime, according to legend, the mission priests found the mines and spent more time mining and smelting the ore than they did in converting the Indians. As the years passed and the Comanches grew more hostile regarding the presence of outsiders in their territory, they made life so unbearable that the priests were forced to abandon the mission, never to return.

During the 1830s, a man named Harp Perry found the mines while traveling through the area. He set up a mining operation and was soon shipping twelve burro loads of silver to San Antonio every three weeks. Again, warring Comanches drove him out of the region. He fled to Mexico. Before leaving, he buried twelve hundred pounds of silver bullion atop a nearby hill. He returned to recover it thirty years later, but the land had changed so dramatically that he was unable to find it.

Legend claims that Jim Bowie located these same mines and, after hiring twenty workers, harvested the rich silver of the San Saba before perishing at the Alamo in 1836. Like those that had arrived before him, he was driven from the area by Indians.

During the summer of 1990, a San Saba County rancher was out on his property searching for some cows that had strayed. He rode by a stream bank that had been undercut by the fast flowing water from a recent flash flood. Exposed along the side of the bank were several silver ingots that had apparently been buried for a long time. He recovered them, twelve in all, cleaned them up, and showed them to a friend who was a banker in Austin. The silver bars, processed and shaped like those associated with the Spanish over two centuries earlier, were placed on display at an Austin bank for several weeks.

Myth or reality? It appears as though the San Saba Mine tale as written by J. Frank Dobie did exist. At this writing, a small group of treasure hunters are petitioning the owner of some land near the San Saba River on which they believe the old mines exist. They seek permission to hunt for them. If found, they will attempt to harvest any silver that might be encountered.

Another tale Dobie related was one he called the Lost Sublett Mine, perhaps the most famous treasure tale in Texas. William Collum Sublett was a hard-luck drifter that settled with his wife and three children in Odessa, Texas, after years of traveling around the

Southwest looking for work. When he was not whitewashing buildings and mopping out saloons, Sublett spent his time prospecting for precious metals in the Guadalupe Mountains, 140 miles to the west. Because the Guadalupes were inhabited by hostile Mescalero Apaches, Odessans regarded Sublett as reckless, even crazy. They called him Old Ben Sublett, and took every opportunity to ridicule him. In response, Sublett promised he would return someday from the mountain range a rich man.

It happened. One afternoon, Sublett drove a rickety buckboard pulled by a skinny horse up to the Mollie Williams Saloon, walked in, and dumped a leather pouch full of gold nuggets onto the bar and ordered drinks for everyone. Thereafter, Sublett traveled to the Guadalupe Mountains every few weeks, always returning with more gold. Though he was often followed, and was occasionally offered money for information about the location of his rich source of gold, Sublett kept the location a secret. Now and then, he dropped hints relative to the location, and on two occasions provided directions to two close friends. One of the friends traveled to the mountain range and returned with several pouches of gold nuggets, but died the following day as a result of a fall from a horse. The second friend also came back from the mountains with a substantial amount of gold, and spent the next three days in a drunken celebratory stupor. When he sobered up, he lost all memory of the location of the gold. He spent the rest of his life trying to locate the source, only to die alone in the mountains years later.

No one knew for certain if Sublett's gold came from a placer deposit or an excavation. Some suggested Sublett discovered a cache of gold nuggets from an earlier stagecoach robbery. A few even advanced the notion that Sublett himself stole the gold but told any who would listen that it was found in the Guadalupe Mountains.

During the 1960s, a young man traveled to the Guadalupes in search of the Lost Sublett Mine. Using information gleaned from researching situation and site, he explored a portion of the southwest-facing slope he regarded as the most promising. On the third day, he found a small, shallow cave, the entrance of which was hidden unless one was standing directly in front of it. Inside the cave, he found several rotted leather pouches, out of which spilled gold nuggets. Nearby, he found an old and rusted ax head on which was scratched the letters "B.S." Could these have been Ben Sublett's initials? Could this small cache of gold nuggets have been the source of Sublett's gold?

The finder plucked as many gold nuggets from the floor of the cave as his pockets would hold. Months later he returned to the area in the hope of retrieving more, but he was never able to relocate the small cave. More than four decades later he continues to search for it. To this day, others arrive in the Guadalupe Mountains from all around the country in search of more of Ben Sublett's gold.

In 2009, a young man made an astounding discovery of a long lost Texas treasure. While reading the book *Lost Treasures in American History* (W.C. Jameson, Taylor Trade Publishing, 2006), he encountered the tale of a Spanish vessel laden with gold and silver coins and ingots that became mired in a river bed. Seeking shelter from a raging hurricane, the ship, bound from Mexico to Spain, attempted to escape the treacherous waves in the Gulf of Mexico by sailing up the swollen Mission River. Once in the calmer water, the ship was carried upstream and then into a tributary by the strong winds, only to become stuck on the shallow bottom. When the storm abated the next day, the Spanish sailors, realizing their predicament, left the ship and undertook the long walk back to the coast where they hoped to signal another vessel and obtain help. Before reaching the coast, however, a band of Karankawa Indians slaughtered them all.

Early settlers to this part of Texas knew about the old ship, now partially buried in the mud and sands of the stream and the adjacent flood plain associated with what has come to be called Barkentine Creek, but they were unaware of the rich cargo that rested inside the sunken hull. In fact, a number of wooden planks were robbed from the partially exposed vessel and used in the construction of some early homes in the area.

For years, the remains of the Spanish vessel could be seen along the bank of the creek, but over time the continued sinking and decay rendered it difficult to locate. Realizing the potential of modern research tools, the young man who read the account opened a Google mapping program on a borrowed computer and, using enhanced satellite photography, searched the region of Texas where Barkentine Creek joins the Mission River. After a few minutes, he spotted what appeared to be the outline of a ship almost completely buried in the ground. After packing a few belongings into his car, he and his girlfriend drove from Southern California to South Texas and made their way to the location he had spotted on the satellite image.

Inspired by what he found, the young man sought the rights and permission to recover the treasure he was certain lay within the rotted hold of the ancient ship. He carried his plea to a Texas court which, in turn, granted him the authority to pursue his recovery operation. His adventure was reported by MSNBC and Fox News, as well as by *Texas Monthly* magazine. At this writing, the logistics pertinent to the recovery of the treasure are still being worked out.

Preparation

Hunting for lost mines and buried treasures is far more involved, and requires considerably more preparation, than hunting for deer, birds, or raccoons. Though my friends who anticipate deer season each year might quibble with this contention, it is a fact that there is precious little actual hunting that takes place during a deer hunt. These days, given the ubiquitous feeders, baited fields, deer blinds, high-powered weapons, four-wheelers, dogs, and other basic and high-tech apparati, the activity called "hunting" amounts to little more than shooting herbivores that are not equipped to shoot back. There is no stalking, no tracking, and little sport is involved. It is recreational shooting, nothing more.

Not so with hunting for lost mines and buried treasures. The serious treasure hunter is faced with significant preparation, much of which involves research devoted to separating truth from folklore. The professional treasure hunter is, in many ways, a kind of detective who is attempting to reconstruct events that may have taken place as many as three centuries earlier. Situation research involves parsing the facts from the myth and determining, as much as possible, the truth associated with a particular treasure or mine. This can include an in-depth review of the available literature on a particular treasure, employing diaries, journals, research papers, newspaper accounts, and other records. The truth is, most of the work involved in a hunt for lost treasure takes place in the library or archives.

Once the situation research phase of the project is completed, the treasure hunter proceeds to site research, which is undertaken in order to familiarize the investigator with the environment to be entered. This can be accomplished by employing sets of research tools, many of which did not exist in Dobie's day. In addition to the always-useful topographic maps and geology maps, Internet tools such as Google and the Acme mapping program have proven very useful. Once situation and site research are completed to the satisfaction of the treasure hunter, an actual search for the lost or buried wealth can then be undertaken.

The environment to be entered will determine the type of equipment and gear to be used. If the destination is a desert, preparation should include accommodations for appropriate dress and water supply, as well as snake bite kits and a supply of sun screen. Mountainous and forested terrain will require different preparations.

Conclusion

As a result of the current popularity and sales of several books (*Buried Treasures of Texas, Buried Treasures of the American Southwest, Legend and Lore of the Guadalupe Mountains*), more and more treasure hunters are entering the mountains, forests, and fields of Texas in search of lost mines and buried treasures. Several have contacted me for advice relative to research and planning, and in this manner I have grown aware of the increased activity within this particular realm of hunting. As with deer, bird, and coon hunting, some of these treasure hunting expeditions have experienced success and many have not.

From the time the nation's economy reached a low point during 2008, more and more interest was directed toward investigating alternate sources of income. The sales of books on lost mines and buried treasures spiked. Data reveals that the purchases of metal detectors and expedition gear among Americans were at an all-time high. Individuals and groups, armed with improved research, search, and recovery tools and techniques, are hunting for many of the legendary troves and lost mines, several of which were first introduced to the public by Dobie and others. At the same time, we learn, applications for hunting licenses have decreased.

For the purist, the quest is at the heart of any hunt. In the case of treasure hunting, the quest continues to lure and inspire.

THE ONE THAT GOT AWAY (OR

SHOULD HAVE): ANECDOTES AND FUNNY STORIES

Lee Haile and a coon

SIERRA TREED

by Lee Haile

One time, while we were building our house on the land in Tarpley and still living in a rent house in Bandera, something crazy happened. We had been working in my shop—probably making things to take to an arts and crafts show to sell. This was in the "downsizing and reorienting" phase of our life, which is a whole story in itself. Well anyway, Karen and I would work sometimes pretty late while the girls, Acayla and Sierra, would play or sleep in a corner of the shop we had fixed up for them, which simply meant that we had a blanket spread out on the ground. The house was just an idea at this time.

We finished up for that night and started home. We have two-and-a-half miles of gravel road to get from our land to the paved road going to Tarpley and then Bandera. Karen was driving the Toyota 4-Runner so I could rest, and the girls were in the back seat. Our two Border Collie dogs were in the back behind the girls. One of the dogs was a young dog that hadn't had much hunting experience, so I was still trying to work with her. We were near the creek when a coon ran across the gravel road and into a mott of live oaks and young cedars not more than fifty yards across.

"Stop," I yelled to Karen, "I want that coon," I said as I was already opening my door. "Let the dogs out," I yelled as I took off running after the coon. It was late winter and the furs were still good, and I wanted to tan out a hide for a new coonskin hat—my other was getting a little old. I jumped the four-foot hog wire, two-bob fence at the edge of the road. I was hollering, barking, growling, and screaming; if I made enough noise and crowded that coon enough I knew he would go up a tree. I didn't have time to grab a light, but the night was bright enough to see a little.

The dogs had caught up with me and figured out which tree the coon had gone up. This was a young grove of oaks and none were over twenty feet tall, and the cedars were half that. While I was getting organized and working on a plan, Sierra and Acayla wandered up. They had jumped out of the truck and followed the dogs into the brush to be part of the excitement. My plan was to climb the tree and make the coon jump out and the dogs could get it. Now, this can get a little crazy even in the daylight, so I told the girls to stay back and stay on the ground, and *don't climb a tree!*

I started up the tree. It forked about three feet off the ground and little limb went off the side. There were not many branches and I had a good idea where that coon was at. The tree didn't grow straight up but went out at a good angle like a lot of oaks do in motts like this, so it was easy to climb. I got way out near the top of this tree, shook it and hollered, and I saw the coon jump out. The fight was on! The coon was growling and squalling, the dogs were growling and barking, and I was yelling encouragement to the dogs, "GET 'IM, GET 'IM, GET 'IM!" It was quite a ruckus!

In the midst of all this noise as I was starting to climb down, I heard one of the girls' very loud and very piercing *scream*! I bailed out of that tree, a combination of jumping and falling to the ground. What I did was grab near the end of the closest limb and jump. Actually there is a method to this. As you fall, the limb slows you down and, more importantly, it keeps you upright. When the limb stops your descent, you grab the next available limb and ride it down. I had perfected this and would jump out of trees from forty feet up to amuse others.

When I got to the ground I made my way through the cedars to the sound of the fight. There had been two more screams during this interval. I came into a very small clearing and saw Sierra standing in the same fork of the tree that both the coon and I had just climbed. The coon was starting back up the tree, and when he got to where Sierra was standing and started trying to climb her legs, she screamed and kicked the coon. Then a dog jumped up and grabbed the coon and down he came. He turned on the dog and the dog let go. The coon then proceeded to climb back up the tree with Sierra.

I got there about the time he got to her and she screamed again (for the fifth time) and kicked at him. I grabbed him by the back and flung him as far as I could away. I grabbed Sierra out of the tree and said, "What are you doing?"

She said, "You said to climb a tree!" I looked over and there was Acayla just a few feet off the ground in another tree.

"No, no, no. I said *don't* climb a tree! You stay on the ground so you can run away, and if a coon climbs a tree he won't have to climb over you!"

She was lucky she did not get bit and they both just thought it was scary and exciting. And I got my new coonskin hat.

Adron Alford and Babe, late 1950s

PORCH HUNTING

by Sue Friday

I can see Grandpa, Adron Alford, sitting on the porch, reared back in his favorite hide-seat straight chair. He has on dusty field boots, frayed-at-the-hem jeans, and is bare chested because he took off his heavy denim jumper to cool off. There is a ring of sweat around his head from his hat. My sister and I, at most 3rd or 4th graders, are fighting over the swing although it is big enough for both of us. Grandpa gives us "the look" and we settle down. For amusement all summer we either read, go to church, help with light farm work, or listen to Grandpa tell stories—always about hunting or fishing or the animals involved.

Today's story is about an ol' boy being chased by a wildcat. "And that ol' boy ran and ran until he couldn't run anymore and fell out on the ground!" Grandpa says, "and the old cat hops up on a log . . ." and Grandpa's hand and arm make the arc of the wildcat jumping onto the log . . . "and looks with his yellow eyes at the ol' boy laying there, gasping for breath, and says . . . ." And here I lose the story. I can see my grandpa clearly, see from his eyes that this will be funny, can hear his voice—and then I can't.

I have no stories of my own because then girls and women in Sabine County didn't hunt with men. No doubt we could have and probably would have done it better and had more fun, but that's a high horse I can ride another time. The stories I heard on that porch are ones I enjoyed then and love all over again every time I hear them retold. They were funny, mythical, fantastic, and sometimes true. They still get told on the porch.

Cousin Troy Pfleider related one at a family dinner recently. A baboon got loose from a traveling show, circus, zoo, or somesuch. Of course, some mighty hunter trapped it and put it in the cage in the back of his pickup. He parked the truck at the local barbershop and invited everyone to come out and marvel. One of the older regulars came out, peered into the cage, and scratched his head.

"Know what this is, Uncle?" he was asked.

"Don't rightly know," he answered, "but from the looks of his rear end he's a domino player!"

Troy's son Joey is a logger and timber buyer. He's as big a yarn teller as his dad and he told me about an old man who had timber he was interested in. Part of the negotiations involved sitting on his porch and trading stories. In this one, the man told of when hogs ran free in the open range. To keep them somewhat tame, he'd take a wooden bucket of feed into the woods and bang it on a trough he'd made of a hollow cypress log. The hogs would come running. This went on awhile until an ivory billed woodpecker moved into the area. They were called Johnny-by-Gods, as in, "Johnny, by God what was that!" Anyway, the Johnny-by-God knocked on the trees all over the bottom and kept the hogs running after what they thought was the sound of the feed bucket. They got so skinny from all the exercise that they weren't fit to eat that year. (And knowing how farmer/hunters think, that may explain why ivory-billed woodpeckers became extinct.)

Many stories involve dogs—which somehow put the soul in hunting. When Grandpa came out on the porch with his gun, his dogs would get so excited that any of the rest of us could stand there with raw meat and they would ignore us. Grandpa kept dogs that earned their keep, either by baying hogs when they needed to be found in the deep woods, treeing squirrels, or finding the coon that was breaking down the corn.

Uncle George Rice kept a pack of fox hounds—just for the fun of hearing them run. Fox hunting happened at night when a group of men would go out in the woods, build a big fire, and stand around and listen to the chase. The night lasted until the fox climbed a tree or denned up, escaping until the next time. Grandpa was usually too tired from farm work to spend the night fox hunting, but we spent many a summer evening sitting on the dark porch listening to the dogs run. "That's ol' Belle out front," he'd say, and I'd nod like I really could distinguish one hound voice from another.

My grandparents lived five miles outside of Hemphill, down Farm Road 944. All of Grandpa's grandchildren were girls, and Leonard, Jimmy, and R. L. Ladner were his substitute grandsons. Leonard and Jimmy were brothers and R. L. their double first cousin. Jimmy passed away several years ago, but until his final illness he hunted daily with a four wheeler as his legs. Leonard and R. L. are respected, solid members of the community now, but all of them were about half-wild as boys.

One summer the three of them and Grandpa, or Uncle Adron as they called him, planned a fishing trip on the nearby creek, which had dried up into holes. They had found a black walnut tree full of nuts and the temptation was too great to pass up. They filled tow sacks with the nuts and beat the green hulls with sticks until they were well bruised. The tow sack was then dropped into a water hole. The walnuts leaked an oil or toxin that paralyzed the fish and they floated to the top. With Grandpa egging them on, the boys jumped in the creek and scooped them up. They came

Seining the Alford pond, 1960s

back with a washtub full of perch and catfish and spent all afternoon cleaning them, enough to feed all three families. My sister
and I had pitched a fit to go with them but were firmly turned
down. We learned later that none had swimsuits, and we would
have seen more boy than was proper.

(A note here: Many of the old methods like deer hunting with
dogs or stunning fish are now illegal. Then, however, hunting and
fishing were based on hundreds of years of tradition and no one
worried much about the way they were done if they produced a
meal.)

R. L. told another fishing story of when he, Leonard, Jimmy,
and James Edward Ener went camping on Housen Bayou. Camping out was truly out: a quilt to sleep on, a fire, and eating whatever you caught. This time they caught a soft-shell turtle and put it
on to cook. After all, they'd been told that turtle tasted "like
chicken." It didn't. The longer it cooked the tougher it got, and
chewing on it didn't make it any better. They had fish by then, but
it was too late to clean them and they left them on a stringer in the
creek. After going hungry all night, the next morning they decided
to clean the fish and have a decent meal. R. L. said that when he
lifted the stringer out of the water—the previous day's work—it
was a long stringer of fish heads. Turtles' revenge!

According to Leonard, the next time they went camping they
went with one of the McGraw boys, whose father had a large
chicken house. He gave them three or four live chickens to take.
They had no cooler and tied the chickens by their legs to trees until
meal times. The chickens, by then pets, went one by one. With
boys, hunger always wins.

Brothers Clarence and Herbert Ladner, the fathers of the boys,
were the most dedicated hunters of the area. For Clarence in particular, breathing and hunting were equally a basic part of life. On
one deer hunting trip he took Uncle Miles McDaniel, and since he
was very old but still liked to hear the dogs run, put him on a
remote stand without much chance of a deer. Of course, that was
the way it ran that day, and they heard the dogs head toward him

and two shots. When Clarence got to him there was no deer, but Uncle Miles was so excited he could barely talk. Clarence looked around and spotted where buckshot had skinned out a place high in a nearby tree. He pointed out to Uncle Miles where he had shot. Uncle Miles found his voice. "That's where that buck was when I was shooting at him!" he snapped.

A couple of porch stories involve Clarence's green '56 Plymouth and the game warden. In the first, Clarence dropped Cleo Gooch and L. G. (initials only as he may still get himself in trouble one day) on their stands and went on and parked the car and turned the dog loose. It began to rain mixed with sleet, and the wind picked up. L. G. eventually decided to head back to the car, shotgun over his shoulder. As it turned out, the game warden's car was also green and L. G. went right up to it, obviously hunting out of season. He was cited and brought before the justice of the peace. L. G. asked for a jury trial, which meant someone went out and rounded up six men hanging around the courthouse. Cleo was put on L. G.'s jury. After deliberating an acceptable amount of time, they found L. G. innocent because of "insufficient evidence."

Another time, Clarence, L. G., and Uncle Adron finished hunting, and put their guns in the back seat and the dog in the trunk. They were ready to leave and the game warden drove up. He glanced in the back seat and saw the guns, but of course that wasn't illegal. He asked if they would open the trunk, thinking he'd find an illegal deer. "Go ahead and look," said Uncle Adron, "but be careful of that wildcat we put in there." They all got out and Clarence handed the warden the keys. As he got the trunk partially open, the dog scrabbled out and the warden jumped back so quick he almost fell down. Evidently, everyone got such a laugh that no one was cited.

Before the practice became illegal, it was the game warden who first explained telephoning fish to Clarence and Herbert. Their father-in-law, Uncle Jody Easley, had an old crank phone and they took it down to the Sabine River. After hooking wires up to the generator and dropping them in the water, they turned the crank, the bell rang, and fish rose to the surface. I saw the largest they caught, a 72 pound catfish. It was ugly, but they ate it anyway. And of course, this probably explains why old telephones seldom turn up in East Texas antique stores.

When R. L. was six he went on Herbert's first deer hunting trip. Herbert had borrowed a double barrel from someone and Uncle Adron, who was on horseback, put them on a good stand. Sure enough, the deer came right at them and Herbert shot twice, wounding it. He would have shot again but he had put squirrel shot in one pocket and buckshot in another and couldn't remember which was which in all the excitement. They tracked the deer to Bull Creek. R. L. said a wounded deer will always go to water and lie there, sometimes with just its nose sticking out. They killed it and pulled it out with Babe, the horse. She wasn't finicky—would even drag a dead hog out of the woods—and they threw it over her back and she hauled it back. Horses worked hard in those days.

The practice at that time was to butcher the deer, divide up the meat, and the one who killed it would turn his back while someone else asked, "Whose is this?" That way the division was deemed fair, as the one naming the owner didn't know who was getting what. Except for one old man who complained that he had gotten the neck the last two hunts. "It's fair," he whined, "but I sure would like to get something better." Naturally, this inspired the others to really fix him. For the next few trips, "Whose is this?" became "And whose is this?" when they got to the neck. He'd get named for the neck once again. "It's fair," he'd say, never catching on.

Hunting and fishing were the main amusements for the men of Sabine County. No TV, Internet, or gambling trips to Biloxi could take their place. It was such a part of everyday life that my cousin Weldon McDaniel tells of wanting to go squirrel hunting after school, taking his squirrel gun on the school bus, and leaving it in the cloak room all day. Imagine that today. As a senior at Hemphill High, the current mayor of Hemphill, Robert Hamilton, put his boat on the top of his car and he and Leonard would skip out early to go fishing. The principal knew all about it—and was probably glad to get rid of them!

And now, on the porch again after over fifty years, R. L. laughs as his arm lifts the string of fish heads from the bayou, but the surprise on his face is the same as it was when he was a boy. Leonard tells about his father asking Uncle Miles McDaniel about the buckshot high in the tree and his face and eyes look up just as his father's did. And I see Grandpa's curved hand describing the wildcat hopping up on the log and wait to hear what it said . . . and I know it will be funny, and possibly profound.

Robert J. (Jack) Duncan

DELIVERANCE II: THE TALE OF A STRANGE ENCOUNTER IN THE BIG THICKET

by Robert J. (*Jack*) Duncan

~ ~

When I met Jim twenty some-odd years ago, he was vice-president of an insurance company. That evening I had dinner with him and another fellow. Over drinks before dinner, he got to telling us about a strange encounter he had experienced in the Big Thicket that was reminiscent of the James Dickey book—and the Burt Reynolds film—*Deliverance.*

The encounter had occurred several years earlier. At the time Jim had lived in Dallas. He wanted to get away from the stress of his job for a few days, to get off by himself in the woods and hunt deer. During deer season, Jim drove to a small town in the Thicket. It was a cold night. He stopped at a hamburger joint to ask directions. The cook insisted that Jim buy at least a burger or two before he would tell him anything.

As Jim was eating, the cook introduced him to another customer, Frank, who was a local hunter. Frank said that he was camped out with some of his kinfolks and invited Jim to join them. Frank and the surly cook seemed to be enjoying a private joke. Jim told us that he had vague reservations from the start, but there was really nothing that he could put his finger on. He didn't have a good solid reason to back out, so he went along. He followed Frank over a winding maze of dirt roads deep into the Thicket.

When Jim was thoroughly "turned around" and had lost all sense of direction, they came to a clearing. Jim said it was the oddest thing: there was a cabin/tent with a smoking stovepipe sticking out its roof. It turned out that the cabin had been made from a big discarded "felt" from a paper mill machine. Even the floor was made of the heavy felt. The thing had a pole frame, and somebody had sewn the felt covering together at the corners. It was maybe fifteen feet square, and it was extremely snug and comfortable, even though the night was quite cold.

Jim said that the hunters seemed to be all the grown menfolk of a big family, the male side of almost a whole clan. There were about a dozen of them, including the grizzled old man of the bunch. Most of them were in the cabin, lying around, some with their boots off. Frank had brought back a couple of bags of hamburgers for them. Now he doled them out.

After they ate, one of the men—the guy had a beard and wore a red flannel shirt—picked up a rifle and pointed it at Jim, almost touching his chest with the end of its barrel.

"Who in the devil invited *you?*" he asked Jim. He seemed to be speaking for several of his kinsmen.

Jim didn't like having a gun pointed at him, but for the moment he was at a loss for words. He hoped that he was simply the victim of a crude prank. Jim thought, *Victim sounds about right*, but he was a lot less sure of the *prank* part.

"Excuse me," the guy said. "Maybe I asked the wrong question. Let me put it to you this way: "*Just who in the hell are you, and what do you think you're doin' here?*"

Jim said he was scared, but he was determined not to take anything off Red Shirt. He realized that he was at a great disadvantage, but something told him that he would be better off if he could conceal his fear. He spoke up on his own behalf, telling Red Shirt that if he knew what was good for him, he would point that damn rifle some other way. Then Jim explained his innocent mission.

Frank chimed in about picking up Jim at the café. He seemed to think the whole thing was amusing. Jim didn't.

Jim told us he thought that maybe they suspected him of being a game warden. They were on what appeared to be public land, but they seemed to consider it their own domain. Jim doubted that *any* of them had a hunting license. Several deer carcasses hung from a tree near the cabin's door, their tongues lolled out. It also crossed Jim's mind that maybe they were operating a whisky still in the woods.

Red Shirt said to the others, "He's liable to have the laws in here on us in no time, Frank. He may claim to be just another city boy out a-huntin', but I'm thinkin' he ain't no such of a damn thing. Let's put the quietus to this business before he nabs us. I don't aim to wind up in the pen, now, damn it! I don't know why in the world you would want to lead him to us."

Frank said that he thought Jim was just some pantywaist weekend sportsman from Dallas that didn't know P-turkey.

They made Jim hand over his car keys and wait outside while the kangaroo court was in session. The felt tent efficiently muffled the voices so that Jim heard only a word or two now and then. Jim thought about running into the woods but he literally didn't know which way to turn, and he remembered hearing stories of people who had been lost in the Big Thicket. He was just about ready to try it anyway when the old man emerged from the tent alone. He walked over to Jim.

"Mister, let's get you out of here," the old man said. "Them boys don't really mean ye no harm, but they're kindly uneasy about you. If I hadn't a-been here, there ain't no tellin' what they would of done. Here's yore keys. Foller me back to town, and *don't you never come back to this part o' the country.*"

Jim looked me in the eye. "I'm here to tell you," he said, "he didn't have to say it twice."

The author at the Texas Folklife Festival, 2010

A THANKSGIVING CATFISH

by Jerry Young

Fishermen and storytellers have a bent for telling whoppers, and this whopper has been told around by one of Texas' truest tale rattlers.

Harley and Hazel Wilson had a passel of kids. Well, just three to be exact. There was Lucille and Arlene, and Harley Jr. They lived on a run-down, no-count piece of land over in Panola County on the Sabine (pronounced "Say Being" by locals) Slough. Why, that piece of land was so poor and run-down and no-count that there was nothing to do with it but donate it to the Baptist Church.

So that's what Harley did.

The Baptist folks were glad to get hold of that piece of land, because being close by the slough and all, it was convenient for baptizing. Well, the Baptists got together and built a church building on the land. But that land was so poor, so run down, so no good that for the church dedication, the deacons had to go up to Marshall and buy fifty pounds of commercial fertilizer before the congregation could raise a tune on that land.

After Harley got shed of that piece of land, he moved Hazel and the kids farther up the Slough to a place called Half Mile Bend. Now, fishing was a whole lot better in Half Mile Bend, and Harley'd rather fish than plow any day. And besides that, Old Slew Fin lived in Half Mile Bend.

Old Slew Fin was one monstrous channel cat. That fish measured out six feet, four inches from the tip of his snout to the end of his tail, and weighed over 146 pounds. That channel cat could tear up a seine net without working up a sweat, and he ate three barbed hooks off a trot line like they were paw paw berries.

You might wonder how Old Slew Fin got his name. Well, Sam Davis owns this brace of full-blooded fish dogs. Those dogs are so full-blooded that they are registered with the National Fish Dog

Society. As the story goes, and I don't have no reason not to believe Sam, it seems that those dogs treed that catfish in his den one Sunday afternoon, and while they were digging him out, one of those dogs accidentally bit off Old Slew's right paddle fin. After that Old Slew Fin always swam a bit to the left, and if you ever hoped to catch that fish, you had to set your hook in the right direction.

Harley surely did like fishing up there on Half Mile Bend. Especially on those fall and spring mornings when the mists come up off that slough. On those mornings, sometimes the mists would be so thick that the fish couldn't tell where the water left off and the mist began, and those fish ended up swimming in the mists. On those mornings, Old Harley'd just sit on the back porch, and when a school of those channel cats came swimming by in the mist, he'd swat the biggest ones over the head with an iron skillet. That was until Hazel made him quit. What happened was, one morning Harley and Hazel's kids were swimming in the mist, and Harley swatted Harley Jr. over the head with that iron skillet, mistaking the boy for a big channel cat.

Now, Harley Jr. never would've won no genius contest before that incident, but Hazel always was convinced that that iron skillet was the reason why Harley Jr. never won any ribbons at the county spelling bee. So, after swatting Harley Jr. with that skillet, Hazel made Harley go down to the slough to do his fishing. Harley found him a spot beneath a big bois d' arc tree there at the edge of the slough to do his fishing.

One fall afternoon, a couple of days before Thanksgiving, Harley was down there with his line out fishing for the family's Thanksgiving catfish. Well, you see, it was a lot easier for Harley to catch a catfish than go out and hunt down a tom gobbler. Besides, Hazel had a way of fixing a Thanksgiving catfish with a good corn-bread and hickory nut stuffing, and served with cranberry sauce and mashed sweet potatoes, it was a feast Hazel and the kids could truly be thankful for.

It was unseasonably warm that day. Had been all fall. In that warm weather, Harley worked up a real sweat leaning against that bois d'arc, and he worked up a real thirst hanging on to the fishing pole. To refresh himself from time to time, Harley'd take a nip of corn drippings from a half-gallon jar wrapped with burlap that he had setting there beside him. Being a good Baptist, Hazel didn't approve of Harley's weakness for corn drippings, so she kept a hard eye out for any backsliding on Harley's part. But that morning, with the jar disguised like the jug he took to the field with him when he went out to plow, Harley'd managed to slip the corn drippings past Hazel's sharp eye.

Sometime late in the afternoon, Harley hadn't caught a thing, but he was sweating hard and he'd worked up a terrible thirst. Old Harley lifted up that half-gallon jar to his lips and was taking a long nip of corn drippings, when out of the comer of his eye he caught sight of a big blue-black cloud coming out of the north.

Now, folks in Texas know a big blue-black cloud coming out of the north means one thing—blue norther. And those blue northers blow through faster than green apples go through Harley Jr. Well, Harley knew he didn't have long to get to the cabin before that norther hit, so he gave his line a yank, and as he did, he felt a tug at the other end of it. Harley looked out across the slough and sure enough—there was Old Slew Fin, a flipping and a flopping in the air, not more than twenty feet above the water, and he was on his way down.

Harley knew if that fish ever hit the water, he was a goner. And sure enough, Old Slew Fin hit the water alright. But it wasn't a splash. It was more like a wump! What happened was that while that fish was in the air that blue norther blew through and froze that slough four inches solid. Well, Harley walked out on the ice, picked up that frozen catfish, and carried it to the cabin.

Old Slew Fin made a fine Thanksgiving catfish that year, although Hazel always said that he needed a bit more salt—kind of like this story.

Robert Flynn at the 2011 TFS meeting

PRANKS IN HUNTING CAMP; OR, THE PHYSIOLOGICAL AND PSYCHOLOGICAL BENEFITS OF ANCIENT RITES PRACTICED IN BUCOLIC AND FRATERNAL SETTINGS

by Robert Flynn

For reasons yet to be explained, God and the Supreme Court placed hunting season during the shortest days of the year. For those who venture into nature to collect something edible rather than to escape TV, that means a lot of non-hunting time in hunting camp. Some hunters fill those hours with eating, drinking, arguing hunting strategies, conjuring visions of the next hunt, playing cards, eating, cooking, tinkering with mechanical devices such as hunting vehicles, cleaning hunting gear (including selected game), cleaning the cabin, and/or cleaning oneself.

While those are meaningful, productive and necessary, the serious hunter also requires creative activities. The two fundamental exercises of the imagination are: One, the preparation, polishing, and delivery of the day's hunting story that includes in detail every animal seen, and the description of the width, breadth, length and points of the bucks' horns with poetic license; and also the enumeration of the number of turkeys, feral hogs, and other game with manly exaggeration. Two, the preparation of the "prank."

BENEFITS OF HUNTING PRANKS

Nonbelievers and other ignorant folks pretend that hunting pranks are sophomoric tricks played by born-again adolescents. Nothing could be farther from the truth. Prank benefits include:

- Rejuvenation of the spirit—brings bounce to legs weary after long hikes looking for game and uplift to the spirits of the disappointed.

- Subjects for conversation—contrary to popular opinion, campfires are not occasion for idle conversations but rather for discourse on the philosophy of hunting, the psychology of rifle calibers, and the chemistry of beer versus bourbon. When the hunting stories grow thin, the prank stories begin.
- Bonding—friends who laugh together are less likely to mistake each other for a turkey behind a cedar bush.
- Heart stimulation—not as great as seeing a Boone and Crockett buck but better than after a stressful day at work coming home to a tired housewife and three cross children.
- Exercise—sometimes for both the pranker, hereafter referred to as the jokester, and the butt of the joke, hereafter referred to as the butt.
- Stimulation of Imaginations—at times when sleep does not come easily, such as when deciding whether to get out of a warm sleeping bag to relieve oneself in hope of getting warm again or trying to doze until the alarm goes off, the jokester can dream of new pranks; the butt can imagine what pranks he/she will face before breakfast.

Best Times for Pranks

Pranks can be played at almost any time, but the experienced jokester knows that jokes are not always appropriate. For example, when a fellow hunter has in his sights the buck he has stalked for days, several pranks will come to the jokester's mind. Leave them there.

Best Pranks for the Right Time

The accomplished jokester knows the pranks most appropriate for specific times.

First cup of coffee: Sleepers are rousing, some have coffee in their hands, some have cigarettes in one hand and coffee in the other, some are out of bed and fully clothed with a cup of coffee in hand. Some are on the move. The first hunter on the move is the butt of the joke.

Appropriate prank: "Can-gun Attack." Requirements: C-ration cans, duct tape, tennis balls, lighter fluid, lighter or matches, second jokester. Directions: With a church key cut holes around the top of a can; with an ice pick punch two small holes opposite each other near the rim at the bottom of the can to make the firing device. Cut out the tops and bottoms of additional cans and tape them to the firing device to form the barrel. Note: For accuracy, make the barrel long. For rapid fire, tape several can-guns together. Place the projectile, a new tennis ball, in the open end of the barrel until it lodges snugly against the receiver. Jokester One holds the can-gun horizontally; Jokester Two squirts lighter fluid into the firing device. Jokester One rotates the can-gun to spread the fluid and allow it to vaporize, and aims the can-gun at the target. Using lighter or matches, Jokester Two ignites the charge. Note: The projectile will travel a short distance at high velocity with enough impact to knock the hat off the butt, but is also effective on house trailers and outhouses. Best usage is to awaken sleeper, startle day dreamer, or alert the inattentive hunter. Another Note: Ribbed cans are not suitable because ribbing relieves pressure on tennis ball. Warning: Avoid shooting at windows or the head of the butt—damage, injury, or retribution may result. Further Warning: Hold can-gun horizontally when preparing to fire so that lighter fluid does not leak onto head, hands, or back of Jokester One, causing them to ignite and Jokester One to overshoot the target. (Can-gun attack is also appropriate for afternoon and REM time.)

Breakfast: Over preferred breakfast—cold cereal, bacon and eggs, toast and jelly, and occasionally hair of the dog—hunters

discuss strategies for the morning hunt or grouse about what went wrong the night before.

Appropriate prank: "Mad Turkey-Hunter." Requirements: camouflage clothing, shotgun, empty box of shotgun shells, BIG firecrackers, fireplace or pit fire. Directions: Place explosives in empty shell box. Jokester, dressed in camouflage, tells again how he had missed a turkey at close range, explains again that he used reloads given him by a friend, and complains again that the shells are worthless while shaking shell box to suggest the reloads are in the box. Jokester declares he is going to throw them away. Other hunters will nod agreement, whereupon the jokester throws the shell box of explosives into the fireplace. Warning: Jokester should place himself near a door or far from it to avoid being run over when the first firecracker explodes. Note: Can also be used at camp fire.

Prehunt: Hunters are leaving cabin and moving to hunting position before dawn.

Appropriate prank(s): "Snarling dog." Requirements: snarling dog alarm that is triggered when moved, ground blind. Directions: After the butt has left the blind on the previous day, set alarm and hang inside blind door. The next morning when the hunter starts to open the door he is greeted by the sound of snarling dogs. Note: Works best on butts who enter a blind before daylight. Another Note: Also works on outhouses. Warning: Do not to use on blinds more than five feet off the ground.

"Blind blind." Requirement: black vinyl. Directions: The evening before, tape black vinyl over all sight openings. Note: Works best if the butt is encouraged to get into the blind before daylight and without a flashlight. Also best on cold, windy mornings when the butt will wait until daylight to open the sliding windows. (Record Wait: Two hours, three and one half minutes.)

"Mannequin poacher." Requirements: mannequin, hunting clothes, broomstick, high stand, shills if necessary. Directions:

Dress mannequin before coming to camp. The previous evening after the hunter has left the stand, place mannequin and broomstick on stand. Note: Works best after breakfast when poachers have been the topic of conversation. If required, shills should express belief that poachers should be shot. Another Note: The butt should be encouraged to approach the stand when only the mannequin silhouette is visible. For added effect, the jokester accompanies the butt until the butt sees the poacher. Jokester then says, "Let's shoot the (insert favorite description here) poacher," and shoots the mannequin.

Noon meal: Some hunters hunt all day, not returning to camp until after dark; others return after the morning hunt to recount the excitement of the morning while preparing lunch.

Appropriate Prank: "Dog poop." Requirements: chunky peanut butter, clean boots, shills. Directions: Jokester complains long and loudly about a dog or dogs in camp. Shills join in. Before eating, the jokester places chunky peanut butter between the heel and sole of his boot. While eating, a shill complains that he can still smell dog poop. Other shills agree. One of them points at the jokester's boot and accuses him of tracking dog poop into the cabin. Jokester denies that it is dog poop. Shills declare that it is. Jokester pokes finger into chunky peanut butter and tastes it to prove it is not dog poop. Jokester runs out of the cabin and makes puking sounds.

Afternoon: Hunters rest during the time after lunch and before the afternoon hunt.

Appropriate prank: "Machine gun." Requirements: gravel, metal roof, veterans of a recent war. Note: Works best when the butts are taking a nap. Directions: Take a handful of gravel and throw it in a spray at the roof. To veteran sleepers it sounds like machine gun fire and is certain to rouse them from deepest slumber. Warning: Ascertain that no weapons are in the house.

Afternoon hunt: Hunters are leaving the cabin for the afternoon hunt.

Appropriate prank: "Trophy Buck." Requirements: old mounted deer head with antlers. Mounted turkey or skull with horns may substitute when necessary. Directions: Place mounted head in heavy brush or other cover. Talk secretively to the butt about a big buck (or long-bearded tom) before or after lunch, describing exactly where it was seen. Note: Works best if the jokester persuades the butt to ride with him so that he can point out the head that is difficult to see.

Campfire: Hunters engage in storytelling between the first drink and dinner.

Appropriate prank: "Jerky treats." Requirements: barbecue flavored rawhide dog chews, resealable plastic bag. Directions: Place dog chews in resealable bag, and as the butts gather to enjoy an after-hunt drink complete with stories, pass the dog chews as you describe how you made jerky last season. Note: Works best if you are enjoying a piece of real jerky, and if the butts have started story telling. A few may furtively discard the chews, but most will work on them for fear of losing their turn in the story telling. Another Note: May be repeated with various treats by using shills. Be certain that one "treat" is slightly different in size or color from the others. Shills cautiously avoid it so that it is the only one remaining for the butt who will refuse it. Warning: After the jerky treat prank, some butts may find it necessary to circle their beds before lying down.

Dinner: After much ado accompanied by mucho mess, the hunters sit together to eat.

Appropriate prank: "Sponge cake." Requirements: sponge cake (preferably lemon or strawberry), kitchen sponge. Directions: Before leaving for camp, bake sponge cake the same color as the kitchen sponge. Remove piece of the cake the same size as the sponge and replace with the sponge before icing the cake. Cut the cake in dimensions approximately the same as the sponge. After arriving at camp, display the cake and proudly announce that it is for dessert after dinner. After everyone has eaten, distribute the sponge cake, making sure that the butt receives the sponge. Note: Shills can heighten the effect if they begin eating before the butt is served and loudly declare how good it is. Another Note: If you have previously employed the jerky treat prank, shills will be necessary.

Liars club: After dinner and before sleep, hunters may stretch the truth a bit.

Appropriate prank: "Rattlesnake in sack." Requirements: armadillo, gunny sack, dark place. Directions: Place an armadillo in the gunny sack and put it in a dark place such as a hall or bathroom, or outside the door to keep it quiet. Be certain that light bulbs are removed so that the dark place remains dark. The butt going to bed or the bathroom or outhouse will bump into it. When kicked, the armadillo will jump straight up. Note: Works best after campfire talk about rattlesnakes. If necessary, a shill can say he put one in a sack. Another shill can remark on the description and size of the rattler.

Bed time: When the butt goes to bed.

Appropriate prank(s): "Recovering light." Requirements: special switch and wiring. If the butt is in a different room than the jokester, a mirror or shill may be necessary to signal when the butt gets in bed. Directions: Wire a separate switch to the light in the butt's room. Wait until the butt turns the light off and gets into bed. Turn light on. Wait until the butt turns the light off and gets into bed. Turn light on. Note: May be repeated.

"Falling bed." Requirement: bunk beds with springs from the bed frame to the wire mesh that holds up the mattress. Directions: remove springs from the bed frame. Reattach with string holding the springs to the frame. When the butt lies down, the string will break and the bed and the butt will fall. Note: Works best on upper bunks. Another Note: Also works best when the butt is a young hunter who springs into upper bunk. Warning: If upper bunk is used, be certain a hunter is not asleep in the lower bunk.

REM time: When all hunters are deep in sleep.

Appropriate prank: "Choo-choo." Requirements: spot light (found at most hunting camps), tape player (found at most hunting camps), recording of steam engine ringing bell and blowing whistle as it approaches a crossing (found in some public libraries, most university libraries with drama departments or radio stations, and commercial radio stations and novelty stores). Directions: Slip outside but leave the cabin door open. Turn on the tape full volume, turn on the spotlight, and—to the sound of train whistle, bells and engine full throttle—run through the cabin flashing the spotlight in the eyes of startled sleepers. Note: Choo-choo works best in remote canyons where there are no trains or tracks. Diesel electric trains may be substituted if necessary. Another Note: Effect can be heightened if you slip back into bed unseen and the following morning tell how you dreamed you were almost run over by a train.

Conclusion: The imaginative hunter can turn idle hours into happy memories equal to the finest fishing stories.

[This article previously appeared in *Texas Sporting Journal.*]

The author with his real trophy buck

Henry and Linda Wolff

FISHING FOR WHOPPERS

by Henry Wolff, Jr.

Whoppers come in many forms, everything from a hamburger to a big fish, but I happen to be particularly fond of the kind that are measured not by taste or size but in the telling, such as the stories that can be heard around a table on a lazy afternoon in a country tavern—or at a fish camp like the one at Indianola that the old fisherman Ed Bell operated for many years.

Known in his time as one of the best tall tale tellers on the Texas Coast, one example would be a story that Bell always credited to a friend, Tex Wilson. It seems that Wilson and his wife had been fishing in some fairly deep water when their boat bogged down.

"It had to be four feet of water for it not to kick up any mud," Bell explained in telling the story. "All at once it just stalled and ol' Tex couldn't figure it out since there weren't any logs or anything there to stop a boat. That was when his wife looked over the bow of the boat and said, 'Good Lord, Tex, cut that thing off and come here and look a minute.' He did and there was a big ol' flounder with his back just flush with the top of the water.

"They had beached on that flounder's back."

While staring at the big fish in disbelief, Bell said they spotted yet another swimming off that was just as big.

"I got curious to see just how big those flounders were, but I didn't go through school far enough to figure it out in algebra or advanced math," Bell would note in telling the story to an appreciative audience. "I had to get me a pencil and a tablet. The way I figured it, a flounder that's twelve inches long, eight inches wide, will weigh about three-quarters of a pound. So I took it from there and after I had worn out two pencils and just about filled the tablet with figures, I got, near as I could, to the exact weight and size of that flounder. It was 48 feet long and 32 feet wide, four feet thick, and weighed 30,000 pounds.

"So, I figured it was a pretty nice flounder."

It was always interesting to hear Bell tell his stories when the weather turned bad and the fishermen would gather inside the rustic camp to swap yarns, or in his later years when he became a regular on the storytelling stage at the Texas Folklife Festival at the Institute of Texan Cultures in San Antonio. His talents at telling tall tales even took him to Washington, D.C. at the Smithsonian Institution during the American Bicentennial Celebration in 1976. He was also prominently featured in Patrick B. Mullen's book from the University of Texas Press, *I Heard the Old Fisherman Say: Folklore of the Texas Gulf Coast*, with the author describing Bell as the best tall tale teller that he had encountered on the Texas Gulf Coast—"a true raconteur who has continued the art of traditional storytelling."

I had fished for many years at Bell's camp at the cut between Powderhorn Lake and Matagorda Bay, but got to know him best after he had become well known for his tall tales and I was writing a newspaper column for the *Victoria Advocate*. I recall once asking him how much truth there was in his stories.

"Not a lot," he replied. "If I put too much truth in them then people will get to believing everything I say."

In his book of Texas coastal folklore, Mullen did some dissecting of Bell as a storyteller, pointing out how his success had to do with four major areas of style – concrete detail, ludicrous images, point of view, and narrative persona. As a newspaper columnist always searching for something to write about, I mostly considered him as being just a damn good story teller. He could hardly open his mouth without making my day, and there just never was any better among those who could spin a good fish tale. He did tell Mullen that he seldom told his tall tales when fishing, however.

"We always had too many interruptions," he said. "We were always catching too many fish."

Some of my favorite spots for catching a good fish story were the country stores and taverns that can be found along the Texas coast and inland counties of the coastal plains, places where the regulars gather when they have nothing better to do or when the weather is just too bad to go fishing. I often stopped at Ruddock's Grocery at Guadalupe just to the southeast of Victoria to listen to Joe Ruddock tell his stories, like one in particular that reminded me a whole lot of Bell's tale about the big flounder. Ruddock said he was running some trotlines in the Guadalupe River below Victoria and had taken "a couple of little twisters off" when he noticed there was something big hooked about midway on one of the lines.

"It was sloshing water up like a geyser," he said, "and made a whirlpool in the river each time it moved."

Ruddock rowed his way up to the fish and started to pull it toward the surface; he could tell that it was rather big, though he thought part of that could have been because he had a heavy sinker on the line. Then he saw the fish's mouth and there was no doubt that it was a whopper. He also noticed that it only had one eye.

"I didn't want to take no old one-eyed catfish home with me," he thought to himself. Then he glanced around to the other side of the boat and there was the other eye.

There was a sign behind the bar at Ruddock's Store that made an impression on me the first time that I walked through the door; it welcomed "fishermen, hunters and all other fancy liars."

One of the secrets of a good fishing tale is that the teller has to get you hooked from the beginning, like another story that I heard being told by one of the regulars at the domino tables at Ruddock's Grocery. Bill Lipscomb said his wife Jessie had been pestering him to take her fishing. They were out in the middle of the Guadalupe River when he pulled out a stick of dynamite that he had brought with him. Although he didn't say it, he had apparently intended to impress Jessie with all the fish that he could catch. It just wasn't his day, and when he threw the dynamite somehow it got hung up on the side of the boat and they nearly capsized as the explosion almost blew them out of the water.

He said Jessie never wanted to go fishing with him again after that.

Another time I ventured over to Vienna in southeastern Lavaca County to a barbecue and bean cook-off at the Lazy J, as good an example as one could hope to find of an old country tavern, where I happened to overhear Rudy Merechka and Andrew Barrera talking about going fishing.

"Maybe tomorrow," Merechka said, "but the wind is out of the southeast and there's probably no water."

"That's when it blows the water in," Barrera countered.

I figured right off that they were fishing partners by the way they were talking, even before they got to telling about the time they brought home a 24-pound catfish. Seems that it was a catch they had made from the freezer at Popeye Fleming's bait stand near Magnolia Beach; the giveaway was that the frozen fish was too long to fit in their cooler and they had to leave the tail sticking out for fear it might break off if they bent it.

"We did trim some of the fin off the tail," Barrera recalled, "but it still wouldn't fit."

When they got home and were telling Barrera's wife about what a good fishing trip they had and showed her their catch, she wanted to know why it was frozen stiff. They told her that they had stopped on the way home and put a quick freeze on it to keep it from spoiling, but for some reason she didn't seem to believe them.

There are just some things that fish tales seem to have in common when it comes to the believing.

One of my favorite of the tales that Ed Bell liked to tell was about a time when he was visiting a friend in Houston. Bell told the man that he would like to go red fishing with him sometime, the red drum being a popular fish on the Texas coast, and a good red fisherman was greatly admired.

"He said that he knew where to fish," Bell recalled in telling the story. "He said that he would be there in the morning real early to pick me up."

His friend arrived about 2:00 a.m. the next morning and began impatiently honking his car horn outside of where Bell was staying.

"That's not real early," Bell said, rubbing his forehead beneath the well-worn captain's hat that was as much a part of his persona as his tall tales. "That's night."

At any rate, they got off in what Bell described as an "awful foggy morning," a Houston fog he further described as being ten times worse than any other fog in Texas. They were driving along in a Model-A Ford toward Galveston, his friend having to lean out of the window on the driver's side to find the stripe in the middle of the highway.

"That's the place," he exclaimed, pulling off the pavement and suddenly bringing the car to a stop.

"I couldn't see a thing except for the marsh grass alongside the road," Bell said, "and it was barely visible." For a brief moment, he thought that he might have seen the shadowy outline of a Brahman bull in the thick fog. His friend got out and baited up his big fishing rig and cast the bait way out.

"I never did hear no splash," Bell said, "but all at once the pole began to bend and I thought for sure that he had roped that Brahman bull."

Instead, his friend pulled in a couple of big red fish. He turned to Bell and asked him if he was going to fish.

"I got so excited that all my fingers turned to thumbs," Bell recalled. "Finally, I got two hooks baited with some ol' dead shrimp." By then his friend had pulled in two more big reds. No sooner had Bell cast out than he hooked two nice eight-pounders.

"You think they can't do some damage," he said, emphasizing what a fight he had in reeling them in.

In all, they caught fourteen big red fish between the two of them before the fog lifted.

"We were ten miles from the bay," Bell explained. "We had been fishing in a fog bank."

Fish tales become whoppers only when big enough to be unbelievable.

Ed Bell

It looks so harmless

ROPING A DEER

[Editor's note: The following has been passed along by email, from many people. If an original contributor can be located, please let me know so proper credit can be awarded. –Untiedt]

Actual letter from someone who farms and writes well:

I had this idea that I was going to rope a deer, put it in a stall, feed it up on corn for a couple of weeks, then kill it and eat it. The first step in this adventure was getting a deer. I figured that, since they congregate at my cattle feeder and do not seem to have much fear of me when we are there (a bold one will sometimes come right up and sniff at the bags of feed while I am in the back of the truck not four feet away), it should not be difficult to rope one, get up to it and toss a bag over its head (to calm it down), then hog tie it and transport it home.

I filled the cattle feeder, then hid down at the end with my rope. The cattle, having seen the roping thing before, stayed well back. They were not having any of it. After about twenty minutes, my deer showed up—three of them. I picked out a likely looking one, stepped out from the end of the feeder, and threw my rope.

The deer just stood there and stared at me. I wrapped the rope around my waist and twisted the end so I would have a good hold. The deer still just stood and stared at me, but you could tell it was mildly concerned about the whole rope situation.

I took a step towards it. It took a step away. I put a little tension on the rope, and then received an education. The first thing that I learned is that, while a deer may just stand there looking at you funny while you rope it, it will be spurred to action when you start pulling on that rope. That deer EXPLODED!

The second thing I learned is that, pound for pound, a deer is a LOT stronger than a cow or a colt. A cow or a colt in that weight range I could fight down with a rope and with some dignity. A deer? No chance.

That thing ran and bucked and twisted and pulled. There was no controlling it, and certainly no getting close to it. As it jerked me off my feet and started dragging me across the ground, it occurred to me that having a deer on a rope was not nearly as good an idea as I had originally imagined. The only up side is that they do not have as much stamina as many other animals.

A brief ten minutes later, it was tired and not nearly as quick to jerk me off my feet and drag me when I managed to get up. It took me a few minutes to realize this, since I was mostly blinded by the blood flowing out of the big gash in my head. At that point, I had lost my taste for corn-fed venison. I just wanted to get that devil creature off the end of that rope.

I figured if I just let it go with the rope hanging around its neck, it would likely die slowly and painfully somewhere. At the time, there was no love at all between me and that deer. At that moment, I hated the thing, and I would venture a guess that the feeling was mutual.

Despite the gash in my head and the several large knots where I had cleverly arrested the deer's momentum by bracing my head against various large rocks as it dragged me across the ground, I could still think clearly enough to recognize that there was a small chance that I shared some tiny amount of responsibility for the situation we were in, so I didn't want the deer to have to suffer a slow death. Therefore, I managed to get it lined back up in between my truck and the feeder—a little trap I had set beforehand—kind of like a squeeze chute. I got it to back in there and I started moving up so I could get my rope back.

Did you know that deer bite? They do! I never in a million years would have thought that a deer would bite somebody, so I was very surprised when I reached up there to grab that rope and the deer grabbed hold of my wrist. Now, when a deer bites you, it is not like being bit by a horse where they just bite you and then let go. A deer bites you and shakes its head—almost like a mad dog.

They bite HARD and it hurts. The proper thing to do when a deer bites you is probably to freeze and draw back slowly. I tried screaming and shaking instead. My method was ineffective. It seemed like the deer was biting and shaking for several minutes, but it was likely only several seconds.

I, being smarter than a deer (though you may be questioning that claim by now), tricked it. While I kept it busy tearing the tendons out of my right arm, I reached up with my left hand and pulled that rope loose. That was when I got my final lesson in deer behavior for the day.

Deer will strike at you with their front feet. They rear right up on their back feet and strike at you at about head and shoulder level, and their hooves are surprisingly sharp. I learned a long time ago that, when an animal—like a horse—strikes at you with their hooves and you can't get away easily, the best thing to do is try to make a loud noise and make an aggressive move towards the animal. This will usually cause them to back down a bit so you can escape.

This was not a horse. This was a deer, so obviously, such trickery would not work. In the course of a millisecond, I devised a different strategy.

I screamed like a woman and tried to turn and run. The reason I had always been told NOT to try to turn and run from a horse that paws at you is that there is a good chance that it will hit you in the back of the head. Deer may not be so different from horses after all, besides being twice as strong and three times as evil, because the second I turned to run, it hit me right in the back of the head and knocked me down.

Now, when a deer paws at you and knocks you down, it does not immediately leave. I suspect it does not recognize that the danger has passed. What they do instead is paw your back and jump up and down on you while you are laying there crying like a little girl and covering your head.

I finally managed to crawl under the truck and the deer went away. So, now I know why when people go deer hunting they bring a rifle with a scope to sort of even the odds.

Jerry Lincecum at the 2010 TFS meeting

TEXAS MENU 1835: VENISON AND HONEY, PRAIRIE CHICKEN, OR BAKED FISH

by Jerry Bryan Lincecum

The autobiography of Gideon Lincecum, my great-great-great grandfather, contains some remarkable accounts of hunting and fishing in unspoiled areas of Texas in 1835. Lincecum's six-month exploration of Texas came about after a good many citizens of Columbus, Mississippi, where he resided and practiced medicine, became interested in migrating to Texas. An emigrating company was organized late in 1834, and Lincecum was appointed physician to an exploring committee charged with traveling to Texas and bringing back a report. He and five other men left Columbus on January 9, 1835, and crossed the Sabine River into Texas on February 3.[1] The following excerpts from Lincecum's autobiography are among many that describe encounters with wildlife in Texas. In 1848, Lincecum moved his family to Long Point, Washington County. His memoirs were written when he was an old man, and most of his accounts of hunting and fishing were first published in The American Sportsman under the title "Personal Reminiscences of an Octogenerian."[2] The following are excerpts of those accounts.

[I recall] our camp at Barton's Bluff on the south side of the Colorado. We had found a bee tree, and while the young men were cutting out the honey, I went off to get a deer, preparatory to one of our grand venison and honey suppers. The big kettle and all our buckets were filled with nice, white honey-comb. I had selected from a drove of twenty or thirty deer, a splendid forked-horn buck. We found a nice camping place, with plenty of good water and wood, and an abundance of green grass for the horses.

Some of the men cut green wood and made a good fire, while others sliced up the good lean parts of the venison into narrow strips; others collected some straight little prairie dogwood (*viburnum dentatum*) rods for broiling sticks, and pressed out each man's tin cup half-full of honey. Neither bread nor salt nor coffee is used at one of these feasts; and for its easy digestive qualities and agreeableness in eating it is most certainly not surpassed by any dish ever set before mankind.

Everything being in readiness, each man trimmed and sharpened at both ends two of the rods, and then running the small end three or four times through one of the slices of venison lengthwise, plants the other end in the ground at the proper distance from the fire, so as to place the meat over good hot coals to broil. He spits another slice of venison on the other stick, and by turning and attending to it, soon has one of the slices thoroughly broiled. This he takes off of the stick and replacing it with another slice sets it over the fire. By this time the piece taken off is sufficiently cool to begin to eat.

The most approved plan for eating is to take the piece of meat in your left hand, your hunting knife in the right, plunge one end of the meat into your cup of honey, deep enough for a mouthful, thrust it between your teeth, and hold it fast while you saw it off with your knife. It is easy enough to see that by the time you consume the first slice the second will be ready, which is to be taken off and replaced with another, as in the first instance, and so on until you have supped up your half cup of honey.

This is enough for any decent hunter to consume; a desire for more would indicate too much animal to be allowed the use of a gun. I have often thought, at the time I was so agreeably feasting in that way, that there could be no better preparation of food for man that is so suitable, so natural, so agreeable and so exactly suited to his constitutional requirements.[3]

[Near present Bastrop] I saw my first prairie hen—a regular pinnated grouse—and succeeded, after following near a mile, and when it was almost too dark to see the sights of my rifle, in killing one of them.

Our old Methodist preacher [Frederick Weaver, a member of the exploring committee] said it looked so much like a chicken it must be good to eat, and if we would agree for him to do so, he would make a try of it for his own supper, and not join us in the venison and honey that time. We still had a kettle full of honey comb, and all went to work making a good fire, for it was blowing up one of those Texas Northers.

As soon as the fire was in proper condition, we were ready for broiling and sopping the venison in the honey, which continued perhaps an hour, and about the time we got through with our satisfactory feast, the old Preacher had set his pan of fried grouse off a little way from the fire and commenced his supper; he had made bread and coffee and promised himself a great repast.

The old fellow was working away a long time; the boys had been out to see about the horses; had fixed their sleeping places and had scuffed and played a long time—9 o'clock—when the old man rose up from the frying pan, wiping his fingers on the long moss, and saying, "Well boys, you may all eat prairie chickens who like. That's the first one that ever I tasted and I am determined it shall be the last."

"Why, papa," asked his son, "was it not well flavored!" "Oh, it tasted well enough," said the old man, "but it was so infernal tough. Why it's a wonder to me that Gid's rifle-ball penetrated the tough old carcass." His son proposed frying some venison for him to piece out his supper with; but the old man refused, on the grounds that he had worried himself down gnawing and pulling at that old grouse, and he was sleepy.[4]

*   *   *

[In early March, the other Mississippians set out on their return journey, but Lincecum was sufficiently interested in the flora and fauna of Texas to continue exploring on his own three months longer, mostly along the coastal plain, provisioning himself with local game and fish.]

Gideon Lincecum

[Along the head branch of the San Bernard River] I got out one of my lines, baited my hook with a chunk of [deer] liver, and threw it into the water. It had not sunk half-way down before it was grabbed, and pulling it up I found a large blue cat had it. He came up to the top of the water quite willingly, and there were two or three more whirling about in the scented water; but my fish finding it was no joke, turned and darted away with such force that he came near getting the line out of my hand. I checked him, however; when he reached the full length of the line, he shot upwards so swiftly, keeping the twanging line tight, that he threw himself a foot or two above the water.

He cut many antics and gyrations before he gave up, and I had to work my way around two or three trees that grew on the bank until I got to a shallow place at the lower end of the big hole, before I could get him out. I dragged him while he was tired, and until he was fairly grounded on the pebbly bottom of the little creek, which I could here leap across. It was with some difficulty that I got him out. I was afraid to trust my little line, so I made it fast to a snag near by and left him panting till I ran and got my lariat from old Ned [Gideon's horse]. I then made a running noose, threw it over his tail, and slipping it to his strong horns in the pectoral fin, drew it down close and then hauled him out and to my camp.

I judged that he would weigh 44 or 45 pounds. He was a whopper, and dwelling as he had in very clear water, his skin was very blue above and as white as the whitest paper beneath. Ned came up from his grazing to see what it was that I had dragged up from the water. He smelt of it, and when it flapped its tail, he jerked up his head and, turning away to his grass, made no remarks.

Having run out of salt by this time, I resolved to try if I could cook the fish in a way that would make it palatable without bread or salt. By the time I had broiled and ate one of the dorsal muscles of a little deer I had shot earlier, I had a large heap of coals and embers. With the axe I chopped off the fish's head, and divided the rest of it lengthwise into equal halves, and cut one of them in two. Then I laid the raw parts together, and winding some long grass around it, opened a hole in the embers, down to the ground, laid in the fish and covered it over with a deep envelope of ashes. I then made a little scaffold over the fire, and placed the remaining half of the fish in small slices, with the venison I had on top of it, and left them there to cure until morning.

When I awoke in the morning, I found the meat and fish on my scaffold dried almost to a bake, and if I had had a little pepper sauce and bread the fish was very nice. I drew out my fish from the embers, and found it still enveloped in the grass which was only scorched a little on the outside. But the fish was thoroughly done, and nearly as dry as good bread. It had absorbed a sufficient quantity of the alkaline principle from the ashes to answer in place of salt, and it was, to say the least of it, a very savory dish. I made a full breakfast from it.

Then, I called up Ned, and after packing up, we set out for another day's journey, having no choice but to leave the nice dried meat and fish and ten or twelve pounds of excellently cooked fish on the ground. I had no way to carry any eatables along.[5]

ENDNOTES

1. Lois Wood Burkhalter. *Gideon Lincecum, 1793–1874: A Biography.* Austin: University of Texas Press, 1965. 35.
2. Gideon Lincecum. "Personal Reminiscences of an Octogenerian." *The American Sportsman.* 12 September 1874–16 January 1875.
3. Jerry Bryan Lincecum and Edward Hake Phillips. *Adventures of a Frontier Naturalist: The Life and Times of Dr. Gideon Lincecum.* College Station: TAMU Press, 1994. 154-155. J. Frank Dobie cited Lincecum's description of how to eat venison and honey in *Tales of Old-Time Texas* (Boston: Little Brown & Co., 1928), 125.
4. Ibid. 155–156.
5. Ibid. 162–163.

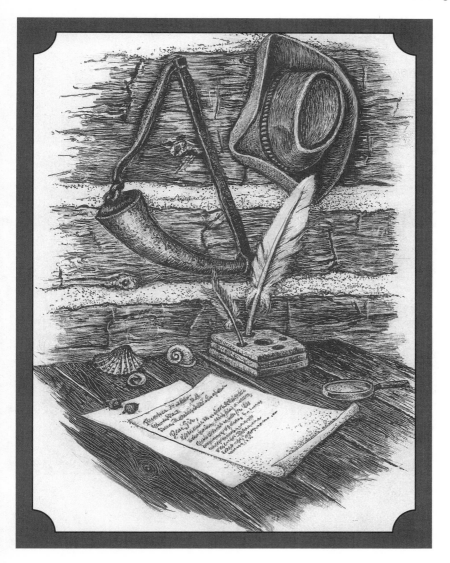

Gideon Lincecum's writing desk as imagined by artist Betsy Warren of Austin

The author's father fishing

FISHERMAN'S PARADISE: "HIS CAP NEVER GOT WET"

by Blaine T. Williams

The Williams family took many an overnight trip to public and private camping areas within driving distance of our home in Arlington, Texas. A college professor's salary didn't afford luxurious accommodations. So, camping out was our usual mode.

The Paluxy River in Glen Rose was a favorite destination. We would wade in the river while searching for dinosaur tracks. A little further downstream, we could swim in a deep corner of the Paluxy that everyone called "Blue Hole."

But my father's love of fishing always brought us back to Fisherman's Paradise, a privately owned stretch of Village Creek, the stream that fed our local lake in what is now southwest Arlington. It took us only twenty minutes or so to get there from home, but it was a cheap and adventurous outing for our seven-member family.

One beautiful summer day, with Dad and Mom in the front seat and all five of us kids plus a friend stuffed into the back, we had turned in from the road, paid our per-carload entry fee, purchased some bait at the old house that served as a combination general store and bait house, eased our beat-up '55 Chevy station wagon across the pasture that led down to the river, to set up a rough camp. We were not alone on this small, twelve-foot-wide creek with two-foot-high banks. Many other families lined the creek, some with much fancier rigs than ours—even a few with travel trailers.

My older brother Wood quickly wandered off looking for mischief. He found it in the form of a cottonmouth water moccasin that had made the mistake of swimming too close to the bank of the stream. Immediately, Wood put the machete that he brought for just such a moment to good use. The snake, however, experienced in dealing with young boys, evaded his efforts. But the commotion got all of our attention. Wood was always up to something exotic, but the idea of a poisonous snake nearby lodged firmly in all our minds. Nevertheless, we were all looking forward to having some bass or crappie for dinner, and would not be deterred by a snake. We all knew that my little sister Joanie was the one who would feed us. Her patience always gave her the advantage in catching fish. But all of us had fun trying.

My father chose to fish at the exact point where Wood had been lashing at the moccasin. Dad was a Little League umpire, and was wearing his black umpire's T-shirt and cap. We were all fishing along the same shoreline, and heard Dad slip, yell out, and then splash into the stream. But before any of us could get there to help, he was already back on dry land! Family lore has it that "his cap never got wet," so hasty was his exit from the water where the moccasin had been seen just thirty minutes before. I am sure that his next few adult Bible-study classes included some "personal testimony" when the subject came to the Sea of Galilee.

After supper, the rain began. Wood, ever the outsider, had pitched a tent. The rest of us were going to sleep in the car or on the ground. It didn't take long for everyone to realize that this rain storm was quickly becoming a gully washer. We all ended up in the car, even Wood. It became quite "cozy" as the hours wore on. We tried to sleep, determined to last out the storm, but the humidity, dank smell, and lack of comfort in the car overwhelmed us all. At last, Dad cranked up the '55 and headed out of Fisherman's Paradise through the rising waters that were now ankle deep.

We had only gone about half-way through the pasture when I was pulled out of my fantasy of a warm, dry bed. From my vantage point on the back seat, I began to see and feel water coming through my favorite hole in the rusted floorboard. (I always enjoyed watching the highway pass by beneath that hole.) At that same moment, the Chevy's engine died—literally flooded. I am sure that the air inside the old '55 turned the color of the Paluxy's Blue Hole as my father realized how his relaxing weekend was progressing. His service in the Navy came in handy, not only as a language resource but also for dealing with the calf-high water he was now forced to slosh through to rouse the owner of the store at Fisherman's Paradise. They both returned with a tractor and reeled in the old '55. Soon we were on our way home.

Over coffee the next morning, my parents read in the paper about other families, also camping at Fisherman's Paradise, whose travel trailers had floated down the river. It turned out that we had survived an historic downpour and were indeed the lucky ones. But we would never let Dad forget that weekend when "his cap never got wet."

Grandpa Mundine

FISHING

by Vicky J. Rose

When the call came from the Texas Folklore Society for papers about hunting and fishing lore, I immediately dismissed it. I never hunted and haven't fished in years. Yet, the more I thought about it, the more I realized what an important hand fishing took in developing my attitude toward life and people.

In those pre-feminist days during the late fifties and early sixties, women with children rarely worked outside the home. I was the middle child of three girls, tow-headed, with wide and trusting eyes. To keep from driving our mother crazy, she kept us busy playing with dolls in the winter, carving doll houses out of cardboard boxes and decorating them with scraps of wallpaper and fabric. In the summer, we were expected to play outdoors. Our only enemies then were snakes and the sticker-burs that infested the deep sandy soil where we lived. My older sister, with her delicate hands and tiny wrists, had an almost abnormal fear of spiders. Although she never grew to love the outdoors as much as I did, she put aside her trepidations, and we spent many hours gathering overgrown vegetables from the garden, placing them in old pots on a bench, and pretending to cook as we added water from the garden hose.

We lived in a hundred-year-old house on fifteen acres two miles outside a small town. Our father was a workaholic who liked to labor alone, so we didn't often accompany him when he checked on his cattle on other acreage he owned. He had strict ideas about what was proper for girls to do, but he allowed us to roam the land our house sat on. His only warning was that we were to stay away from the fence of our neighbors, carefully explaining that they had an old, mentally challenged son who wouldn't hurt us, but he did not want us to bother him. Forty years later I learned another reason he did not want us close to the fence—the neighbor's son had developed a fondness for cows our father did not want us to witness.

In the heat of the summer, however, we forgot our fear of snakes and spiders and with friends swam in our tank—what everyone outside of Texas calls a pond. The water was muddy and the color of an anemic orange. We scared the snakes away with our noise, but the fish often nibbled at our toes. When friends weren't around, I would walk the two miles into town to my grandparents' tiny house, the remnant of an old hotel. Sometimes my grandfather would take me fishing with him, something I enjoyed immensely because it let me spend time with him. I liked to talk too much occasionally, as most children do, and Grandpa would tell me we had to be perfectly quiet when we fished because we didn't want to scare the fish away. Years later when my husband took me fishing, he asked why I was so silent. I looked at him in surprise. Didn't this city boy I married know anything? When I repeated Grandpa's edict, he burst into laughter, explaining we didn't have to be *that* quiet. Poor Grandpa! He must have been desperate trying to shut up his little chatterbox of a grand-daughter.

Behind my grandparents' house resided a family with many children. They were "townies," and had a much more *laissez faire* attitude about life than I was used to. One of the girls my age often came to play with me when she saw I was in town, and sometimes we would imitate television shows. Rusty had round, slightly bulging eyes and brilliant, even, white teeth. A stout girl, she would jump behind the steering wheel in my grandfather's old truck and play *Green Hornet*. She always wanted to be Kato because he got to drive. I sat on the other side and tried to pretend I was the Green Hornet, but I never could get the hang of it. Other times, she would suggest we play *Gomer Pyle*. She would be Sergeant Carter and yell and order me around, while I grinned sheepishly like Gomer and looked dumb. I was better at being Gomer Pyle than the Green Hornet.

One day, to my relief, she suggested instead we walk to a small tank on some land my grandfather leased down the road. We stomped through wispy grass and weeds in those happy, carefree days before fire-ants, and once at the tank saw an unusual sight. Dozens of small fish were jumping in and out of the water, swimming and leaping from one end of the tank to the other. They leapt in time like marching soldiers, in and out of the water until they reached the other side. In one coordinated swift move, they turned and swam back, jumping in and out of the water to the other end of the tank, repeating it over and over again.

Rusty and I turned to one another wide-eyed and opened-mouthed. "Let's try to catch some!" she said, and I eagerly agreed. We looked around until we found an old fishing net my sometimes careless grandfather had left behind. It would be easy, we thought; all we would have to do would be stand at the edge of the water, and the fish would just jump into our net.

It didn't turn out that way. Laughing, talking, we took turns grabbing for the fish with our net. All the din and ruckus we made did not deter the fish from their fantastic hurdling through the air and swimming from one end of the tank to the other. Nor did they allow themselves to be caught in the net. Rusty and I spent hours trying to catch those fish, a seemingly easy task that turned out to be impossible. Finally, exhausted, we gave up and went back home.

To our chagrin, no one believed our story about the jumping fish. Repeatedly, we tried to describe what we saw and were met with disbelief. We finally gave up trying to get anyone to believe us. Years later when I attempted to explain it to my then husband, he agreed the fish were probably mullets, but reserved judgment on the leaping part of my account.

Rusty and I took different paths in life and drifted apart. She's gone now, and can no longer back up my story. When someone repeats a questionable tale, I remember Grandpa's subterfuge and realize even the people we love don't always tell the exact truth. And yet, there were those mullets. . . .

Uncle Earl and one of his coon dogs

CANEY CREEK NIGHT HUNTING: A SAGA OF DIRE SITUATIONS AND SCARED PRAYERS

by Wildwood Dean Price

One of the most memorable coon hunts I ever remember going on got underway late one Saturday evening in 1957. It was early autumn, and the day was clear, cool, and damp—the kind of dampness that a coon dog can really work a trail on.

By the time I arrived at Uncle Earl's, he and Joe Choice had unpenned the dogs and were getting ready to leave for a hunt on Caney Creek. The usual discussion broke out between Uncle Earl and Joe Choice as to where we could get the best hunt.

This time, Joe Choice won the argument.

"We ain't been to the old railroad bridge that crosses Caney in a coon's age. Everyone is taking bets that I can't climb that giant cottonwood tree that grows there. I wanna prove to myself that I can climb Goliath; that's what everyone is calling that old tree. That's where I wanna go."

It was final; Uncle Earl wanted to see if Joe Choice could climb Goliath, too.

Although I had been taught to respect my elders, when we were out in the woods coon hunting, Uncle Earl and Joe Choice considered me their equal. So it was that they refused for me to call them anything but Earl and Joe, which I did.

It was getting dark by the time we reached the branch that crossed the road where we intended to start the dogs. Joe pulled his pickup off the road into the bar ditch. Trailer and old Queenie and the rest of the dogs were rattling their chains. When the truck stopped, two of Joe's dogs, Jake and Lady, jumped out and their chains got tangled; they were choking themselves. Joe rushed to untangle them and in the excitement, he forgot to turn the pickup's lights off.

Earl snapped Trailer, a beautiful black and tan, to his leash. Joe led his dogs on a chain to which they were snapped individually. That way he could release them as he saw fit. We led the dogs off into the woods and down into a branch before Earl unsnapped Trailer's chain and told him, "We're after coons," and then sent him on his way. It was slap-dab-dark when Trailer hit a cold trail and bawled for the first time. As soon as Trailer struck trail, Joe unsnapped Queenie.

The rest of the dogs would have to wait their turn. When Queenie and Trailer worked the cold trail into something hotter, Joe would release the rest of his dogs and they would go straight to Trailer and Queenie.

Trailer's slow, drawling bawl echoed through the creek bottom, and then Queenie joined him with her clear bell-like voice. Pretty soon the trail warmed up, and first one dog and then the other sounded their voices in anticipation of seeing the coon. Joe released the rest of his dogs, except Jude. Jude remained on the leash as punishment for treeing a coon when a coon wasn't in the tree.

We sat down on a log and waited. I built a small fire. We had been listening for what seemed like hours to Trailer and Queenie cold-trailing, and now that the other dogs joined in, Trailer hushed his bawling. My mind wandered.

Trailer's the smartest coon dog ever . . . he knows what Earl wants him to hunt . . . he knows when to bark . . . he's saving his voice 'til they tree the coon.

Trailer had gained himself a reputation for his voice. There was none more resonate, none louder nor sweeter than Trailer's. Earl claimed that on a cold, clear night you could hear him treed five miles away.

The pack of dogs pushed the coon faster and faster; we finally had a race on our hands.

"It's a hot race to the finish now. They're hot on his tail. They're pushin' him 'cross Caney," Earl hollered above the noise.

"Yep—I hope to that giant cottonwood on the other side of the creek," Joe said.

Suddenly the tone of Queenie's voice changed, and Trailer joined her.

"They're treed!" Earl announced.

It was a duplicate of the way it always was: When Joe heard Earl announce, "They're treed," he took off. He never needed a light because he had what he called night eyes. Earl was right on his heels with the lantern, and I was keeping up the best way I could. I was used to following crashing sounds and the ever-dimming lantern light.

I heard Earl holler from somewhere up ahead, "They're on the other side of the creek in Goliath."

I arrived at Goliath, and there Earl and Joe were, standing on the creek bank urging the dogs into a tizzy.

"Get him, Trailer," Earl hollered.

"Get him, Queenie," Joe echoed.

Joe encouraged each dog in his pack by name: "Get'em Jake, get'em Lady; get'em Bow." They ended the chant with a flurry: "Get-em, get-em, get-em." With every "Get-em," the dogs jumped higher and higher.

Jude whined on the leash.

The dogs clawed and bit chunks of bark from the tree. Growls and barks filled the air. There was a silent oath between Joe and Earl—made to their dogs. They would never drag them away from their tree without first whipping their prey out for them to fight. If need be they would chop at a hollow tree all night, just to fell it and deliver a coon to their pack of dogs. No obstacle was too big to keep them from honoring their oath to their dogs. As far as Earl was concerned, the obstacle facing them was not Goliath, the giant cottonwood tree; it was the long deep hole of water between them and Goliath.

Long ago, there had been a railroad bridge at this point on Caney Creek. The train hadn't operated along those tracks in years, and the abandoned bridge had caved into the creek. The caved-in bridge partially dammed the creek and created the longest, deepest hole of water anywhere on Caney Creek. All the crossties from the railroad track had wound up in the water and created ideal dens for cottonmouth moccasins. Over the years they had raised their young there, and the place had become infested with big moccasins. Some people called the place "Cottonmouth Hole."

"Neither Goliath nor Cottonmouth Moccasins are gonna stop me," Joe bragged, "If I can get some help from Earl and you, Dean."

Goliath was not just any tree; all the old-timers claimed that Goliath was the biggest cottonwood tree in all of Caney Creek bottom, and maybe even Texas. The old-timers all laughed about Goliath being so big that any varmint in its right mind was too afraid to climb it. "Any varmint, that is, except Joe Choice," Earl always claimed.

Joe had very long, very thick and very hard toenails, made for climbing, he thought. Anyone who had seen Joe climb a big tree believed him. He would walk up to a tree, look up to see how far it was to the first limb, and then bear-hug it, hook his toenails into the bark, and shinny plum to the top without stopping. "Joe Choice can climb so fast, you can't keep your light on him," I always bragged.

Joe would tuck his head, embarrassed-like, and say, "I'm fast . . . but I ain't that fast."

Joe barked orders. "Earl, you and me will shuck our overalls and swim over there. I'll shinny up Goliath while you hold the dogs, and then I'll whoop that coon out. Dean, you start us a warmin' fire."

"Hey, wait a minute," Earl protested. "I ain't 'bout to swim that creek with all of them cottonmouths in there. Frost ain't hibernated 'em yet. I'll walk down the creek bank, find a crossing, and come back up the creek to the tree. But I ain't takin' my britches off," he added.

"Nope. All that'll take too long," Joe said as he clicked his overall's suspenders open. "That coon ain't gonna wait that long. He'll climb across the treetops and be gone." Joe stripped down to his pure white boxer shorts and scolded, "You and Dean get a move on."

Caney Creek heads in the black-land region of southern Fannin County. The rains through the centuries displaced the black dirt from Caney Creek's watershed and deposited it in a thick black coating along the creek's banks. We heard a big splash, and the next thing we knew Joe was scaling the creek bank on the other side. Joe's body—being about the same color as the creek bank—left nothing to see except the white blur of his bleached boxer shorts as he climbed up the muddy creek bank.

"Look," Earl laughed, "there goes a pair of boxer shorts with no one in 'em."

"Get a move on, Earl," Joe hollered from across the creek, where he stood bear-hugging the tree in preparation for the climb. "The coon's on the move, and if he goes in a holler, I'm gonna see to it that you saw Goliath down by yourself.

Earl ran down the creek, found himself a place to cross, and then ran back up the creek. I built us a warming fire. Finally, Earl got to the tree where Joe was and got all the dogs under control. He held Trailer and Queenie with one hand and Jake, Lady, and Bow with his other hand. He tied Jude to a sapling.

The moon was full, and it silhouetted Joe as he passed through its beam on his way to the top of Goliath. The big legs on his white boxer shorts flapped like wings in the gentle breeze. Joe was at least fifty feet up the tree when all silence broke out.

"Why are you so quiet, up there, Joe?" Earl hollered.

"Do you hear that buzzin' that's coming from up here in this tree with me?"

Earl cupped his hands and placed them around his ears. "Yeah . . . I hear a buzzing. What's causin' it?"

"I can't hear anything," I hollered from across the creek.

"Honeybees," Joe screamed. "They are down below me. I've clumb up past 'em."

"Climb back down—fast as you can," Earl advised.

"I can't. I can't stand to go down through 'em."

"Give it up, Joe; you have got to climb back down through 'em," Earl pleaded.

"Too many of 'em . . . sounds like a cream separator whirrin' down there. What am I gonna do?"

"Turn a loose, and jump out," I advised from across the creek.

"I can't do it, Dean. Earl can't hold the dogs off of me."

Earl got sarcastic. "You gotta choose, Joe. Stick it out, bail out, or climb down; **you can't fly**."

"Augh. They're swarmin' inside my shorts . . . Lordeeeee!" Joe's voice, for the first time ever, trembled with fear.

If you've ever seen a critter whooped out of a tree and seen him hit the ground among a pack of frenzied dogs, you will appreciate Joe's concern. That split second before the dogs recognized him had the potential—in Joe's mind—of being more dangerous than a fifty-foot freefall.

"I can't stay up here with 'em. Dean, dad-nab-it, get yourself on across that creek and help Earl hold them dogs off of me, and I'll jump out."

"Whaa . . . Oh my, they're inside my drawers. Aaaghh! They're eatin' my butt up. Oh, have mercy . . . Lordeeeee!"

"Break you a limb off and swat at 'em," Earl chided.

"I'm swattin' at 'em with both hands.

Aaaghh! I'm . . . f-a-l-l-i-n-g!" His voice trailed along behind him as he sped toward the ground.

I gotta help Earl.

I was there, reaching for the dogs, but I was too late. The dogs lunged toward the spot where Joe was fixing to hit the ground. Earl toppled over and he went sliding topsy-turvy down the slick bank toward Cottonmouth Hole.

Whomp! Joe hit the ground right in front of the growling, gnarling dogs.

Instantly the dogs recognized Joe and started licking him all over the face. I could have sworn they were laughing. Jude was doing his part; he was on top competing for a lick, his tangled chain and uprooted sapling making matters worse. I parted the dogs and slapped Joe's cheeks and blew in his face. He didn't respond.

I looked down at his dull, sooty face and chanted a scared prayer: "Is he dead? Please, don't let him be dead. Is he dead? Please, don't let him be dead!"

He just lay there limp. I cried. Joe roused up a little and gasped for air; wheezing sounds filled his throat and lungs as he tried to replace the air that the ground had jousted out of him. He moaned and groaned and rolled around on the ground with one of his big hands on each cheek of his butt. Between wheezes he started to mumble a little.

My pleading eyes met his. "Are you gonna be okay?" Joe mumbled something, and then his eyes rolled back in his head, and he passed out again. I slapped him and fanned him . . . and prayed, like I had heard Mother pray.

He revived a little and got up on his knees. "Where's Earl? I need air!"

The dull, sooty appearance of the skin on his face was leaving, and he was getting his sheen back.

He's beautiful.

"I'm coming, Joe." Earl scampered up the creek bank as wet as a drowned rat and as pale as a ghost. Clawing and scratching, he finally reached the top of the muddy bank and with one jump was by Joe's side.

"Are you gonna be Okay?"

"Don't know. My butt's on fire . . . full of bee stingers. Waugh. . . !"

Earl pulled a Case trapper's knife from his overalls pocket, grabbed Joe with one hand, held the knife with the other hand and opened it with his teeth. "Roll over, Joe. I'll dig the stingers out," he commanded.

Pain and fear filled the whites of Joe's eyes when he saw the glint of the moon reflecting from the long, pointed, super-sharp knife blade. His eyes rolled back in his head. "Whoa! Put it up! You ain't gonna dig them stingers out of me with that thing. Minnie'll do it. Y'all just get me home." Joe wasn't wheezing anymore. The sound of Earl trying to open the knife with his teeth must've caused him to refill his lungs with air.

It was late, and the fun of the hunt had vanished. I helped Joe gather himself up off the ground and offered my services. "Joe, I'll drive your pickup and take you and your dogs home."

"Trailer and me—we'll walk home, Dean. You get Joe home to Minnie as fast as you can. Dovie and I will come over in the morning to check on you Joe."

"Come on, Joe," I beckoned as I held out my hand.

"I ain't gonna go nowhere without my overalls. You know me better than that, Dean."

"Whew," Earl sighed, "If that doesn't beat a hen a peckin' with a wooden bill. Your overalls are still on the other side of the creek." We all laughed as we looked across the creek. There Joe's overalls were hanging on a limb by my big crackling fire.

As far as crossing Caney Creek and fetching Joe's overalls, Joe can't; Earl won't . . . I must.

I stood there facing Cottonmouth Hole and said a scared prayer, this time for myself. "Lord . . . please, help me cross over. Help me not make them Cottonmouth Moccasins mad, and help this night to hurry and get over."

It didn't take me long to fetch Joe's overalls. He squiggled down in them, fastened the suspenders, and left the side vents open so his butt could get air.

The dogs knew the hunt was over and raced out into the night toward the pickup. When we got there, the dogs had sprawled out in the bed and were waiting on us. Joe crawled up in the bed with them and lay down on his side. I crawled in the cab, turned the key on, and hit the starter button—nothing. I glanced at the light switch; it was pulled out.

Joe left the lights on.

Through the woods it was about three miles to Joe's house—if there was nothing wrong with you. In Joe's case it must've seemed like twenty miles.

There wasn't anything we could do. Joe had to get home and get the stingers out of his behind. We walked the three miles to Joe's house making very little talk.

Joe offered the daybed on the screened-in back porch, but I was content sleeping on the front porch with the dogs. I was too tired to walk around to the back of the house and open the screen door. I lay down and propped my head on the woodbox without taking my wet overalls off. I faintly remember seeing Joe come to the door and issue a word of warning: "You go on to sleep now. I'll not stand for any peepin' through the window."

The last time I took a friend to see Goliath, a rotten log was all that remained. The evidence of a railroad bridge ever being there was all but gone. Uncle Earl is gone. Joe Choice is gone. Trailer and Queenie are gone. I talked to a man over in Oklahoma a few months ago who had bought one of Trailer and Queenie's pups back in 1959. He said he gave Uncle Earl $500 for the pup way back then. He said, "Earl and Trailer, and Joe and Queenie were the best coon hunters that ever lived."

Uncle Earl and Trailer, 1956

Francis Edward Abernethy is Professor Emeritus of English at Stephen F. Austin State University and Editor Emeritus of the Texas Folklore Society.

Len Ainsworth indulges his interest in things "Texas" via involvement in the National Ranching Heritage Center, the National Cowboy Symposium and Celebration, and by dealing in collectible books through his Adobe Book Collection (www.adobebookcollection .com). He is a member of a local Westerners corral, TSHA, TFS, and is a frequent contributor to the RHA quarterly *Ranch Record*. He is Emeritus Professor and Vice-Provost of Texas Tech University.

Randy Cameron is a native Texan and a retired journalism instructor. He is now a fly fishing guide in Colorado, where he lives on the Rio Grande River in the San Juan Mountains with his wife Mary and son Will.

Mary Margaret Dougherty Campbell, a sixth-generation Texan, holds a B.A. and an M.A. in English from Texas Tech University, and also an M.S. in Educational Administration from Texas A & M University, Corpus Christi. She has presented papers at the South Central Modern Language Association, the Conference of College Teachers of English, the Texas/Southwest Popular Culture Association, the Popular Culture Association, the National Cowboy Symposium and Celebration, and the South Texas Ranching Heritage Festival. She has had articles published in *English in Texas, South Texas Traveler, South Texas Catholic*, and *Cowboy Magazine*, and has essays in three TFS publications: *The Family Saga, Folklore: In All of Us, In All We Do, Death Lore: Texas Rituals, Superstitions, and Legends of the Hereafter*, and *Celebrating 100 Years of the Texas Folklore Society 1909-2009*. Her poems have appeared in *English in Texas, American Cowboy, Rope Burns*, four volumes of the *Texas Poetry Calendar*, and

Big Land, Big Sky, Big Hair: The Best of the Texas Poetry Calendar. She is a petroleum landman and the Executive Director of George West Storyfest. Currently, she serves the TFS as President.

Kenneth W. Davis, a past-president and Fellow of the Texas Folklore Society, sometimes wanders about West Texas in search of lore worthy of preservation. He remains interested in oral narration and folk communal activities.

Robert J. (Jack) Duncan has taught at Collin College and Grayson County College and has worked in other capacities for two community colleges. He was president of the Texas Folklore Society in 1980, and is a life member of the Texas State Historical Association. Jack is a widely published freelance writer, in both scholarly and popular periodicals, including *Reader's Digest.* For the past eleven years, he has worked as a writer/editor/researcher for Retractable Technologies, Inc., a manufacturer of safety needle medical devices in Little Elm. A lifelong learner, Jack continues to take graduate courses at UNT in a variety of disciplines. He has lived in McKinney most of his life. He is married to his high school sweetheart, the former Elizabeth Ann Harris; they have two sons and five teenage grandsons. Jack and Elizabeth have belonged to the Texas Folklore Society for four decades.

Bob Dunn of Garland is a native Texan whose passion is collecting information about the state and the unique people who formed it and still live here. This intense interest has led him, on regular travels through the state, to amass what may be one of the largest and most varied private libraries of Texana in the state. His Lone Star Library in Stephenville is housed on the second floor of the Literary Lion book store, where researchers are welcome to explore its content without charge.

Robert Flynn is the author of thirteen books, including nine novels. *Echoes of Glory* received a Spur Award from Western Writers of

America for best long novel in 2010. Flynn's newest novel is *Jade: Outlaw*.

Sue Friday is a native of Houston but lives and writes on a farm outside Charlotte, North Carolina. She and her late husband, Tom, rescued her grandparents' dogtrot home near Hemphill, Texas, several years ago. The porch and hall were left open as the place to continue the tradition of outside family gatherings and storytelling. "Porch Hunting" is her third article for the Texas Folklore Society.

Riley Froh was born in Luling, Texas, and spent his teen years there enjoying the 1950s. He is descended from original settlers of the town. His great-grandfather drove cattle up the Chisholm Trail, and his great-great-grandfather was a noted Texas Ranger. He holds bachelor's and master's degrees from Southwest Texas State College (now Texas State University), and is retired back to Luling after teaching Texas history, U.S. history, and British Literature for forty years at San Jacinto College. He is the author of *Wildcatter Extraordinary, Edgar B. Davis*, and *Sequences in Business Capitalism*, as well as several articles on Texas history and folklore. His numerous short stories have appeared in *Louis Lamour Western Magazine*, various Western Writers of America anthologies, and other literary journals. Currently, he is writing the popular column "To and Froh" for the Luling *Newsboy* ("Caldwell County's Finest Newspaper"). He is married to Mary Binz of San Antonio, Texas, whose father was well known in the Alamo City as a horse trainer and trick rider. Mary is also retired from San Jacinto College. Their son, Noble King Froh, continues the cowboy tradition of both families.

Nina Vansickle Marshall Garrett was born in 1926 in Pushmataha County, Oklahoma. In 1944, she graduated from the Boswell High School in Choctaw County, Oklahoma, as the class Salutatorian. During 1945, she worked at the Douglas Aircraft

Plant near Oklahoma City building airplanes. In December of that year she married William Marshall, a high school classmate, after he returned from military service in Europe. They settled in Bonham, Texas, and raised four daughters: Linda, Joy, Mary Ann, and Billie Gail. Nina worked in a doctor's office for twenty-six years before she retired in 1988. After the death of Mr. Marshall, Nina married Theo Garrett, a long-time friend. Always an avid reader, Nina loves to study genealogy and write family stories. As a member of Telling Our Stories at Austin College in Sherman, Texas, she has attained several awards. She entered a contest of TOS with her first published story about her family traveling to Arizona and California in 1934. She was awarded $100 for her entry.

Lee Haile is from Tarpley, Texas. He is an entertainer, performing at dude ranches, festivals, schools, and parties throughout the state. He sings old songs, recites cowboy poetry, and is especially known for his storytelling. He is a woodworker also, and has a saw mill and enjoys going from tree to finished furniture for clients. He and his family have been members of the TFS since he gave his first paper on folk toys when he was in college in 1982. He has also been the Folk Toy Maker at the Texas Folklife Festival since 1987.

Jim Harris is a past-president of the Texas Folklore Society and a retired college teacher of English. He has been director of the Lea County Museum in Lovington, New Mexico, since 2002. He and his wife Mary have been married since 1965. They have one son, Hawk, who lives in Elgin, Texas. A lifelong fisherman, Jim has published a number of articles, stories, poems, and books.

W. C. Jameson is the award-winning author of more than sixty books, 1,500 articles and essays, 300 songs, and dozens of poems. His prominence as a professional fortune hunter has led to a series of best-selling books, as well as consulting with the *Unsolved Mysteries* television show and the Travel Channel. He served as an advisor for the film *National Treasure*, starring Nicolas Cage, and appears in an interview on the DVD. He has written the sound-tracks for two PBS documentaries and one feature film. His music has been heard on NPR, and he wrote and performed in the musical *Whatever Happened to the Outlaw, Jesse James?* Jameson has acted in five films and has been interviewed on The History Channel, The Travel Channel, PBS, and *Nightline*. When not working on a book, he tours the country conducting writing workshops and performing his music at folk festivals, concerts, roadhouses, and on television. He lives in Llano, Texas.

James B. Kelly credits his experience and training in the Corps of Cadets at Texas A & M University and a lifetime spent hunting in Texas and all over the world as the beacons that have guided his life. He was born in Ft. Worth, and grew up and was educated in the public schools in Sinton, Texas. He graduated from Texas A & M University in 1952, and was commissioned into the U.S. Army that same year, serving during the Korean Conflict with the 30th Regimental Combat Team of the 3rd Infantry Division. He became a successful insurance and banking executive and office developer in Houston, as well as a rancher in Washington County, Texas. He is a dedicated A & M supporter and was elected to the Corps of Cadets Hall of Honor in 2005. He attended his first TFS annual meeting in 2000.

Jerry B. Lincecum, a sixth-generation Texan, is Emeritus Professor of English at Austin College. He holds the B.A. in English from Texas A & M University and the M.A. and Ph.D. degrees from Duke University. A past-president of the Texas Folklore Society, he has presented many papers at annual meetings of the Society and co-edited *The Family Saga: A Collection of Texas Family Legends* for the TFS in 2003. Since 1990, he and Dr. Peggy Redshaw have directed "Telling Our Stories," a humanities project at Austin College that aids older adults in writing their autobiographies and family histories. He also serves as a trainer and editor for the Legacy program at Home Hospice of Grayson County, which collects the life stories of Hospice patients and publishes them in booklet form.

W. Frank Mayhew is a native of Conway, Arkansas, now living in Texas for the third time. His first Texas experience was shortly after graduating from Southern Arkansas University when he was hired to teach biology and coach football at Marshall, Texas. His second experience came after leaving Marshall for Pine Bluff, Arkansas, to take a "temporary" job with the Southern Pacific Railroad, where he stayed for twenty-one years. Southern Pacific had the very good sense to transfer him to Houston. However, never one to leave a good thing alone, the SP then transferred him to Atlanta, Georgia. It was while in Atlanta that he was hired away by the Norfolk Southern Railroad, who immediately sent him to Dallas, where he remained until he retired some ten years later. Several years before retiring from the rail industry, he secured the necessary credentials that would allow him to return to his first love, teaching, this time at the collegiate level. He started his second tenure in teaching the same month he retired, first at Texas Woman's University in Denton as an Adjunct History Professor, and later on at Collin College in McKinney as Professor of American & Texas History, which he still teaches today. He has been married to his first love, Shelby Lea Mayhew, for forty-seven years.

Lowell McCormack lives in Gainesville, Texas. She has two children, three grandchildren, and four great-grandchildren. She is 80+ years old and has been married to Paul McCormack for over sixty years. She was Chief Financial Officer of Dallas Title Company for seventeen years, retiring in 1983. While working there, she earned a masters degree in graphoanalysis (handwriting analysis) and became a Certified Questioned Document Examiner. Several of her articles were published in the journal *Graphoanalysis*. For a period of almost a year before it went out of business, she published a column entitled "Your Handwriting is You" in the weekly *Cooke County Leader*. Earning an associate of arts degree from Cooke County College (now NCTC) in 1992, Lowell became a Certified Art Instructor for Grumbacher Art Supplies. She was Treasurer of South Central Art Guild for seven years, a founding member of Gainesville Area Visual Arts, and Secretary of Cooke County Arts Council. Active in organizations in Gainesville, Lowell was the first woman member of the Kiwanis Club, becoming its first woman President in 1991. Her membership in other organizations includes Cooke County Heritage Society, Cross Timbers Genealogical Association, and MENSA. While attending North Central Texas College she won several awards for her writing. After joining Cross Timbers Genealogical Society, she became interested in writing her family's history. Her first book, *Memories of Growing Up in the Coney Family*, has been published, and many of her stories were included in the Texas State Historical Society's "My Texas" web page. She meets regularly with the "Telling Our Stories" group under the leadership of Professor Jerry Lincecum of Austin College, and has had several stories published in their book collections.

Clyde "Chip" Morgan is a recruiter and educator in the insurance industry, living in West Texas and dove/quail hunting the Rolling Plains area northwest of Abilene. Since early adolescence, he has trained and hunted American Pointers. Gracie was his first Labrador Retriever. "Rattlesnake at the Ants in the Pants" is the fifth in a compilation of five separate tales he has written about the life of Gracie, who came to him six years ago via a rescue. She was raised in a pen with two potbellied pigs. Her previous owners possessed a menagerie that also included a raccoon, two prairie dogs, a seven-toed momma cat with seven kittens, and a big red dog named Rusty. Only Rusty and the seven-toed momma cat got to stay; the rest had to go. The rescue was his wife's idea and he reluctantly agreed. This fall, two weeks into the dove season, Gracie suddenly passed. The day before, she showed no apparent illness or weakness when helping to retrieve a limit of mourning dove. The next morning she was found in her kennel, looking as if she were asleep. The printing of "Rattlesnake at the Ants in the Pants" is a wonderful epitaph to a great dog.

Charlie Oden is an old folklore junkie who lives with Paul Sartain, his daughter, and her family in Irving, Texas. He became a folklore junkie after he experienced a number of detention halls in high school, during which time he read all of J. Frank Dobie's books that were in the school library; he read them because they were the same kind of stories Charlie's mom and dad told. He worked for over forty years for the T&NO (SP) Railroad, where much folklore was generated by operating employees as they worked transporting passengers and freight hither, thither, and yon to their destinations. He has collected and written some of this vast field of lore, and he is a member of the Houston Folklore Society, Texas Folklore Society, Southwest Celtic Music Association, and a former member of the Central Texas Story Telling Guild and the Canadian Folk Music Society. If you know any clean tall tales, please contact him through the TFS. He probably will be willing to swap tall tales with you.

Dean Price was born to Joe and Sybil Price in the Red River Valley in 1941. He grew up in his dad's footsteps and learned how to tie hoop nets, how to rig them and fish them, how to build river boats and read the river, and how to trap fur-bearing animals and make leather, rawhide, and leather with fur on. His father taught him the uses of all the native plants along Red River. "Every thing has a duty in life," was his dad's favorite saying, and he adheres to that philosophy as well. He has continued to rely on nature and Red River to survive and support his family. He designs works of art and furniture from dogwood, rattan, willow, and other raw materials from nature, receiving the Texas Forestry Association's award for architectural excellence in wood design in 1998. He has authored two books: *Treasure River*, an historical novel about the Red River published in 2006, and *River of Dreams*, his memoirs about growing up on Red River, published in 2008. His passion is playing traditional bones, and he is responsible for developing the double handed, center pivoting bois d'arc "ClickySticks" that gives the player four contact points and two tones, instead of the traditional two contact monotone ones (and he has a patent pending, issued 11/12/2010 [Patent Pending 404,945] for ClickSticks).

Ruth Cleveland Riddels was born in the Pleasant Valley Community, east of Rotan, Texas, on a very small dry-land cotton farm, the ninth of ten children. She attended the two-room school built on a corner of the farm until 1945, when the school closed. For another year, she attended another community school which closed, and then she went to Rotan schools. She is a graduate of Howard Payne College (now University) in Brownwood, Texas. She retired from Chrysler Corporation, and has two children and two grandchildren. She is a long-time resident of Farmers Branch, Texas, and currently resides in Lewisville, Texas. She joined the Texas Folklore Society in 1986, and has attended all annual meetings since that time. Her daughter is also a member of the TFS.

Vicky J. Rose is a native Texan whose ancestors came to Texas with Stephen F. Austin, prayed within the sounds of gunfire at San Jacinto, stood up with Sam Houston in the Texas Legislature to oppose secession, and were murdered by marauding Indians on the plains near Waco and the streets of Bastrop. It's no wonder she loves Texas folklore! Vicky lives in Central Texas with her son Dan and numerous pets, all of whom are always ready to hear another tall Texas tale.

Jean G. Schnitz was born in Spur, Texas. She graduated from Raymondville High School in 1948, and from Texas College of Arts and Industries College (now Texas A & M University) in Kingsville in 1952. She and Lew Schnitz were married in 1953; they have three sons and four grandchildren. A retired legal secretary, she lives near Boerne. Jean served two separate terms on the Texas A & I University Alumni Board. She was President of the Nueces County Legal Secretaries Association in Corpus Christi in 1980. She was a participant in the Texas Folklife Festival in San Antonio, for her 29th year, in 2010. Since 1990 she has presented nine papers to the Texas Folklore Society, most of which were subsequently published in TFS annual publications. She became a Director on the Board of the Texas Folklore Society in 2002, and presided as President at the 91st annual meeting in San Antonio in April of 2007.

Thad Sitton is an historian of anthropological background and training, specializing in studies of rural Texas during the first half of the twentieth century. As a student of what he terms "the Southern side of Texas history and lifeways," he has published books about rural schools, free-range stockmen, hunters, mule-era cotton farmers, sawmill towns, county sheriffs, and independent African-American farming communities. Several of his essays on the history of hunting and fishing have appeared in *Texas Parks and Wildlife* magazine. A native of Lufkin, Texas, he now lives in Austin.

Blaine T. Williams has a degree in political science and a paralegal certification from the University of Texas at Arlington. He develops software, trains staff, and consults with city, county, and non-profit housing rehabilitation programs. Raised by a father who is a sociology professor and a mother who worked for the United Way, he was exposed to an eclectic range of information and people during his formative years. This has given him an appreciation for the range of storytelling and storytellers who appear at the annual Texas Folklore Society meetings.

John Wolf completed public school in Marshall, Texas, and an undergraduate and two graduate degrees at Stephen F. Austin State University. After his time in the Angelina Cat and Coon Hunting Association, he and his new wife bid farewell to East Texas and moved to the Metroplex, where he completed a Ph.D. in psychology and then accepted employment in Lubbock as a psychologist with the U. S. Department of Veterans Affairs. The future of which he speaks in the story held two children, four grandchildren, service in the United States Naval Reserve, twenty years of PT teaching at South Plains College, and a thirty-two-year career with the VA. He retired in 2005, and his retirement incarnation includes avid collecting of Western Americana and Texana, membership in the Texas Folklore Society and the West Texas Historical Association, as well as the Llano Estacado Corral of Westerners International, and the opportunity to meet and appreciate many wonderful writers of western history and folklore. Encouraged by Dr. Abernethy and Dr. Kenneth Davis, this is his first effort at writing other than numerous professional publications.

Henry Wolff, Jr. is a long-time Texas journalist whose career embraced some fifty years. In 2009, he retired from the *Victoria Advocate*, Texas' second oldest existing daily newspaper, where his "Henry's Journal" column appeared for three decades. During that time he wrote more than 6,000 columns about the people, places, history, and culture of Texas—particularly of South Texas and the Texas Coastal Plains. He is a former president of the Texas Folklore Society and of the South Texas Historical Association. He has served on the boards of the South Texas Zoological Society and the German-Texan Heritage Society, and was also a long-time vice-chairman of the Victoria County Historical Commission.

Jerry Young grew up in Oklahoma but crossed the Big Red because Texas paid $700 more a year for teachers. He holds a B.A. from Oklahoma Baptist University and an M.A. from the University of North Texas, and he did doctoral studies at East Texas State University. He taught high school speech and theatre in Sherman High School and Pemberton High School (Marshall), and he taught English and speech in Honey Grove High School. In 1980, he became Director of Curriculum and Instruction for Kaufman ISD. Overlapping his last years at Kaufman and his retirement years, he taught speech communications as an adjunct instructor with the Dallas County Community College District. He also taught two continuing education classes with DCCCD for folks wanting to learn the art of storytelling. Throughout his career, he maintained an active life as director or actor in community theatres, professional theatre, television, and film. His writing resume includes a variety of church and educational publications. He grew up in a family of storytellers, so it was not a stretch for him to join the cadre of Texas and Oklahoma storytellers. He is a past-president and treasurer of the Tejas Storytelling Association Board of Directors, and he has been a member of the Texas Folklore Society for fifteen years. He and his wife Barbara live in Mesquite, Texas. Their four children are scattered around the country; their eight grandchildren check in regularly, and their five great-grandchildren are just downright fun.

INDEX